WORKS ISSUED BY
THE HAKLUYT SOCIETY

———

THE HAKLUYT HANDBOOK
VOLUME II

SECOND SERIES
NO. 145

ISSUED FOR 1974

The Hakluyt Handbook

Edited by
D. B. QUINN

VOLUME II

THE HAKLUYT SOCIETY
LONDON
1974

Library of Congress Catalogue Card Number: 72–87176

ISBN 0 521 08694 9   vol. 1
0 521 20211 6   vol. 2
0 521 20212 4   set of two vols.

Printed in Great Britain
at the University Printing House, Cambridge
(Brooke Crutchley, University Printer)

Published by the Hakluyt Society
c/o British Museum
London WC1B 3DG

Contents

VOLUME II

PART FOUR
CONTENTS AND SOURCES OF
THE THREE MAJOR WORKS
By A. M. and D. B. QUINN

PART FIVE
HAKLUYT'S BOOKS AND SOURCES

By D. B. QUINN, C. E. ARMSTRONG and
R. A. SKELTON

CONTENTS

INDEXES

By A. M. QUINN

Illustrations

Usages and abbreviations

'u' and 'v', 'i' and 'j' have been retained in their contemporary usage except for citations of the titles of Hakluyt's *Divers voyages* (1582), *Principall navigations* (1589), and *Principal navigations* (1598–1600).

English books are published in London unless otherwise stated.

References to Hakluyt's works are to the original editions throughout. For convenience of reference a concordance of *Principal navigations* (1598–1600) with *Principal navigations* (1903–5) is given on pp. xii–xiii.

Arber, *Transcript*. Edward Arber, ed., *A transcript of the registers of the Company of Stationers of London, 1554–1640*, 5 vols. (1875–94)

Atkinson, G. Atkinson, *La littérature géographique française de la renaissance* (Paris, 1927). *Supplément* (1936)

B.M. British Museum (now British Library, Reference Division)

BSA. Bibliographical Society of America

DNB. Dictionary of national biography

DV. Richard Hakluyt, *Divers voyages touching the discoverie of America* (1582)

Lumley [with a number]. *The Lumley library. The catalogue of 1609*, edited by Sears Jayne and Francis R. Johnson (1956)

N.H.L. Naval Historical Library, formerly Admiralty Library

N.R.S. Navy Records Society

O.E.D. Oxford English dictionary

Parks, *Hakluyt*. George Bruner Parks, *Richard Hakluyt and the English voyages* (New York, 1928; reissued with corrections 1961)

PN (1589). Richard Hakluyt, *Principall navigations* (1589)

PN (1598–1600 & 1599–1600). Richard Hakluyt, *Principal navigations* (1598–1600 and 1599–1600)

P.R.O. Public Record Office

Quinn, *Gilbert.* D. B. Quinn, ed., *The voyages and colonising enterprises of Sir Humphrey Gilbert,* 2 vols. (1940)

Quinn, *Richard Hakluyt editor.* D. B. Quinn, *Richard Hakluyt editor,* introductory to facsimiles of *Divers voyages* (1582) and *A shorte and briefe narration of the two navigations to Newe Fraunce* (1580), 2 vols. (Amsterdam, 1967)

Quinn, *Roanoke voyages.* D. B. Quinn, ed., *The Roanoke voyages, 1584-90,* 2 vols. (Cambridge, 1955)

Quinn and Cheshire, *Parmenius.* D. B. Quinn and N. M. Cheshire, *The new found land of Stephen Parmenius* (Toronto, 1972)

Quinn and Skelton, edd., *PN (1589)* (1965). D. B. Quinn and R. A. Skelton, edd. Richard Hakluyt, *Principall navigations (1589).* 2 vols. (Cambridge, 1965)

S.T.C. *Short-title catalogue of English books, 1476-1640,* edd. A. W. Pollard and G. R. Redgrave (1926)

Taylor, *Hakluyts.* E. G. R. Taylor, ed., *The original writings and correspondence of the two Richard Hakluyts,* 2 vols. (1935)

Concordance between *Principal navigations* (3 vols., 1598–1600) and *Principal navigations* (12 vols., 1903–5)

Concordance between *Principal navigations* (3 vols., 1598–1600)
and *Principal navigations* (12 vols., 1903–5) (*cont.*)

PART FOUR

CONTENTS AND SOURCES OF THE THREE MAJOR WORKS

A. M. and D. B. QUINN

Introductory Notes

The lists which follow are the first which attempt to assign all the items in Hakluyt's three documentary collections, *Divers voyages* (1582), *Principall navigations* (1589) and *Principal navigations* (1598–1600), to their sources and to follow through the re-publication of certain items from 1582 to 1600. They are to a considerable extent tentative working lists rather than definitive ones. In the case of *Divers voyages* (1582) much of the evidence has already been presented by D. B. Quinn in *Richard Hakluyt editor* (1967). For *Principall navigations* (1589) a first attempt to survey the sources in detail has been made in the introduction, by D. B. Quinn and R. A. Skelton, to the facsimile edition (1965), and this has now been developed. No attempt has been made hitherto to put together what is known about the sources of *Principal navigations* (1598–1600) and this remains the most provisional of the three lists.

When Hakluyt used materials from printed sources he sometimes gave sufficient reference to make clear which edition was employed for his text and/or translation. On other occasions he gave indications of what book it was but not the edition, so that it may or may not be possible to pin down his source to a specific publication. In still other instances he gave little or no indication he had used a printed source and it has had to be searched for, though not always found, especially since news pamphlets on which he may have relied have totally disappeared. In these circumstances it has been thought safer to use the word 'from' a particular volume only for cases where it is certain or virtually certain that Hakluyt used that particular edition, and 'in' for those cases where the reference may or may not be to the edition he used. The number of untraced references to printed sources is thought to be small, but it may well be that further scrutiny or research will alter a number of 'in' references to 'from' references, as well as filling a number of gaps.

The position with regard to manuscript sources is very different. A limited number of manuscripts which Hakluyt used, or probably used, are still in existence, but these, as may be seen from the 'Chronology' (I, 263–331), cover only a handful of those he assembled. At various times he was clearly accommodated with texts by statesmen like Walsingham and Burghley; he was provided with documents closely relating to their own enterprises by voyagers or voyage entrepreneurs like Ralegh, Drake, Hawkins and Cavendish; he was given access to company records by men like Michael Lok, Edward Osborne and Richard Staper; he was able to obtain narratives from participants in voyages, without necessarily having contact with their principals (though if he had to pay for such aid he may have been subsidized by some of his backers); he took down or arranged to have taken down oral accounts which were then written up for publication; he used his own correspondence and that of his elder cousin, Richard Hakluyt, lawyer, as well as reports which one or other of them had supplied to the organizers and promoters of commercial or exploring expeditions. He picked up odds and ends from graveyards and other haunts of antiquaries. Sometimes his friends seem to have sent him notes of interesting items for which they gave no source and for which he found none; clearly by 1598 he had a circle of correspondents who helped him, as well as young men like John Pory (and Philip Jones in the earlier, pre-1589, stage) who located documents for him as well as translating and sub-editing texts. But so very often our knowledge is imprecise or lacking. We have naturally associated with his published versions any manuscripts which we know, or strongly suspect, were used by him, but most of the surviving papers are ones which may or may not, could or could not, have been employed by him. In the latter case we have used the non-committal phrase 'represented in' before the location. He does, however, give us clues in his preliminaries about persons who gave him certain types of document and these have been used, together with internal indications of a non-specific type, to indicate or suggest in some tentative manner where he may have obtained his materials even though clear evidence may not exist. The value of such guesses is bound to vary very much and an ingenious critic can no doubt, in some cases, suggest various more likely alternatives which have been passed over. Yet it is hoped that even the less likely guesses may help to stimulate criticism and research so that gradually a fuller conspectus of Hakluyt's manuscript – and oral – sources can be arrived at. It may be worth saying that reference to secondary materials and modern editions has been made only where they throw some necessary light on dating or offer clues to the existence of manuscripts which have not been consulted.

The form in which the contents and sources have been presented needs explanation. Hakluyt gave no table of contents in *Divers voyages* and so the items have been simply presented *seriatim*, but both in 1589 and in 1598-1600 he gave very full lists of items printed – missing only a very occasional small piece. These tables of contents have been used as the framework for the following lists. It seemed important for the understanding of the articulation of the works that this should be done. Hakluyt has been criticized by literary historians and later collection-compilers alike for putting in with voyage narratives a wide selection of historical documents relating to the background or context of the actual movement of men or ships. His arrangement of his tables of contents shows that he was very conscious that he was attempting to satisfy a dual readership, the one interested in the events, the other in causes and circumstances. Hakluyt, therefore, not only arranged his materials regionally in both editions, but distinguished in his contents lists between the voyages and the *pièces justificatives* with which he surrounded them. He did this consistently, region by region, in 1589 and in the volumes of 1598 and 1599, but in 1600 he changed his plans and broke down his lists of voyages and the appropriate subsidiary documents into no less than fourteen different sub-categories. In all cases his own arrangement has been retained: so have his indications of pagination, which means that the reader of the second edition in the 1903–5 printing must use the concordance on pp. xii–xiii, remembering that in this edition the original pagination of the 1598–1600 edition is retained in the side-notes. For the 1589 edition the existence of the indexed facsimile of 1965 should obviate any difficulties of this sort. The lists of contents and sources can, in this way, be of use in the analysis of Hakluyt's objectives in putting his collections together and can give a clearer view of the various types of sources used than a continuous listing would have done. It is hoped that these lists will be effectively integrated by the index to the book.

24

Divers voyages (1582)

[Hakluyt obtained this document with nos. 10 and 12 from Cyprian Lucar, whose father Emmanuel Lucar had been the executor of Robert Thorne the younger, d. 1532, and from whom they derived. Manuscript versions without the maps are in B.M., Cotton MS Vitellius C. VII, ff. 329–45; and Lansdowne MS 100, ff. 65–80v; Hatfield House, Cecil Papers 245/5; see H.M.C., *Cecil*, I (1883), p. 6 (no. 29).]

[10] 'The booke made by...Robert Thorne in the yeere 1527. in Siuill to Doctour Ley...'   B3v
[From the same source as no. 9 and associated with it in the three surviving MSS.]

[11] Hakluyt's note on the source of the Thorne materials, with a note of the despatch of two ships on 20 May 1527.   D4
[The 1527 item was taken from Richard Grafton, *A chronicle at large...of the affayres of Englande* (1569), p. 1149.]

[12] 'This is the forme of a Mappe sent 1527. from Siuill...by maister Robert Thorne marchaunt, to Doctor Ley...'   [facing D4v]
[Obtained by Hakluyt with nos. 9 and 10, but no MS version is now extant.]

[13] 'To the most Christian king of Fraunce, Fraunces the first. The relation of Iohn Verarzanus a Florentine, of the lande by him discouered..., written in Diepe the eight of Iuly 1524.'   - A1
[Translated by Hakluyt from Ramusio, *Navigationi et viaggi*, III (1556), ff. 420–2v.]

[14] Map of the Arctic and sub-Arctic regions, dedicated by Michael Lok to Philip Sidney.   [facing B3v]
[Compiled by Lok for Hakluyt: see pp. 56–7, 65 above.]

[15] 'The discouerie of the Isles of Frisland, Iseland, Engroueland, Estotiland, Drogeo and Icaria, made by M. Nicholas Zeno, Knight, and M. Antonio his brother.'   B4v
[Translated by Hakluyt from Ramusio, *Navigationi et viaggi*, II (1574), ff. 225v–37v (having first appeared in Nicolò Zeno, *De i commentarii del viaggio in Persia di M. Caterino Zeno...Et dello scoprimento dell' Isole Frislanda, Eslanda, Engronelanda, Estotilanda, et Icaria, fatto...da due fratelli Zeni, M. Nicolò...e M. Antonio* (Venice, 1558).]

[16] 'The true and last discouerie of Florida made by Captaine
Iohn Ribault in the yeere 1562...'   E2
    [Reprinted by Hakluyt from Jean Ribault, *The whole and true
discouerye of Terra Florida* [1563].]

[17] 'Notes in writing besides more priuie by mouth that were
giuen by a Gentleman, Anno. 1580. to M. Arthur Pette and to
M. Charles Iackman, sent by the marchants of the Muscouie
companie for the discouerie of the northeast strayte...'   H1
    [Hakluyt attributed these notes, when he reprinted them in *PN*
(1589), pp. 460–6, to his elder cousin, the lawyer, whom he
described as 'M. Richard Hakluyt of Eiton in the countie of
Hereford, Esquire'.]

[18] Notes framed by a Gentleman heretofore to bee giuen to one
that prepared for a discouerie, and went not...'   K1
    [Hakluyt attributed these notes to his cousin the lawyer, when he
reprinted them in *PN* (1589), pp. 636–8, as 'Notes framed by
M. Richard Hakluyt of the middle Temple Esquire, giuen to
certaine Gentlemen that went with M. Frobisher in his North-
west discouerie for their directions...']

[19] 'The names of certain commodities growing in part of
America, not presently inhabited by any Christians from Florida
Northward...'   K4
    [Compiled by Hakluyt himself and not subsequently reprinted.]

25

Principall navigations (1589)

The order of all the voyages comprised in this whole worke in generall, together with the names of the persons, the Authors of them, and the annotations of the course of yeeres and quarters of the worlde, wherein they were perfourmed.

[A]   *The voyages of the first part to the South and Southeast regions.*

1. The voyage of Helena, the Empresse, daughter of Coelus King of Britaine, and mother of Constantine the great, to Ierusalem. Anno 337.   Pagina 1. 2
    From John Bale, *Scriptorum illustrium maioris Brytanniae...catalogus* (Basle, 1557–9), I, 31–2 (I, xxxv).
    Latin and English.

2. The voyage of Constantine the great, Emperour and King of Britaine, into Greece, Egypt, Persia, and Asia. An. 339.   [pages] 2. 3
    From John Bale, *Scriptorum illustrium maioris Brytanniae...catalogus* (Basle, 1557–9), I, 32–3 (I, xxxvi).
    Latin and English.

3. The voyage of Pelagius Cambrius vnder Maximus King of the Britaines into Egypt, and Syria. An. 390.   [pages] 3. 4
    From John Bale, *Scriptorum illustrium maioris Brytanniae...catalogus* (Basle, 1557–9), I, 36–7 (I, xxxviii).
    Latin and English.

4. The voyage of Iohn Erigen vnder Alphred to Athens. An. 858.
                                                                   [page] 4
    From John Bale, *Scriptorum illustrium maioris Brytanniae...catalogus* (Basle, 1557–9), I, 124–5 (II, xxiv).
    Latin and English.

5. The voyage of Andrew Whiteman, alias Leucander, vnder Canutus the Dane to Palestine. An. 1020.   [page] 5
    From John Bale, *Scriptorum illustrium maioris Brytanniae...catalogus* (Basle, 1557–9), I, 151 (II, xliv).
    Latin and English.

6. The voyage of Athelarde of Bathe vnder H. the first to Egypt & Arabia. An. 1130. [page] 5

From John Bale, *Scriptorum illustrium maioris Brytanniae...catalogus* (Basle, 1557–9), I, 183–4 (II, lxix).
Latin and English.

7. The voyage of William Archbishoppe of Tyre, vnder Henrie the first to Hierusalem, and the cittie of Tyre in Phoenice. An. 1132 [pages] 5. 6

From John Bale, *Scriptorum illustrium maioris Brytanniae...catalogus* (Basle, 1557–9), II, 150 (XIII, lxix).
Latin and English.

8. The voyage of Robert Ketenensis vnder King Steuen, to Dalmatia, Greece, and Asia. An. 1143. [page] 6

From John Bale, *Scriptorum illustrium maioris Brytanniae...catalogus* (Basle, 1557–9), I, 191 (II, lxxx).
Latin and English.

9. The voyage of Richard the first King of England into Asia for the recouerie of Ierusalem out of the hands of the Sarracens. Anno. 1190. [page] 6

From John Foxe, *Actes and monuments*, I (4th ed. 1583), 242–6, 248.

10. The voyage of Baldwine Archbishop of Canterburie, into Syria and Palestina with king Richard. An. 1190. [page] 14

From John Bale, *Scriptorum illustrium maioris Brytanniae...catalogus* (Basle, 1557–9), I, 228–9 (III, xxvii).
Latin and English.

11. The voyage of Richard surnamed Canonicus, vnder king Richard into Syria and Palestina. An. 1190. [page] 15

From John Bale, *Scriptorum illustrium maioris Brytanniae...catalogus* (Basle, 1557–9), I, 242 (III, xliv)
Latin and English.

12. The voyage of Guilielmus surnamed Peregrinus, vnder king Richard also into Palestina. An. 1190. [page] 15

From John Bale, *Scriptorum illustrium maioris Brytanniae...catalogus* (Basle, 1557–9), I, 242 (III, xlv).
Latin and English.

13. The voyage of Hubert Walter, bishop of Sarum, vnder king Richard also into Syria. An. 1190. [page] 16

From John Bale, *Scriptorum illustrium maioris Brytanniae...catalogus*
(Basle, 1557–9), I, 248–9 (III, lvi).
Latin and English.

14. The voyage of Robert Curson a noble man of England, and
cardinall, vnder Henry the third to Damiata in Aegypt. An. 1218.
[page] 17
From John Bale, *Scriptorum illustrium maioris Brytanniae...catalogus*
(Basle, 1557–9), I, 267–8 (III, lxxix).
Latin and English.

15. The voyage of Rainulfe Glanuill a valiant noble man, and Earle
of Chester, vnder Henrie the third to Damiata in Aegypt also. An.
1218.   [page] 17
From John Bale, *Scriptorum illustrium maioris Brytanniae...catalogus*
(Basle, 1557–9), I, 279 (III, xciii).
Latin and English.

16. The voyage of William Longespee, in English Longsword, a
noble man of England into Aegypt and Asia, with Lewes the French
king. An. 1248.   [pages] 17. 18 [*recte* 17–19]
Adapted and translated from *Matthaei Paris...Angli, historia maior*
(London, 1571), pp. 973, 986, 1041–2, 1046, 1050–2.

17. The voyage of prince Edward, the sonne of king Henrie the third
into Asia. An. 1270.   [page] 20
Derived from Walter of Guisborough. (See *Chronicle*, ed. Harry
Rothwell (Camden, 3rd ser., LXXXIX (1957)), pp. 203–13).
[Hakluyt's text has not been identified.]

18. The voyage of Robert Turneham, vnder ye sayd Prince Edward
into Syria. An. 1270.   [page] 23
From John Bale, *Scriptorum illustrium maioris Brytanniae...catalogus*
(Basle, 1557–9), II, 153 (XIII, lxxxii).
Latin and English.

19. The voyage of Iohn Mandeuil knight in Latin, begun in the
raigne of Edwarde the 2. Anno. 1322. continued for the space of 33.
yeeres, and ended in the raigne of Edwarde the 3. from England to
Iudea, and from thence to India, China, Tartaria, and as farre as 33.
degrees to the south of the Aequinoctiall.   [page] 25
Text identified with *Liber pñs cui⁹ fert⁹ iohañes de mādeuille militari'*

ordis agit de diuerſ patrijs (n.d., n.p. B.M., IA. 47355).
[Reprinted in *Hakluyt's collection of the early voyages of the English nation* (London, 1810), II, 77–138.]
Latin only.

20. The voyage of Macham, the first discouerer of the Island of
Madera, vnder Edward the third. An. 1344.   [page] 80
  From Antonio Galvão, *Tradado . . . dos diuersos & desuayrados caminhos, por onde nos tempos passados a pimenta & especearia veyo da India ás nossas partes* (Lisbon, 1563).
  [In the edition of 1571 *Tratato . . . dos diuersos & desuayrados caminhos* (Lisbon, 1571), ff. 15–15v.]

21. The voyage of Thomas Windam vnder Edward the 6. to Guinea,
and the kingdome of Benin. An. 1553.   [page] 83
  From Richard Eden, *The decades of the newe worlde or west India* (1555), pp. 345–8.

22. The voyage of Robert Gaynsh vnder Queene Mary to Guinea.
An. 1554.   [page] 89
  From Richard Eden, *The decades of the newe worlde or west India* (1555), pp. 349–60.

23. The voyage of William Towerson marchant of London, vnder
Queene Mary to Guinea. An. 1555.   [page] 98
  From manuscript; first printed in *PN* (1589).

24. The voyage of William Towerson aforesaid, the second time to
Guinea, and the Castle of Mina. An. 1556.   [page] 112
  From manuscript; first printed in *PN* (1589).

25. The voyage of William Towerson aforesayd, the third time to
the coaste of Guinea, and the riuer of Sestos. An. 1557.   [page] 120
  From manuscript; first printed in *PN* (1589).

26. The first voyage of Robert Baker to Guinea. An. 1562.   [page] 130
  Probably from *The brefe Dyscource of Roberte Baker in Gynney India Portyngyule and Fraunce &c.*; a news pamphlet licensed to Frances Coldoke (1568).
  [No copy is now known to survive. It was entered in the Stationers' Register in 1568 (Arber, *Transcript*, I, 363).]

27. The voyage of the sayd Robert Baker to Guinea the second time.
an. 1563.   [page] 135

Probably from *The brefe Dyscource of Roberte Baker* (1568).
[As previous item.]

28. The voyage of George Fenner, to Guinie, & to the Islands of
Cape Verde. An. 1566. [By Walter Wren.]   [page] 142
   From manuscript; first printed in *PN* (1589).

29. The voyage of Thomas Steeuens, round about the Cape of
Bona Speranza, to Goa in the East India. An. 1579.   [page] 180
   From manuscript; first printed in *PN* (1589).
   [This had reached Hakluyt from his elder cousin, the lawyer
   Richard Hakluyt, by 1583.]

30. The voyage of Laurence Aldersey, to the cities of Ierusalem &
Tripolis. An. 1581. [By Laurence Aldersey.]   [page] 177
   From manuscript; first printed in *PN* (1589).

31. The voyage of William Huddie, to Rio Grande in Guinie, set
out by Edward Cotton of Southampton. An. 1583.   [page] 187
   From manuscript; first printed in *PN* (1589).
   [Probably given to Hakluyt by Edward Cotton.]

32. The voyage of Zacheus Hellier, in the Iesus of London to
Tripolis in Barbarie. An. 1584. [By Thomas Sanders, or Saunders.]
                                                    [page] 192
   From Thomas Saunders, *A true and breefe discourse of a most lament-
   able voiage, made latelie to Tripolie in Barbarie, in a ship named the Iesus*
   (1587) [S.T.C. 21778.]

33. The voyage of Iohn Newberie, and Ralfe Fitche, to Tripolis in
Syria, Aleppo, Babylon, Balsara, Ormuz, Goa. An. 1583.   [page] 208
   [This refers to the letters listed in B 38-43 below.]

34. The voyage of Iohn Evesham into Egypt. An. 1586.   [page] 222
   From manuscript; first printed in *PN* (1589).

35. The voyage of Laurence Aldersey, to the cities of Alexandria,
and Cairo in Egypt. An. 1586.   [page] 224
   From manuscript; first printed in *PN* (1589).

36. The voyage of Edward Wilkinson, with the Marchant Royall
to Tripolis in Syria. Anno 1586. [By Philip Jones.]   [page] 227
   [It would appear that this was a reprint of a news pamphlet

Newes from Turkey, A true report in verse of a sea fight in the straightes by 5 Shipps of London against 11 Gallies & 2 Frigattes of the King of Spaine (1586), of which no copy has survived. See W. A. Jackson, 'Humphrey Dyson's library', BSA, *Papers*, XLIII (1949), 285.]

37. The voyage of Iohn Eldred, to Tripolis in Syria by sea, and from thence by lande and riuer to Babylon, and Balsara. An. 1583.

[page] 231

From manuscript; first printed in *PN* (1589).
[From Levant Company archives or Eldred's personal collection?]

38. The late voyage of Anthonie Ingram and his companie, to the kingdome and cittie of Benyn in Africa. An. 1588. [By the chief factor on the voyage.] [page] 818

From manuscript; first printed in *PN* (1589).·

[B] *The Ambassages, letters, Priuileges, and other necessarie matters of circumstance appertaining to the voyages of the first part.*

1. An annotation concerning the voyage of Baldwine Archbishop of Canterburie, taken out of Giraldus Cambrensis in his Itinerarium Cambrie. [1190] pag. 14

From Luigi Ponticus Virunii, ed., *Pontici Virunnii...Britannicae historiae libri sex...Itinerarium Cambriae auctore Sil. Giraldo Cam-brense cum annotationibus D. Poveli* (1585), f. 229.
Latin and English.

2. The life of Sir Iohn Mandeuil knight, written by M. Bale.

[*floruit* 1332–72] [page] 23

From John Bale, *Scriptorum illustrium maioris Brytanniae...catalogus* (Basle, 1557–9), I, 478–9 (VI, xlvi).
Latin and English.

3. The tombe and Epitaph of Sir Iohn Mandeuill in the citie of Liege noted by Ortelius in his Itinerarium Belgij. [17 November 1371.] [page] 77

From Abraham Ortelius, *Itinerarium per nonnullas Galliae Belgicae partes* (Antwerp, 1584), pp. 15–16.
Latin only.

4. The dedication of his [Sir John Mandeville's] voyage to king Edward the 3. [page] 25

Latin only. [Preface to no. A. 19 above.]

5. An admonition of Richard Hakluyt touching the new impression
and purgation of Mandeuil.   [page] 77
   First printed in *PN* (1589).
   Latin only.
   [Hakluyt's caveat about the reliability of no. A. 19 above.]

6. Certaine places alleaged out of the naturall historie of Plinie
agreeing with Mandeuil in his reports of the diuers shapes of men.   [page] 77
   From Pliny, *Naturalis historia*, vi, 30; vii, 2.
   Latin only.

7. A note concerning the aide and assistance of English merchants
giuen to king Iohn the first of Portugall for the winning of Ceut in
Barbarie. [1415.]   [page] 79
   From Thomas Walsingham, *Historia breuis...ab Edwardo primo,
   ad Henricum quintum* (1574), p. 440.
   Latin and English.

8. The ambassage of Iohn the 2. of Portugall sent to Edward the 4.
king of England, to stay Iohn Tintam and William Fabian English-
men, preparing for a voyage to Guinie. [1481.]   [page] 81
   From Garcia de Resende, *Lyuro das obras* (Lisbon, 1545), sig.
   C2v–3r.
   Portuguese and English.

9. The maner of entring of Soliman the great Turke, with his armie
into Aleppo in Syria, marching into Persia against the great Sophie.
[1553].   [page] 81
   From manuscript; first printed in *PN* (1589).
   [Possibly given to Hakluyt by Anthony Jenkinson with no. 11
   below.]

10. The presents giuen to the great Turke at that time by his Bashaes,
and the Venetian Consul in Tripolis. [1553].   [page] 82
   From manuscript; first printed in *PN* (1589).
   [Possibly given to Hakluyt by Anthony Jenkinson with no. 11
   below.]

11. The safe conduct giuen by the great Turke to Anthonie Ienkin-
son at Aleppo in Syria. [1553]   [page] 82
   From manuscript; first printed in *PN* (1589).
   Translated.
   [Hakluyt notes that Jenkinson gave him the Turkish and French

CONTENTS AND SOURCES OF THE THREE MAJOR WORKS

versions: he would have been able to translate only from the latter.
Our main authority for the Turkish correspondence is Paul
Wittek, 'The Turkish documents in Hakluyt's "Voyages",'
Bulletin of the Institute of Historical Research, XIX (1942–3), 121–39,
in which this and fifteen other items are discussed. See also
pp. 184–6 above.]

12. A briefe description of Africa. [page] 84
From Richard Eden, *The decades of the newe worlde or west India*
(1555), p. 344.

13. The commodities and wares that are most desired in Guinie
betwixt Sierra Leone, and the furthest place of the Mine. [page] 130
From manuscript; first printed in *PN* (1589).

14. The woorthie enterprise of Iohn Foxe, in deliuering 266.
Christians out of the captiuitie of the Turkes at Alexandria. [1563–
79.] [page] 150
From a printed version entered in Stationers' Register 23 July 1579.
[Arber, *Transcript*, II, 357. No copy has survived, but an edition
of 1608, Anthony Munday, *The admirable deliuerance of 226 christians*,
S.T.C. 18258, is extant.]

15. The Ambassage of Edmund Hogan merchant of London and
sworne Esquier of her Maiesties person, from her highnesse to Mully
Abdelmelek Emperour of Marocco, and king of Fez and Sus. [1577.]
[page] 156
From manuscript; first printed in *PN* (1589).
[Probably given by Hogan after his return either to Richard
Hakluyt or to his elder cousin.]

16. The letters of the great Turke sent to the Queenes most excellent
Maiestie from Constantinople. [15 March 1579. In text A.H. 987
is misprinted 937.] [page] 163
From manuscript; first printed in *PN* (1589).
In English.
[This probably came to Hakluyt from Richard Staper. It is repre-
sented in P.R.O., S.P. Foreign, Turkey, S.P. 97/1, f. 1 (*Cal. S.P.
For., 1578–9*, pp. 453–4), and in B.M., Cotton MS, Nero B. VIII,
ff. 50–1 (Latin).]

17. The letters of the Queenes Maiestie to the great Turke in answere
of his letters. [25 October 1579.] [page] 164

From manuscript; first printed in *PN* (1589).
Latin and English.
[Represented in P.R.O., S.P. Foreign, Turkey, S.P. 97/1/f. 1 (*Cal S.P. For., 1579–80*, pp. 76–7), and in Cotton MS, Nero B. VIII, f. 51 (Latin).]

18. The large priuileges of the great Turke granted to the English merchants trading in his dominions. [June 1580.]   [pages] 166. 168
From manuscript; first printed in *PN* (1589).
Latin and English.
[This may have reached Hakluyt from Richard Staper. It is represented (as of 1 June 1581) in P.R.O., S.P. Foreign, Turkey, S.P. 97/1, ff. 5–8, and Treaty Papers, S.P. 103/72, f. 3. The Turkish firman is Bodleian, Laud MS, Or. 67, ff. 81–5; see p. 185 above. John Sanderson had a copy (B.M., Lansdowne MS 241, ff. 380–2), so copies were probably issued to Levant Company officers on duty in Turkey.]

19. The second letters of her Maiestie to the great Turke, promising a redresse of the disorders of Peter Baker of Ratcliffe committed in the Leuant. [26 June 1581.]   [page] 171
From manuscript; first printed in *PN* (1589).
In English.
[Represented in Latin in P.R.O., S.P. Turkey, S.P. 97/1, f. 16; *Cal. S.P. For., 1581–2*, p. 221.]

20. The letters patents granted by her Maiestie to Sir Edward Osborne, M. Richard Staper, and certaine other merchants of London for their trade into the dominions of the great Turke. [11 September 1581.]   [page] 172
From manuscript; first printed in *PN* (1589).
In English.

21. Her Maiesties commission vnder her great seale to M. William Harebrown, authorizing him her Ambassadour in Turkie. [20 November 1582.]   [page] 176
From manuscript; first printed in *PN* (1589).
Latin and English.

22. The third letters of her Maiestie to the great Turke, in commen-dation of M. Harebrowne. [15 November 1582.]   [page] 183
From manuscript; first printed in *PN* (1589).
Latin and English.

From manuscript; first printed in *PN* (1589).
In English.
[This probably came to Hakluyt from Richard Staper.]

31. A letter of Master Harebrown, written to the foresaid king of
Tripolis, to the same purpose. [15 January 1585.]   [page] 202
From manuscript; first printed in *PN* (1589).
Italian and English.
[From Levant Company archives?]

32. A note of the yeerely totall summe allowed by the great Turke,
out of his treasurie, to the officers of his Seraglio or Court.   [page] 203
From manuscript; first printed in *PN* (1589).

33. The Great Turke his chiefe officers.   [page] 205
From manuscript; first printed in *PN* (1589).
No. 32 continued.

34. The Great Turkes yeerely reuenue.   [page] 206
From manuscript; first printed in *PN* (1589).
No. 32 continued.

35. The allowance of the Great Turke to Christian Ambassadors,
resident at Constantinople.   [page] 207
From manuscript; first printed in *PN* (1589).
No. 32 continued.

36. A letter of the Queenes Maiestie, written to Yeladin el Kubar,
king of Cambaia. [February 1583.]
From manuscript; first printed in *PN* (1589).
In English.

37. A letter written by her Maiestie, to the king of China. [February
1583.]   [page] 207
From manuscript; first printed in *PN* (1589).
In English.

38. A letter of Iohn Newberie, written from Aleppo in Syria, to
Richard Hakluyt of Oxford. [28 May 1583.]   [page] 208
From Hakluyt's own collection; first printed in *PN* (1589).

39. A letter of Iohn Newberie, written to Leonard Poore of London,
from Aleppo. [29 May 1583.]   [page] 208
From manuscript; first printed in *PN* (1589).
[Hakluyt probably collected nos. 39, 40, 41, 42, and 43 from the

recipients. He did not succeed in obtaining Newbery's to —,
from Baghdad, 15 July 1583, and Basra, 15 August 1583, now
represented in B.M., Lansdowne MS 241, ff. 388v–389, or Newbery to Walsingham, 30 May 1583, P.R.O., S.P. 97/1, 28, *Cal.
S.P. For. 1583*, p. 371.]

48. The description of the Island of Sancta Helena, frequented by
the Portingals, in their returne from the East India. [page] 222
From manuscript; first printed in *PN* (1589).
[A section of no. 47 above.]

49. The valiant fight performed in the voyage from Turkie, by 5.
ships of London, against 11. gallies, and two frigats of the king of
Spaines at Pantalarea in the Leuant. [1586.] [page] 227
[Probably based on a lost news pamphlet, see pp. 345–6 above,
where it appears as 'The voyage of Edward Wilkinson'.]

50. The letters patents granted by her Maiestie to certaine noble men,
and marchants of London, for a trade to Barbarie. [5 July 1585.] [page] 234
From manuscript; first printed in *PN* (1589).
[Enrolled, P.R.O., Patent Roll 27 Eliz., pt. 13, C. 66/1266.]

51. The ambassage of Henrie Roberts, sworne Esquire of her
Maiesties person, from her Highnes to Mully Hamet, Emperour of
Marocco, king of Fes and Sus. [1585–9.] [page] 237
From manuscript; first printed in *PN* (1589).
[Possibly given by Roberts to Hakluyt on his return.]

52. The edict of the Emperour of Marocco [Mouley Ahmed
El-Mansour] in fauour of all English men trading in his dominions.
[10/17 March 1588.] [page] 231 [*recte* 237]
From manuscript; first printed in *PN* (1589).
Spanish and English.
[Probably obtained from Richard Staper. For the date see H. de
Castries, *Les sources inédites de l'histoire du Maroc* (1ᵉ. série: Angle-
terre), I (1918), 490–1.]

53. A letter of the said Emperour [Mouley Ahmed El-Mansour]
written to the Earle of Lecester. [11/21 August 1588.] [page] 238
From manuscript; first printed in *PN* (1589).
Spanish and English.
[Possibly obtained from Richard Staper. For the date see H. de
Castries, *Sources inédites pour l'histoire du Maroc*, I (1918), 506–7.]

54. A letter of the Queenes Maiestie, written to the said Emperour of
Marocco. [20 July 1587.] [page] 238
From manuscript; first printed in *PN* (1589).
Spanish and English.
[Possibly obtained from Richard Staper.]

55. The letters patents granted by her Maiestie, to certaine marchants of Exceter, and others of the West parts, and of London, for a trade to the riuers of Senega, and Gambia in Guinie. [3 May 1588.]
[page] 241 [*recte* 240]
From manuscript; first printed in *PN* (1589).
[Enrolled, P.R.O., Patent Roll 30 Eliz., pt. 9, C66/1312.]

[C]   *The voyages of the second part made to the North and Northeast quarters.*

1. The voyage of Arthur king of Britaine to Island, and the most northeasterne partes of Europa. Anno. 517.   Pag. 243. 244
From Geoffrey of Monmouth, in Jerome Commelin, ed., *Rerum Britannicarum...scriptores* (Heidelberg, 1587), conflated from pp. 67, 69, 70, 73.
Latin and English.

2. The voyage of Malgo king of Britaine, to Island, Gotland, Orkney, Denmarke and Norway. An. 580.   [page] 244
From Geoffrey of Monmouth, in Commelin, *Rerum Britannicarum...scriptores* (Heidelberg, 1587), p. 84.
Latin and English.

3. The voyage of king Edgar with 4000. ships round about his large Monarchie. Anno 973.   [page] 245
From John Dee, *General and rare memorials pertayning to the perfect arte of nauigation* (London, 1577), pp. 54–60.

4. The voyage of Nicholaus de Linna a Franciscan Frier, and an excellent Mathematician of Oxford, to all the regions situate vnder the North pole. An. 1360.   [page] 248
Inscription from Gerard Mercator, *World Map* (1569).
Latin and English.

5. The voyage of Sir Hugh Willoughbie knight wherein he vnfortunately perished at Arzina reca in Lapland. An. 1553   [page] 265
From manuscript; first printed in *PN* (1589).
[Represented in B.M., Cotton MS, Otho E. VIII, ff. 11–16v. Hakluyt apparently printed it from this manuscript, but it is not known in whose possession it then was.]

6. The voyage of Richard Chanceler Pilot Maior the first discouerer by sea of the kingdome of Moscouia. An. 1553.   [page] 280

13. The Letters of the Emperour of Russia sent to king Edward the sixt, by Richard Chanceler. [page] 292
    From manuscript; first printed in *PN* (1589).
    In English.
    [Copies in English are in B.M., Cotton MS, Otho E. VIII, ff. 49–50; Lansdowne MS 141, f. 342.]

14. The coynes, weights, and measures vsed in Russia. [By John Hasse.] [page] 293
    From manuscript; first printed in *PN* (1589).
    [From Muscovy Company archives?]

15. The commission giuen to the Marchants Agents, resiant in Russia. [page] 295
    From manuscript; first published in *PN* (1589).
    [From Muscovy Company archives?]

16. The othe ministred to the seruants of the Moscouie company. [page] 299
    Continuation of no. 15.

17. The Letter of George Killingworth the first Agent in Russia, written to the companie. [page] 299
    From manuscript; first printed in *PN* (1589).
    [From Muscovy Company archives?]

18. The first Priuileges graunted by the Emperour of Russia to the English marchants. [page] 302
    From manuscript; first printed in *PN* (1589).
    [From Muscovy Company archives?]

19. The Charter of the marchants of the Moscouia companie, graunted by Queene Marie. [page] 304
    From manuscript; first printed in *PN* (1589).
    [Represented in B.M., Cotton MS, Otho E. VIII, ff. 49–50; Lansdowne MS 141, ff. 263–72; enrolled P.R.O., Patent Roll, 1 and 2 Philip and Mary, pt. 3, C. 66/883, m. 31; *Cal. P.R., 1554–5*, pp. 55–60.]

20. Instructions giuen to the Pursers of the Moscouie voyages. [1556.] [page] 309
    From manuscript; first printed in *PN* (1589).
    [From Muscovy Company archives?]

21. A discourse of the honourable receiuing into England of the first Ambassadour from the Emperour of Russia.   [page] 321
From manuscript; first printed in *PN* (1589).
[Authenticated by the notary John Incent, to whom it has some, times been attributed. J. Hamel, *England and Russia* (1854), p. 12, attributed it to Robert Best, who had qualifications as an inter, preter. This was accepted by E. D. Morgan and C. H. Coote, *Early voyages and travels to Russia and Persia*, II (1886), 355, and has often been adopted subsequently, e.g. by A. Cross, *Russia under western eyes, 1517–1825* (1971), p. 381. The document was signed by a number of leading members of the Muscovy Com, pany.]

22. The description of Russia with the customes and maners of the Inhabitants.   [page] 339
A continuation of no. 21.

23. The letters of the Queenes Maiestie written to the Emperour of Russia, requesting licence and safe conduct for Anthonie Ienkinson to passe through his Dominions into Persia. [25 April 1561.]   [page] 359
From manuscript; first printed in *PN* (1589).
Latin and English.
[Represented, in Latin, in the Queen's register of Latin letters, 1558–68, B.M., Royal MS, 13. B. I, f. 47.]

24. The letter of the Queenes Maiestie to the great Sophie of Persia, sent by Anthonie Ienkinson. [25 April 1561.]   [page] 361
From manuscript; first printed in *PN* (1589).
Latin and English.
[The letter of 25 April 1561 to Tahmasp I, Sophi of Persia, is represented in both languages in the Queen's register of Latin letters, 1558–68, B.M., Royal MS, 13. B. I, f. 49.]

25. The priuileges giuen by Obdolowcan king of Hircania, to the companie of English marchants trading in Russia obteined by Anthonie Ienkinson. [1563.]   [page] 374
From manuscript; first printed in *PN* (1589).

26. Certaine letters of Arthur Edwards written out of Russia, Media, and Persia, to the companie of Moscouie marchants in London. [1565–7.]   [pages] 376. 377. 380. 384
Pp. 367, 377, 380 are from manuscript, first printed in *PN* (1589):

p. 384 is printed in part in Richard Willes, *The history of trauayle in the west and east Indies* (1577), ff. 322v–333.

27. The distances of diuers places in Russia. [page] 385
From manuscript; first printed in *PN* (1589).
[From Arthur Edwards or Muscovy Company archives.]

28. The way and distances from Saint Nicholas in Russia to the Caspian Sea. [page] 386
From manuscript; first printed in *PN* (1589).
[As no. 27 above.]

29. Notes and obseruations gathered by Richard Iohnson of the seuerall wayes from Russia to Cathay ouer land. [page] 388
From manuscript; first printed in *PN* (1589).
[Largely from Muscovy Company archives?]

30. An Act for the Corporation of marchants Aduenturers for the discouering of newe trades, made in the eight yeere of the Queenes Maiestie. [page] 397
As a private act it does not appear in *Statutes of the Realm*. It was published as 'An Act made 8 Eliz for the Corporacion of Marchants adventurers for the discouerie of newe Trades of the Muscouy company, printed in folio' in 1566. No copy is known to survive. [W. A. Jackson, 'Humphrey Dyson's library' in BSA, *Papers*, XLIII (1949), 285.]

31. The priuileges graunted by the Emperour of Russia to the English marchants obteined by Anthonie Ienkinson. [22 September 1567.] [page] 397
From manuscript; first printed in *PN* (1589).
[Hakluyt may have obtained this from Jenkinson. Represented in B.M., Lansdowne MS 141, ff. 273–8 (and see *Cal. S.P. Dom., 1547–80*, p. 229), but this was not written until *c.* 1610.]

32. The Ambassage of Thomas Randolfe Esquire from the Queenes Maiestie to the Emperour of Russia. [1568.] [page] 399
From manuscript; first printed in *PN* (1589).
[This may possibly have reached Hakluyt from Lord Burghley.]

33. The priuileges graunted to the English marchants at M. Randolfe his sute. [1569.] [page] 402
From manuscript; first printed in *PN* (1589).

[Represented in B.M., Lansdowne MS 141, ff. 278–84v, but this was not written until *c.* 1610.]

34. A commission graunted by M. Randolfe for a discouerie to the Northeast by Sea. [1 August 1568, but '1588' in text.]   [page] 406
   From manuscript; first printed in *PN* (1589).
   [Represented in B.M., Lansdowne MS 10, ff. 132–2v.]

35. Instructions giuen to the discouerers in that action. ['Necessarie notes']   [page] 407
   A continuation of no. 34. [Also represented in Lansdowne MS 10, ff. 133–4v.]

36. Certaine letters in verse writ out of Moscouia by George Tur⸗ beruill, Secretarie to M. Randolfe, touching the state of the countrey and manners of the people.   [pages] 408 409.
   From George Turberville, *Tragical tales* (London, 1587); appended as 'Epitaphes and Sonnettes'.

37. Notes concerning the fourth English voyage into Persia.   [page] 416
   From Richard Willes, *The history of trauayle in the west and east Indies* (1577), ff. 333–6.

38. Obseruations of the Sophie of Persia, and of the religion of the Persians. [By Geffrey Ducket.]   [page] 422
   From Richard Willes, *The history of trauayle in the west and east Indies* (1577), ff. 324v–328v.
   [Closely related is Ducket's 'A Resolution of serten demawndes towching the passage owt of the Cuntrye of Russia into Persia, with sum notes of that cuntry and the maners of the people there', B.M., Additional MS 48151, ff. 169–74v.]

39. The Ambassage of Anthonie Ienkinson from the Queenes Maiestie to the Emperour of Russia in the yeere 1571.   [page] 426
   From manuscript; first printed in *PN* (1589).
   [Represented in B.M., Lansdowne MS 100, ff. 112–125v, a longer version.]

40. A briefe rehearsall of all the trauailes of Anthonie Ienkinson.   [page] 436
   From manuscript; first printed in *PN* (1589).
   [This may have been written by Jenkinson for either of the Richard Hakluyts.]

41. A note of all the necessarie instruments and appurtenances belonging to the killing of the Whale. [page] 437
From manuscript; first printed in *PN* (1589).
[A short note, appended to the list, was given by William Borough to Hakluyt.]

42. The deposition of William Burrowgh to certain interrogatories mooued vnto him concerning the Narue and Kegor. [23 June 1576.] [page] 438
From manuscript; first printed in *PN* (1589).
[Probably given by Borough to Hakluyt. The deposition made in the course of a dispute between the Muscovy Company and Alderman William Bond, over trading by the latter to Narva, the matter being taken to the Privy Council and Bond imprisoned. See T. S. Willan, *The Muscovy merchants of 1555* (1953), p. 81.]

43. The reasons of William Burrowgh, to diswade the vse of a trade to the Narue by way through Sweden. [page] 439
From manuscript; first printed in *PN* (1589).
[Probably given by Borough to Hakluyt.]

44. The latitudes and Meridian altitudes of diuers places in Russia from the North to the South. [page] 453
From manuscript; first printed in *PN* (1589).
[Appended to no. A. 20 above, this also apparently came to Hakluyt from William Borough.]

45. Directions giuen by Richard Hakluyt Esquire to Morgan Hubblethorne Dyer, sent into Persia. [1579.] [page] 454
From manuscript; first printed in *PN* (1589).
[Given by Richard Hakluyt, lawyer, to his cousin for publication.]

46. A commission giuen by Sir Rowland Hayward Knight, and George Barne Aldermen, and Gouernour of the Moscouie com/panie, to Arthur Pet, and Charles Iackman, for the discouerie by Sea towards Cathay. [1580.] [page] 455
From manuscript; first printed in *PN* (1589).
[From Muscovy Company archives?]

47. Rules, and orders giuen to be obserued by them in that dis/couerie. [By William Borough.] [page] 458
From manuscript; first printed in *PN* (1589).
[Probably given to Hakluyt by Borough.]

48. Breefe aduises giuen them by M. Iohn Dee, to that purpose.

[page] 459

From manuscript; first printed in *PN* (1859).
[Represented in B.M., Lansdowne MS 122, ff. 29–30v, and B.M., Cotton MS Otho E. VIII, ff. 79–80.]

49. Instructions giuen them by Richard Hakluit Esquire to that purpose also. [page] 460

Reprinted from *DV* (1852), sig. ²H1–²I4, described as 'Notes in writing, besides more priuie by mouth, that were giuen by a Gentleman, Anno 1580. to M. Arthure Pette and to M. Charles Iackman...' Their author is now identified as 'M. Richard Hakluyt, of Eiton in the countie of Hereford, Esquire.'

50. A Iornall of their discouerie written by Nicholas Chaunceller.

[page] 476

From manuscript; first printed in *PN* (1589).
[Represented in B.M., Cotton MS, Otho E. VIII, ff. 68–78.]

51. The letter of Gerrardus Mercator, to Richard Hakluyt of Oxeford touching that discouerie. [28 July 1580.] [page] 483

From manuscript; first printed in *PN* (1589).
Latin and English. [No other text is known.]

52. The opinion of William Burrough sent to a friend requiring his iudgement, for the fittest time of the departure of our ships towardes Saint Nicholas in Russia. [page] 487

From manuscript; first printed in *PN* (1589).
[Probably given to Hakluyt by William Borough.]

53. The Queenes Maiesties Commission giuen to Sir Ierom Bowes, authorising him her highnesses Ambassador with the Emperour of Moscouia. [4 June 1588.] [page] 487

From manuscript; first printed in *PN* (1589).
Latin and English.
[Represented in P.R.O., State Papers, Foreign, Russia, S.P. 91/1, ff. 6–15.]

54. The Queenes Maiesties letters written to the Emperour by Sir Ierom Bowes, in his commendation. [19 June 1588.] [page] 489

From manuscript; first printed in *PN* (1589).
Latin and English.

55. The discourse of the Ambassage of Sir Ierom Bowes, to the foresayd Emperour. [page] 491
From manuscript; first printed in *PN* (1589).
[State I, pp. 491–505, was withdrawn and cancelled: it was replaced by State II, pp. 491–501. See above p. 000, and Quinn and Skelton, edd., *PN* (1589), I (1965), xxiii–iv.]

56. The manner of preferring of sutes in Russia. [page] 490
From manuscript; first printed in *PN* (1589).
[From Muscovy Company archives?]

57. A letter of Henry Lane, to William Sanderson marchant of London, contayning a briefe discourse of all things passed in our Northerne discoueries for the space of 33. yeres. [Between 1583 and 1589.] [page] 500 [*recte* 496]
From manuscript; first printed in *PN* (1589).
[Presumably given by William Sanderson to Hakluyt. Lane records that he has already 'lent out to others. . copies of mine old letters to content one that meant to please many'. The person was probably Hakluyt, and Lane, consequently, is one source for his Muscovy Company materials.]

58. The late Ambassage of Giles Fletcher Doctor of the Ciuil laws from her Maiestie to the Emperour of Russia. [1588.] [page] 502 [*recte* 498]
From manuscript; first printed in *PN* (1589).
[A summary of Fletcher's achievement and a list of the chapters of the first version of his still unpublished 'Of the Russe common wealth'. Hakluyt may, possibly, have received these from Fletcher himself.]

59. The most solemne and magnificent Coronation of Pheodore Iuanowich the New Emperour of Russia obserued by Ierom Horsey. [page] 819
From manuscript; first printed in *PN* (1589).
[Directly from Horsey or from Muscovy Company archives?]

60. The priuiledges graunted by the newe Emperour to the English marchants, and obtained by the foresaid Ierom Horsey. [1586.] [page] 823
From manuscript; first printed in *PN* (1589).
[Directly from Horsey or from Muscovy Company archives?]

61. The honorable testimonies of diuers strangers, touching the notable discoueries of the English made in the Northeast parts.

[page] 504

(a) Reprinted from G. B. Ramusio, *Delle navigationi et viaggi*, II (Venice, 1582), f. 17v.
Italian and English.

(b) Gerald Mercator, *World Map* (1569).
Latin and English.

(c) J. Osorio da Fonseca, *De rebus Emmanuelis Lusitaniae regis* (Cologne, 1574)
[Hakluyt says that the passage was taken from Johannes Metellus Sequanus (Jean Metal), who wrote a dedicatory epistle to this edition. It would fit in with his general survey of European expansion which he includes but it is not to be found in the copies in B.M. and Bodl. It may be that it was cancelled at some stage in the book's history.]
Latin and English.

[E] *The voyages of the third and last part, made to the West, Southwest and Northwest regions.*

1. The voyage of Madoc the sonne of Owen Gwinned prince of Northwales to the West Indies. Anno. 1170.   Pagina 506.
From David Powell, ed., Caradoc of Llancarfan, *The historie of Cambria* (1584), pp. 227–9.

2. The voyage of Sebastian Cabot, borne in the citie of Bristol, wherein hee discouered a mightie tracte of land from the circle Arctike to Florida. An. 1494.   [page] 512.
From Giovanni Baptista Ramusio, *Delle navigationi et viaggi*, I (1550), ff. 398–403. Reprinted from Richard Eden, *The decades of the newe worlde or west India* (1555), pp. 255–6.

3. The voyage of Sir Thomas Pert knight, and Sebastian Cabot to Brasil, Saint Domingo, and Saint Iohn de Porto Ricco. An. 1516.   [page] 515.
A commentary by Richard Hakluyt based on Richard Eden, *A treatyse of the newe India* (1553); Robert Thorne, 'A declaration of the Indies' (in *DV* (1582)); and G. Fernández de Oviedo, *Historia natural de las Indias* (1526) (from Ramusio, *Delle navigationi et viaggi*).

4. The voyage of the two ships, whereof one was called the *Dominus Vobiscum,* for discouerie of the North partes. An. 1527. [page] 517. Compiled by Richard Hakluyt from Richard Grafton, *A chronicle* (1568), and Edward Hall, *The vnion of...York and Lancaster* (1548); and with reference to Robert Thorne, 'A declaration of the Indies' and 'The booke made...to Doctor Ley,' taken from *DV* (1582).

5. The voyage of Master Hore, and diuers other gentlemen, to New⁄ found land, and Cape Briton. An. 1526. [For 1536.] And in the 28. yere of king Henry the eight. [page] 517.
From manuscript; first printed in *PN* (1589).
[Compiled by Richard Hakluyt from information collected by himself and by his elder cousin.]

6. The voyage made by William Hawkins, father to Sir Iohn Haw⁄ kins to Brasil. Anno 1530. [page] 520.
From manuscript; first printed in *PN* (1589).
[From information supplied by Sir John Hawkins.]

7. The voyage of Sir Iohn Hawkins to the West Indies. An. 1562. [page] 521.
From manuscript; first printed in *PN* (1589).
[Probably written by Hakluyt from information obtained from John Hawkins; see p. 237 above.]

8. The voyage of Roger Bodenham to Saint Iohn de Vllua in the Bay of Mexico. Anno 1564. [page] 522.
From manuscript; first printed in *PN* (1589).
[Possibly given by Bodenham to the younger Hakluyt or to his elder cousin.]

9. The second voyage of Sir Iohn Hawkins to the coast of Guinea first, and then to Noua Hispania. An. 1564. [By John Sparke.] [page] 523.
From manuscript; first printed in *PN* (1589).
[Probably obtained from John Hawkins.]

10. The third voyage of Sir Iohn Hawkins made with the Iesus of Lubecke, one of her Maiesties Ships to the West India. An. 1567. [page] 553.
From John Hawkins, *A true declaration of the troublesome voyage* (1569).

11. The voyage of Dauid Ingram from the bay of Mexico ouer land neere to the Cape Briton. An. 1561. [page] 557.
Reprinted from David Ingram, *A true discourse of the aduentures & trauailes* (1583); no known surviving copy.

12. The voyage of Robert Tomson marchant into Noua Hispania out of Spaine. An. 1555. [page] 580.
From manuscript; first printed in *PN* (1589).
[Apparently obtained from the elder Hakluyt.]

13. The voyage of Iohn Chilton into the West India, with many memorable things concerning the state thereof. An. 1568. [page] 588.
From manuscript; first printed in *PN* (1589).
[Apparently obtained from the elder Hakluyt: represented in B.M., Additional MS 22904, in an expanded form.]

14. The voyage of Sir Francis Drake to Nombre de Dios, and Dariene. An. 1572. [page] 594.
From manuscript; first printed in *PN* (1589).
[Part of the 'Relation' of Lopes Vas, the Portuguese pilot taken by Cumberland's ships in the Plate in 1587, parts of which are given on pp. 595-6 and 673-4 (nos. 15, 21). The document was given in full in the second edition; see pp. 458 below.]

15. The voyage of Iohn Oxnam of Plymmouth to the West India, and ouer the streight of Dariene into the South sea. An. 1575. [page] 595.
[A further instalment of the 'Relation' of Lopes Vas (see nos. 14 and 21).]

16. The first voyage of Sir Martin Frobisher to the North west. An. 1576. [page] 615.
From manuscript; first printed in *PN* (1589).
[Obtained either from Frobisher or Michael Lok.]

17. The second voyage of Sir Martin Frobisher to the same coastes. An. 1577. [page] 622.
Reprinted from Dionyse Settle, *A true reporte of the laste voyage... by Capteine Frobisher* (1577).

18. The third and last voyage of Sir Martin Frobisher, to Meta Incognita. An. 1578. [page] 630.
Reprinted from Thomas Ellis, *A true report of the third and last voyage into Meta Incognita* (1578).

19. The voyage of Christopher Hare, with the Minion of London
to Brasil. An. 1580. [By Thomas Grigges.]   [page] 641.
From manuscript; first printed in *PN* (1589).

20. The voyage of Edward Fenton, and Luke Ward, as farre as
34 degrees of Southerlie latitude. An. 1582. [By Luke Ward.] [page] 647.
From manuscript; first printed in *PN* (1589).

21. The voyage of Iohn Drake, after his separation from Master
Fenton, at the Iland of Sancta Catelina, to the ryver of Plate. An.
1583.   [page] 639. [*recte* 673]
From manuscript; first printed in *PN* (1589).
[Part of the 'Relation' of Lopes Vas. The other parts were given
above pp. 594–6 (nos. 14, 15), see p. 234 above.]

22. The voyage of Sir Humfrie Gilbert knight, to the coastes of
America. An. 1583. [By Edward Hayes.]   [page] 679.
From manuscript; first printed in *PN* (1589).
[Most probably obtained from Hayes, who was closely in touch
with Hakluyt.]

23. The voyage of Philip Amadas, and Arthur Barlowe to Virginia,
at the charge, and direction of Sir Walter Raleigh. An. 1584.   [page] 728.
From manuscript; first printed in *PN* (1589).
[Obtained either from Sir Walter Ralegh or Thomas Harriot.]

24. The voyage of Sir Richard Greenuile to Virginia, for Sir Walter
Raleigh. Anno 1585.   [page] 733.
From manuscript; first printed in *PN* (1589).
[Obtained either from Sir Walter Ralegh or from Thomas Harriot.]

25. The voyage made at the direction of Sir Walter Raleigh, the
third time to Virginia. An. 1586.   [page] 147. [*recte* 747]
From a manuscript compiled by Hakluyt. First printed in *PN*
(1589).

26. The voyage of Edward Stafford, and Iohn White, set out by the
aforesaid Sir Walter Raleigh the fourth time to Virginia. An.
1587.   [page] 764.
From manuscript; first printed in *PN* (1589).
[Probably obtained from John White.]

27. The voyage of Iohn Dauis, for the discouerie of the Northwest
passage. An. 1585.   [page] 776.

From manuscript; first printed in *PN* (1589).
[Obtained either from John Davis or William Sanderson.]

28. The second voyage of Iohn Dauis in the foresaid attempt. An.
1586.   [page] 781.
From manuscript; first printed in *PN* (1589).
[Obtained either from John Davis or William Sanderson.]

29. The voyage of Richard Pope master of the Barke called the
Sunn⁄shine, sent another way for the discouerie of the passage by
Iohn Dauis in his second voyage. An. 1586. [By Henry Morgan.]
                                                                 [page] 787.
From manuscript; first printed in *PN* (1589).
[Obtained either from William Sanderson, whose servant Morgan
was, or from John Davis.]

30. The third voyage of Iohn Dauis in his former enterprise, wherein
hee discouered 200. leagues more to the North⁄west, then master
Frobisher. An. 1587. [By John Janes.]   [page] 789.
From manuscript; first printed in *PN* (1589).
[Obtained either from John Davis or William Sanderson.]

31. The voyage of Robert Withrington, and Christopher Lister, as
farre as 44. degrees to the South of the Equinoctiall, set out by the
right honorable the Earle of Cumberland. An. 1586. [By John
Sarracoll or Saracould.]   [page] 793.
From manuscript; first printed in *PN* (1589).
[Hakluyt had probably access to the original signed copy in B.M.,
Lansdowne MS 100, ff. 30–51 ('This note was coppied out of my
boke by Iⁿᵒ Frost...By me Iⁿᵒ Saracould'). From the published
version Saracould's criticisms of Withrington have been deleted;
see p. 242 above.]

32. The famous voyage of M. Thomas Candish Esquire round about
the globe of the earth, in the space of two yeeres and lesse then two
moneths begunne in the yeere 1586. [By N. H.]   [page] 809.
From manuscript; first printed in *PN* (1589).
[Apparently obtained from Thomas Cavendish. The possibility
that the initials should be M. H. for M[aster Robert] H[ues] is
discussed above, p. 229, though precise information is lacking.]

33 The voyage of William Michelson, and William Mace, with a
ship called the Dogge, to the bay of Mexico. An. 1589.   [page] 817.

From manuscript; first printed in *PN* (1589).
[Apparently obtained from Edward Wilkinson of Tower Hill, London, to whom letters about this matter were directed. See K. R. Andrews, *English privateering voyages*, p. 51, and pp. 237–8 above.

[F]   *The discourses, letters, priuiledges, relations and other materiall circumstances incident to the voyages of the third part.*

1. The offer of the discouerie of the West Indies by Christopher Columbus, to king Henry the seuenth, and the kings acceptation of the offer.   Pag. 507, 508
From Fernando Colon, *Historie del S. D. Fernando Colombo... vita...dell' Ammiraglio D. Christoforo Colombo* (Venice, 1571), ff. 31–31v.
Italian and English.

2. A testimonie of Ferdinando Columbus, touching the same offer.
[page] 509
From Fernando Colon, *Historie del S.D. Fernando Colombe...vita ...dell' Ammiraglio D. Christoforo Colombo* (Venice, 1571), f. 120v.
Italian and English.

3. The letters patents of King Henry the seuenth, graunted vnto Iohn Cabot, and his 3. sonnes, Lewes, Sebastian, and Santius, for the discouerie of newe lands. [5 March 1496.]   [page] 509
Reprinted from *DV* (1582).
Latin and English.

4. A record of the Rolles touching the voyage of Iohn Cabot, and Sebastian his sonne. [3 February 1498.]   [page] 511
First printed in *PN* (1589); from a Privy Seal Docquet Book, apparently no longer extant.
[The warrant is P.R.O. Warrants for the Issue of the Great Seal, C.82/173, Feb. 13 Henry VII; see Williamson, *Cabot voyages* (1962), 226–7.]

5. A testimonie of Sebastian Cabot his discouerie of the West India, in his mappe cut by Clement Adams, and to be seen in her Maiesties priuie gallerie at Westminster.   [page] 511
Legend from the reprint of the Cabot map of 1544, 'sett out' in London by Clement Adams, apparently in 1549, of which no copy survives.

6. A testimonie of Baptista Ramusius, Secretarie to the estate of
Venice, touching Sebastian Cabot.   [page] 513
Reprinted from DV (1582).

7. A testimonie of Sebastian Cabot his voyage in the 6. chap. of
the 3. Decade of Peter Martyr of Angleria.   [page] 513
From Richard Hakluyt's edition of Peter Martyr, *De orbe nouo* ...
decades (Paris, 1587), decade 3, ch. 6, pp. 232–3.
Latin and English.

8. The confession of Francis Lopez de Gomara a Spaniard, touching the discouerie of a great part of the West India by the English.
                                                     [page] 514
From Francisco López de Gómara, *La historia de las Indias* (Cara-
goça [Zaragoza], 1552), f. xx. Translated.

9. A record of Robert Fabian in his Chronicle not yet printed, of
Sebastian Cabots first discouerie.   [page] 515
Reprinted from DV (1582): he now states that this manuscript was
in the possession of John Stow.

10. Another record of the said Robert Fabian, concerning 3. Sau-
ages brought into England, and presented to the King by Sebastian
Cabot.   [page] 515
Reprinted from DV (1582) (also from the MS in Stow's possession).

11. The large pension graunted by king Edward the sixt, to Sebastian
Cabot, constituting him graund Pilot of England. [6 January 1549.]
From manuscript; first printed in PN (1589).   [page] 159 [*recte* 519]
Latin and English.
[From P.R.O., Patent Roll 2 Edward VI, part 2, m 32, C 66/809;
see Rymer, *Foedera*, xv (1713), 181; *Cal. P.R. 1547–8*, p. 320.]

12. An acte against the exaction of money or any other thing, by any
officer for licence to traffike into Iseland and New found land, made
in Anno 2. Edward 6.   [page] 521
2 and 3 Edward VI, C 6.

13. The arriuall and curtesie of syr Iohn Hawkins to the distressed
French men in Florida, confessed by Laudoniere the French captaine
in the discourse of his voyage.   [page] 543
Reprinted from René de Laudonnière, *A notable historie containing
foure voyages made by certayne French captaynes vnto Florida* (1587);
translated by R. Hakluyt.

14. A relation of the commodities of Noua Hispania, & the maners of the Inhabitants, written by Henry Hawkes marchant, who liued 5. yeeres in the countrie.   **[page] 545**
> From manuscript; first printed in *PN* (1589).
> [Apparently obtained from the elder Richard Hakluyt.]

15. The relation of Dauid Ingram concerning his trauaile in the countrie of America.   **[page] 557**
> Repeated from no. E. 11 above.

16. The discourse of Miles Philips, one of syr Iohn Hawkins companie, set on shore in the bay of Mexico, concerning the bloodie and most tyrannous cruelties of the Spaniards, vsed against him and his fellowe Englishmen at Mexico.   **[page] 562**
> From manuscript; first printed in *PN* (1589).
> [Probably obtained from Philips after his return to England in February 1582 or February 1583.]

17. The discourse of syr Humfrie Gilbert knight, to prooue a passage by the Northwest to Cathaya, and the East Indies.   **[page] 597**
> Reprinted from Humphrey Gilbert, *A discourse of a discouerie for a new passage to Cataia* (1576).

18. The discourse of Richard Willes to the same purpose. [Namely to prove the existence of a Northwest passage.]   **[page] 610**
> Reprinted from Richard Willes, *The history of trauayle in the West and East Indies* (1577), ff. 230–6.

19. The relation of Thomas Wiars, concerning ye discouerie of a great Iland, situate in 57. degrees of latitude.   **[page] 634 [*recte* 635]**
> From manuscript; first printed in *PN* (1589).
> [Possibly obtained from Frobisher or Michael Lok.]

20. The notes of Richard Hakluyt Esquire, deliuered for instruction to certaine gentlemen of master Frobishers companie.   **[page] 636**
> Reprinted from *DV* (1582) (where it might appear they were contributed by the elder Hakluyt to Sir Humphrey Gilbert's 1578 expedition).

21. A letter written to master Richard Staper merchant of London, by Iohn Whithall, dwelling at Santos in Brasill.   **[page] 638**
> From manuscript; first printed in *PN* (1589).
> [Probably obtained from Staper.]

22. The same letter answered by diuers merchants of London, and sent to him [John Whithall] in the Minion of London.   [page] 640
   From manuscript; first printed in *PN* (1589).
   [Also possibly from Richard Staper.]

   [22a. Not in list of Contents (and not in Index).]
The famous voyage of Sir Francis Drake into the South Sea, and there hence about the whole Globe of the Earth, begun in the yeere of our Lord, 1577.
   [Without pagination; signed Mmm 4-6 [7-9]; printed after com-pletion of the rest of the book.]
   From manuscript, as condensed by Hakluyt; first printed in *PN* (1589).
   [See W. H. Kerr, 'The treatment of Drake's circumnavigation in Hakluyt's "Voyages",' BSA, *Papers*, xxxiv (1940), 281–302; Quinn and Skelton, edd., *PN (1589)*, 1 (1965), xxii–iii, liv–vi.]

23. Instructions giuen by the right honorable the Lords of the Counsel to Edward Fenton, for the orders to be obserued in the voyage recommended vnto him. [9 April 1582.]   [page] 644
   From manuscript; first printed in *PN* (1589).

24. A letter written to Richard Hakluyt Esquire, of the middle temple, by Anthonie Parkhurst, conteyning a true report of the state and commodities of Newe found land. [13 November 1578.]
                                                                    [page] 674
   From manuscript; first printed in *PN* (1589).
   [Given to Richard Hakluyt by his elder cousin.]

25. The letters patents graunted by her Maiestie to syr Humfrie Gilbert knight, for the inhabiting and planting of America. [11 June 1578.]   [page] 677
   From manuscript; first printed in *PN* (1589).
   [Enrolled P.R.O., Patent Roll 21 Eliz., part 4, m., C.66/1178, mm. 8–9.]

26. The letters of Stephanus Parmenius a learned Hungarian, to Richard Hakluyt of Oxford from Newfound land touching the state of that Countrie. [6 August 1583.]   [page] 697
   From manuscript; first printed in *PN* (1589).
   Latin and English.

[See D. B. Quinn and N. M. Cheshire, *The new found land of Stephen Parmenius* (Toronto, 1972), pp. 168–85.]

27. The confession of Richard Clarke of Waymouth Master of the Admiral ship of Sir Humfrey Gilberts fleete, written in excuse of that fault of casting away the ship and men, imputed to his ouersight.

[page] 700

From manuscript; first printed in *PN* (1589).
[Probably obtained from Clarke.]

28. The discourse of Sir George Peccham Knight touching the possession of the Newfound landes taken in the right of the Crowne of England, of her Maiesties lawfull title thereunto, and of the commodities that would insue to this Realme by planting in them.

[page] 701

Reprinted from Sir George Peckham, *A true reporte of the late discoueries of the Newfound Landes* (1583).

29. A letter of Thomas Aldworth Marchant, and then Maior of Bristoll to the right honorable Sir Francis Walsingham, touching a voyage intended for westerne discoueries. [27 March 1583.]   [page] 718
From manuscript; first printed in *PN* (1589).
[Apparently obtained from Walsingham.]

30. The discourse of Master Christopher Carlile to satisfie and incourage our Marchants, and people in general about the action of planting in America.   [page] 718
Reprinted from Christopher Carleill, *A discourse vpon the entended voyage to the hethermoste partes of America* [1583] (represented in John Carter Brown Library), or *A breef and sommarie discourse vppon the entended voyage to the hethermoste partes of America* [1583] (represented in Westminster Chapter Library, CB. 17 (3).)
[Neither edition is in S.T.C.: 'A briefe and summary discourse' is represented in MS in P.R.O., State Papers, Domestic, Elizabeth, S.P. 12/87 and 88; and 'Articles set doune by the Comities' in both P.R.O., C.O.1/1, 1, and B.M., Lansdowne MS 37, ff. 164–5.]

31. The letters Patents granted by the Queenes Maiestie to Sir Walter Raleigh Knight for the discouering, and inhabiting of new Countries, to continue the space of 6. yeres and no more. [25 March 1584.]   [page] 725
From manuscript; first printed in *PN* (1589).

[Hakluyt appears to have been allowed by Ralegh to copy the original. His version has verbal differences from the enrolment on P.R.O., Patent Roll, 26 Eliz., pt. 1, mm. 38–40, C.66/1237. See Quinn, *Roanoke voyages*, 1, 82–9.]

32. An accompt of the particularities of the imployment of the English men left in Virginia vnder the charge and gouernment of Ralfe Lane, written by himselfe. [page] 737
> From manuscript; first printed in *PN* (1589).
> [Probably obtained from either Ralegh or Harriot.]

33. The discourse of Thomas Harriots, touching Virginia. [page] 748
> Reprinted from Thomas Hariot, *A briefe and true report of the new found land of Virginia* (1588).

34. The letters Patents of the Queens Maiestie granted to Adrian Glibert [Gilbert] and others for the search of the northwest passage. [6 February 1584.] [page] 774
> From manuscript; first printed in *PN* (1589).
> [Possibly obtained from John Davis or William Sanderson. Enrolled P.R.O., Patent Roll, 26 Eliz. part 8, C.66/1243.]

35. A letter of Iohn Dauis written to William Sanderson touching his 2. voyage of discouerie. [14 October 1586.] [page] 786
> From manuscript; first printed in *PN* (1589).
> [Probably obtained from William Sanderson.]

36. His [John Davis'] 2. letter written to the foresaid William Sanderson touching the discouerie of his third attempt. [16 September 1587.] [page] 792
> From manuscript; first printed in *PN* (1589).
> [Probably obtained from Sanderson.]

37. The letter of Ralfe Lane written from Virginia to Richard Hakluyt of the Temple, concerning the state thereof. [3 September 1585.] [page] 793
> From manuscript; first printed in *PN* (1589).
> [Obtained from the elder Hakluyt.]

38. A verie exact and perfect description of the distances from place to place from the riuer of Plate till you come to the end of the Streight of Magelan, and againe from the riuer of Plate to Pette Guarras northward. [page] 803

From manuscript; first printed in PN (1589).
[Apparently obtained from Lopes Vas, see p. 456 below.]

39. A letter of Master Thomas Candish to the right honorable the
Lord Chamberlaine touching the successe of his voyage about the
world. [9 September 1588.]   [page] 808
From manuscript; first printed in PN (1589).
[This may have been obtained from Lord Hunsdon, but there
were identical letters to other persons in circulation (and in print
in the Netherlands). It is possible that Hakluyt took it from a
printed broadsheet, a copy of which has not survived.]

40. The names of the Kings or Princes of Iaua at the time of our
Englishmens being there.   [page] 813
From manuscript; first printed in PN (1589).
[Probably obtained from Cavendish.]

41. Certaine wordes of the naturall language of Iaua learned and
obserued by our men there.   [page] 813
From manuscript; first printed in PN (1589).
[Probably obtained from Cavendish.]

42. Certaine notes, and references taken out of the large Mappe of
China brought home by Master Thomas Candish.   [page] 813
Compiled from material supplied by Thomas Cavendish; first
printed in PN (1589).
[For the map see p. 53 above. It is suggested above, p. 220, that
the materials on the map were probably obtained from a Chinese
gazetteer.]

43. An assignment from Sir Walter Raleigh to diuers gentlemen,
and Marchants of London, for continuing the inhabitations of the
English in Virginia. [7 March 1589.]   [page] 815
Probably from Hakluyt's own copy as he was one of the assignees;
first printed in PN (1589).

[44. Not in table of Contents.]
The voyage set foorth by Master Iohn Newton, and Master Iohn
Bird Marchants of London to the kingdome and Citie of Benin in
Africa...in the yeere, 1588.   [page] 818
From manuscript; first printed in PN (1589).
[Reaching Hakluyt shortly before his collection went to press,
this was probably given to him by one of the promoters.]

26

Principal navigations
(1598-1600)

Volume I

[A] *A Catalogue of the Voyages of this first volume, made to the North and Northeast quarters.*

1. The voyage of Arthur K. of Britaine to Island and the most Northeastern parts of Europe, Anno 517.   pag. 1.
Reprinted from *PN* (1589).

2. The voyage of Malgo king of Britaine to Island, Gotland, Orkney, Denmark and Norway, Anno 580.   pag. 3.
Reprinted from *PN* (1589).

3. The conquest of the Isles of Anglesey and Man by Edwin the Saxon king of Northumberland, Anno 624.   [page] 3.
From Bede, 'Ecclesiasticae historiae gentis Anglorum', bk. II, chapters 5, 9, in J. Commelin, ed., *Rerum Britannicarum...scriptores* (Heidelburg, 1587), pp. 179–80, 182–3.
Latin and English.

4. The voyage of Bertus into Ireland, Anno. 684.   [page] 4.
From Bede, bk. IV, chapter 26, in Commelin (1587), p. 245.
Latin and English.

5. The voyage of Octher to the North parts beyond Norway about the yeere 890.   [page] 4.
From Paulus Orosius, *Historia adversum Paganos*, as translated and modified by King Alfred who added sections on Ohthere and Wulfstan.
[Hakluyt apparently used Alfred's text, now B.M., Cotton MS, Tiberius B. 1, ff. 7 *et seq.*, but it is not known either whether it was already in the possession of Robert Bruce Cotton at this time, or whether Hakluyt did the translation from Anglo-Saxon for himself.]

6. The second voyage of Octher into the Sound of Denmarke.   [page] 5.
As no. 5 above.

7. Wolstans Nauigation into the East sea, or the Sound of Denmarke.
[page] 6.
As no. 5 above.

8. The voyage of King Edgar with 4000, shippes round about his
large Monarchie, Anno 973.   [page] 6.
Reprinted from *PN* (1589).

9. The voyage of Edmund and Edward the sonnes of King Edmund
Ironside, into Hungary, Anno 1017.   [page] 9.
From Florentinus Wigorniensis, *Chronicon ex chronicis*, ed. Lord
William Howard (1592), p. 391.
Latin and English.

10. The mariage of the daughter of Harald vnto Ieruslaus duke of
Russia in his owne Countrey, Anno 1067.   [page] 16.
From Saxo, Grammaticus, *Danica historia libris xvi* (Frankfurt,
1576), p. 187.
Translated.

11. The voyage of a certaine Englishman into Tartaria, and from
thence into Poland and Hungary, Anno 1243.   [page] 20.
From Matthew Paris, *Matthaei Paris monachi Albanensis, Angli
historia maior*, ed. Matthew Parker (1571), pp. 818–21. [Lumley
no. 1322.]
Translated.

12. The long and wonderfull voyage of Frier Iohn de Plano Carpini,
Anno 1246.   [pages] 21, 37, 53.
Transcribed and translated by Hakluyt in Lord Lumley's library
from what is now B.M., Royal MS 13. A XIV, ff. 198–212 (Ch.
i–viii of the 'Historia Mongalorum').
Latin and English.

13. The iournall of Frier William de Rubricis, Anno 1253.
[pages] 71, 93.
Transcribed and translated by Hakluyt in Lord Lumley's library
from what is now B.M., Royal MS 14. C. XIII, ff. 225–36.
Latin and English.

14. The voyage of Nicolaus de Linna a Franciscan Frier, and an

excellent Mathematician of Oxford to all the Regions situate
vnder the North-pole, Anno 1360.   [page] 121.
  Reprinted from *PN* (1589).

15. The voyage of Henry Earle of Derby, afterward King of England,
into Prussia and Letto, Anno 1390.   [page] 122.
  From Thomas Walsingham, *Historia breuis* (1574), p. 377. [Lumley
  no. 1479.]
  Latin and English.

16. The voyage of Thomas of Woodstock duke of Glocester into
Prussia, Anno 1391.   [page] 123.
  From Thomas Walsingham, *Historia breuis* (1574), p. 379.
  Latin and English.

17. The voyage of sir Hugh Willoughby knight, wherein he
vnfortunately perished at Arzina Reca in Lapland, Anno 1553.
                                        [page] 232. [*recte* 231]
  Reprinted from *PN* (1589).

18. The voyage of Richard Chanceller Pilote maior, the first discouerer by sea of the kingdome of Moscouia, Anno 1553. [pages] 237, 243.
  Reprinted from *PN* (1589).

19. The voyage of Stephen Burrough toward the Riuer of Ob,
intending the discouery of the Northeast passage, Anno 1556. [page] 274.
  Reprinted from *PN* (1589).

20. The landing of Richard Iohnson among the Samoeds, Anno
1556.   [page] 283.
  From manuscript. First printed in *PN*, 1 (1598).
  [From Muscovy Company archives?]

21. The voyage of the aforesaide Stephen Burrough from Colmogro
in Russia to Wardhouse, in search of certaine English ships not
heard-of the yeere before, Anno 1557.   [page] 290.
  Reprinted from *PN* (1589).

22. The voyage of M. Anthony Ienkinson into Russia, wherein
Osep Napea, first Ambassadour from the Emperour of Moscouia to
Queene Mary, was transported into his Countrey, Anno 1557.
                                              [pages] 301, 314.
  Reprinted from *PN* (1589).

23. The voyage of M. Anthony Ienkinson from the Citie of Mosco in Russia to Boghar in Bactria, Anno 1558.   [page] 324.
Reprinted from *PN* (1589).

24. The voyage of M. Anthony Ienkinson through Russia, and ouer the Caspian sea into Persia, Anno 1561.   [page] 343.
Reprinted from *PN* (1589).

25. The voyage of Thomas Alcock, George Wrenne, and Richard Cheyney, seruants vnto the Company of Moscouy Merchants in London, into Persia, Anno 1563.   [page] 353.
Reprinted from *PN* (1589).

26. The voyage of Richard Iohnson, Alexander Kitchin, and Arthur Edwards seruants to the foresaid company into Persia, Anno 1565.   [page] 354.
Reprinted from *PN* (1589).

27. The voyage of Thomas Southam and Iohn Sparke by land and riuer from Colmogro to Nouogrod in Russia, Anno 1566.   [page] 365.
Reprinted from *PN* (1589).

28. The voyage of M. Anthony Ienkinson into Russia the third time, Anno 1566.   [page] 372.
Reprinted from *PN* (1589).

29. The voyage of Arthur Edwards Agent for the Moscouy company, Iohn Sparke, Laurence Chapman, Christopher Faucet, and Richard Pingle, seruants, into Persia, Anno 1568.   [page] 389.
Reprinted from *PN* (1589).

30. The voyage of Thomas Banister and Geffrey Ducket, Agents for the Moscouy Company, into Persia the fift time, Anno 1569.
[page] 394.
Reprinted from *PN* (1589).

31. The voyage of William Burrough Captaine of 13. English ships to the Narue in Liefland, Anno 1570.   [page] 401.
Reprinted from *PN* (1589).

32. The voyage of M. Anthony Ienkinson into Russia the fourth time, Anno 1571.   [page] 402.
Reprinted from *PN* (1589).

33. The voyage of Christopher Burrough into Persia the sixt time, Anno 1579.   [page] 419.
Reprinted from *PN* (1589).

34. The voyage of Arthur Pet and Charles Iackman, sent to discouer the Northeast seas beyond the Iland of Vaigats, Anno 1580.   [page] 445.
Reprinted from *PN* (1589).

35. The voyage of Master Ierome Horsey ouer land from Mosco in Russia to England, Anno 1584.   [pages] 469, 470.
Reprinted from *PN* (1589).

36. A voyage to the Northeast, performed by certaine Russes, and translated out of Sigismundus ab Herberstein.   [page] 492.
From Siegmund von Herbertstein, *Rerum Muscouitarum commentarii* (Basel, 1571), ff. 65 (Rizam), 69v–70 (Rizam), 80–84, 86–90.
Translated.

37. A voyage to Sibier and the Riuer of Ob, by land, declared in a letter written to Gerardus Mercator.   [pages] 510, 511, & 512.
From manuscript. First printed in *PN*, 1 (1958). [See also B. 148, p. 402 below.]
Latin and English.
[It is not known how Hakluyt obtained this letter: no other text is known. See M. van Durme, *Correspondance Mercatorienne* (1959), p. 164.]

38. The vanquishing of the Spanish Armada, Anno 1588.   [page] 591.
From Emanuel van Meteren, *Historia Belgica* (Cologne, Arnold Mylius?, 1597?), or *Idem* (Antwerp, n.d.), pp. 470–85.
English translation from the Latin.
[Though it is possible this came from one of the German editions of 1596, 1597 or 1598, it may well be that van Meteren supplied it directly to Hakluyt, in advance of the Latin edition, for him to translate. See John Parker, *Van Meteren's Virginia, 1607–12* (Minneapolis, 1961), pp. 12–17, 87–8.]

39. The honourable voyage to Cadiz, Anno 1596.   [page] 607.
From manuscript. First printed in *PN*, 1 (1598).
For its attempted suppression about September 1599, see p. 312 above.
[Abbreviated, apparently by Hakluyt himself, from the narrative

by Dr Roger Marbecke, the original of which is B.M., Sloane MS 226. It bears a close resemblance to 'A Breife & a true discourse of the late honorable voyage vnto Spaine & of the wynning, Sackinge & burning of the famous towne of Cadiz...' in Stowe MS 159, ff. 353–69v. Another closely associated version is Bodl., Rawlinson MS D. 124, ff. 1–29. See J. Corbett, *The successors of Drake* (1900), pp. 440, 442–4.]

[B] *The Ambassages, Treatises, Priuiledges, Letters, and other obseruations, depending vpon the Voyages of this first Volume.*

1. Two testimonies of Galfridus Monumetensis in his history of the Kings of Brittaine, concerning the conquests of King Arther.

pagina. 1.

Reprinted from *PN* (1589).

2. A testimony of M. Lombard in his 'Αρχαιονομία, touching the right and appendances of the Crowne of the king of Britaine.   pag. 2.
Reprinted from *PN* (1589).

3. A Chronicle of the Kings of Man, taken out of M. Camdens Chorographie.   [page] 10.
From William Camden, *Britannia* (1594), pp. 685–96. [Lumley no. 1167.]
Translated.

4. The ancient state of the shipping of the Cinque Ports.   [page] 17.
From William Lambard, *Perambulation of Kent* (1596), pp. 114–24.

5. Libellus historicus Iohannis de Plano Carpini.   [page] 21.
Transcribed by Hakluyt in Lord Lumley's library from what is now B.M., Royal MS 13. A. xiv.
Latin and English.

6. Part of the great Charter graunted by King Edward the first, to the Barons of the Cinque Ports. [17 June 1278.]   [page] 117.
[Represented in P.R.O., Charter Roll 6 Edw. I m. 3., C. 53/66; *Cal. Ch. R. 1257–1300*, p. 209.]
Translated.

7. The rolle of the huge Fleete of Edward the thirde before Caleis.
[page] 118.
Hakluyt claims to have obtained this from the account of William

Norwel, keeper of the wardrobe, 21 April, 18 Edward III to 24
November, 21° [1344–7].
[This account of William de Northwell is not now among
Exchequer Accounts Various (E.101) in P.R.O.]
Translated.

8. The summe of expences layde out in the siege of Caleis.   [page] 121.
Continuation of no. 7.

9. A note of Thomas Walsingham touching King Edward the
thirde his huge Fleete of 1100. ships, wherewith he passed ouer vnto
Caleis, Anno, 1359.   [page] 121.
From Thomas Walsingham, *Historia breuis* (1576), p. 166.
Latin and English.

10. Certaine verses of Geffrey Chaucer, concerning the long Voyages,
and valiant exploits of the English knights in his dayes.   [page] 124.
In *The workes of our antient and lerned English poet, Geffrey Chaucer,
newly printed* (1598). Prologue to the Knight's Tale, sig. A2,
The letter of Cupid, f. 329.

11. A testimonie out of Cornelius Tacitus, prouing London to haue
bene a famous Mart-towne in the raigne of Nero the Emperour.
                                                              [page] 124.
From Cornelius Tacitus, *Annales*, bk. xiv.

12. A testimony out of venerable Beda, proouing London to haue
bene a Citie of great traffique in his time.   [page] 125.
In Bede, bk. II, ch. 3, in Commelin, *Rerum Britannicarum...
scriptores* (1587), p. 178. [Lumley 1007 was Louvain, 1566.]
Latin and English.

13. The league betweene Carolus Magnus and Offa King of Mercia,
concerning the safe trade of English Merchants.   [page] 125.
From William of Malmesbury, *De gestis Regum Anglorum*, bk. I,
ch. 4, in Sir Henry Savile, *Rerum Anglicarum scriptores post Bedam*
(1591), f. 17 [with some rearrangement of the material]. [Lumley
952.]
Latin and English.

14. An ancient testimony translated out of the olde Saxon Lawes,
conteyning the aduancement of Merchants, for their thrice crossing
the wide seas.   [page] 126.

From William Lambard, *Perambulation of Kent* (1596), pp. 500–1.

15. A testimony of certaine Priuileges obteined for the English and
Danish Merchants by Canutus the King of England. [page] 126.
From William of Malmesbury, *De gestis Regum Anglorum*, bk.
2, ch. xi (not ix as in text), in Savile, *Rerum Anglicarum scriptores*,
f. 41v.
Latin and English.

16. The flourishing state of Merchandise in the City of London in
the dayes of Wilhelmus Malmesburiensis. [page] 227.
From William of Malmesbury, *De gestis Pontificum Anglorum*, bk.
xxi, in Savile, *Rerum Anglicarum scriptores* (1596), f. 133v.
Latin and English.

17. A testimony of the said Wil, of Malmesbury concerning traffique
to Bristow in his time. [page] 127.
From William of Malmesbury, *De gestis Pontificum Anglorum*, bk.
iv, in Savile, *Rerum Anglicarum scriptores* (1596), f. 161.
Latin and English.

18. The league betweene Henry the second, and Frederick Barborossa
Emperour of Germany, partly touching trade of Merchandise.
[page] 128.
In Otto I, bishop of Frisingen, *De rebus gestis Friderici Imperatoris*,
bk. I, ch. 7, in Christian Wurtisen, *Germaniae historicorum illustrium*
(Frankfurt, 1585), pp. 479–80. [Lumley 1355 was Strasbourg,
1515.]
Latin and English.

19. A generall safe conduct granted by King Iohn to all forreine
Merchants. [page] 129.
Copied by Hakluyt from a record in the Tower of London.
Latin and English.

20. The letters of King Henry the third, vnto Haquinus king of
Norwey. [Haakon V, 1299–1319; 10 October I Henry III, 1217.]
[pages] 129, 130.
From manuscript. First printed in *PN*, I (1598).
Latin and English.
[Enrolled, Patent Roll, 2 Henry III, m.8; *Cal. Patent R.*, *1216–25*,
p. 133; *Diplomatiarum Norwegicum*, XIX, pt. I (1910), ed. A.
Bugge, p. 95.]

21. A mandate for the king of Norway his ship called, The Cog.
[13 Henry III.]   [page] 130.
  From manuscript; first printed in *PN*, 1 (1598).
  Latin and English.
  [Enrolled in Close Roll, 13 Henry III, m. 2; *Cal. Close R.
  1227–31*, p. 218; *Diplomatarium Norwegicum*, XIX, pt. 1 (1910),
  ed. A. Bugge, p. 138.]

22. A Charter granted for the behalfe of the Merchants of Colen, in
the 20. yeere of Henry the thirde. [8 November 1235.]   [page] 131.
  Hakluyt claimed to have copied it from Charter Roll, 18 Edward I.
  Latin and English.
  [Enrolled in P.R.O., Patent Roll, 20 Henry III, C.66/46, m. 14;
  Cal. P.R. 1232–47, p. 130.]

23. The Charter of Lubeck granted for seuen yeeres in the time of
Henry the third. [23 December 1266.]   [pages] 131, 132.
  Latin and English.
  [Enrolled in P.R.O., Patent Roll, 51 Henry III, C.66/85, m.31;
  Cal. P.R. 1266–72, p. 20.]

24. A Charter of the Merchants of Almaine, or the Stilyard,
merchants. [44 Henry III, confirmed 1 and 29 Edward I.]   [page] 132.
  Latin and English.
  [Represented in B.M., Cotton MS, Vespasian B. VIII, ff. 87ff. The
  Confirmation of 7 December 1317 is enrolled in P.R.O., Charter
  Roll, 11 Edward III, C.53/124, m.10; *Cal. Ch. R. 1300–26*,
  p. 371.

25. A mandate of King Edward the first concerning outlandish
Merchants. [3 Edward I.]   [page] 133.
  Latin and English.

26. King Edw. the first his great Charter granted to forreine Mer,
chants, Anno Dom. 1303. [1 February 1303]   [page] 133.
  [Enrolled in P.R.O., Chamber Roll, 31 Edward I, C.53/89, m.4;
  Cal. Ch. R., 1300–26, p. 33.]
  Latin and English.

27. The letters of Edward the second vnto Haquinus King of
Norway, concerning certain English Merchants arrested in Norway.
[16 April 1313.]   [page] 138.

[Enrolled, Close Roll, 6 Edw. II, m.7d.; *Cal. Close R., 1307–13,* p. 576.]
Latin and English.

28. Another letter of Edw. the second vnto the said Haquinus for the merchants aforesaid. [1313.]   [page] 139.
[Enrolled, Close Roll, 6 Edw. II, m.7d., *Cal. Close R., 1307–13,* p. 576.]
Latin and English.

29. A third letter of King Edward the second to the said Haquinus in the behalfe of our English merchants. [3 April 1313.]   [page] 140.
[Enrolled, Close Roll, 6 Edw. II, m.7d., *Cal. Close R., Edw. II, 1307–13,* p. 577; *Diplomatiarum Norwegicum,* XIX, pt.1 (1910), ed. A. Bugge, pp. 607–9.]
Latin and English.

30. An Ordinance for the Staple to be holden at one certaine place. [13 Edward II.]   [pages] 142, 143.
[Represented in B.M., Royal MS 19.A. XIV, ff. 67v–76; and Cotton MS, Nero C.1, f. 72ff. See *Statutes of the realm,* I (1816), 332–43.]
Latin and English.

31. A Catalogue of the great Masters of Prussia.   [page] 144.
In Sebastian Münster, *Cosmographia universalis* (Basel, 1572), ch. 484, pp. 928–32. [Lumley 2498 was Cologne, 1575, and Lumley 2495, Basel, 1582.]
Translated.

32. The Oration or speach of the Ambassadours sent from Conradus de Zolner, Master generall of the land of Prussia, vnto Richard the second, king of England. [1388.]   [page] 148.
From manuscript. First printed in *PN,* I (1598). Represented in B.M., Cotton MS, Nero B. II, ff. 6–7.
[The latter is a collection of transcripts relating to Poland and the Baltic countries, covering 1387–1600. Each page is headed 'Polonia', and some original documents are inserted. Hakluyt is likely to have seen some of the documents from which it was compiled or to have used it before the collection had been completed. If he did use it, and it was already in Cotton's hands, it would be evidence of their collaboration. References to the documenta-

tion of the embassy are in *Diplomatic correspondence of Richard II,* ed. Edouard Perroy (1933), p. 213.]

33. An agreement made by the Ambassadours of England and Prussia, confirmed by king Richard the second. [22 October 1390.] [page] 150.
From manuscript. First printed in *PN,* 1 (1598). [Represented in B.M., Additional MS 48009, pp. 21–5, and Cotton MS, Nero B. II, ff. 8–9v. See *Diplomatic correspondence of Richard II,* ed. E. Perroy (1933), pp. 212–13.]
Translated.

34. The letters of Conradus de Iungingen, Master generall of Prussia, vnto Rich. the second. [22 February 1398.] [page] 153.
From manuscript. First printed in *PN,* 1 (1598).
[Represented in Edinburgh University MS Laing 351, f. 59; see *Diplomatic correspondence of Richard II,* ed. E. Perroy (1933), p. 256; and also in B.M., Additional MS 48009, pp. 319–22.]
Translated.

35. A briefe relation of William Esturmy and Iohn Kington, con-cerning their Ambassages into Prussia and to the Hans-townes. [page] 154.
From manuscript. First printed in *PN,* 1 (1598). [Represented in B.M., Cotton MS, Nero B. II, ff. 58–60 and Additional MS 48009, pp. 194–9.]
Translated.

36. Certaine Articles of complaint exhibited by the Liuonians. [page] 156. [Part of no. 35 above.] Represented in B.M., Additional MS 48009, pp. 200–1.]

37. Other complaints exhibited by the Cities of the Hans. [page] 156. [Also part of no. 35 above, represented in B.M., Additional MS 48009, pp. 201–3.]

38. Compositions and Ordinances concluded betweene the Am-bassadours of Prussia, and the Chanceller and Treasurer of England, Anno 1403. [page] 157.
From manuscript. First printed in *PN,* 1 (1598). [Represented in B.M., Cotton MS, Nero B. II, ff. 15–16, and Additional MS 48009, pp. 233–4.]
Translated.

39. The letters of the Chancellet and Treasurer of England vnto Conradus de Iungingen, master generall of Prussia. [1 June 1404.]

[page] 158.

From manuscript. First printed in PN, 1 (1598).
Translated.

40. The letters of king Henry the fourth vnto Conradus de Iungingen, the master generall of Prussia for entercourse of traffique. [16 July 1404.]

[page] 159.

From manuscript. First printed in PN, 1 (1598). [Represented in B.M., Cotton MS, Nero B. 11, ff. 30–30v. and in Additional MS 48009, pp. 60–3.]
Translated.

41. The letters of Conradus de Iungingen vnto king Henry the fourth. [16 July 1404.]

[page] 160.

From manuscript. First printed in PN, 1 (1598). [Represented in B.M., Cotton MS, Nero B. 11, ff. 31–31v and Additional MS 48009, pp. 62–3.]
Translated.

42. An agreement made betweene king Henry the fourth, and Conradus de Iungingen. [8 October 1405.]

[page] 161.

From manuscript. First printed in PN, 1 (1598). [Represented in Cotton MS, Nero B. 11, ff. 33–5 and Additional MS 48009, pp. 25–31.]
Translated.

43. An agreement betweene king Henry the fourth, and the Hans-townes. [15 December 1405.]

[page] 164.

From manuscript. First printed in PN, 1 (1598). [Represented in Cotton MS, Nero B. 11, ff. 35–7.]
Translated.

44. A testimonie out of Albertus Krantzius concerning the surprise of Bergen in Norway, wherein 21. houses of the English merchants were burnt.

[page] 169

In Albertus Krantz 'Historia rerum gestarum regni Norwagiae' in Alberti Krantzii rerum Germanicarium historici clarissi (Frankfurt, 1580), 2nd numeration, pp. 419–20. [Lumley 939 was Strasbourg, 1546.]
Translated.

From manuscript. First printed in *PN*, I (1598).
Latin and English.
[Enrolled P.R.O., Patent Roll 5 Henry IV, pt. 2, m.17, C.66/371;
Cal. P.R. 1401–5, p. 394.]

52. A note touching the mighty ships of king Henry the fift, taken
out of a Chronicle in the Trinitie Church of Winchester.   [page] 185.
   Latin only.
   [This Hyde Abbey Chronicle has not been identified.]

53. A branch of a Statute made in the eight yeere of Henry the 6,
for the trade to Norway, Sweueland, Denmarke and Finmarke.
[1429–30.]   [page] 186.
   8 Henry VI, c. 2. [See *Statutes of the realm*, II, 239.]

54. Another branch of a Statute made in the 10. yeere of king
   Henry the sixt concerning the state of English merchants in the
   dominions of the king of Denmarke. [1431–2.]   [page] 186.
   10 Henry VI, c. 3. [See *Statutes of the realm*, II, 273.]

55. Libellus de politia conseruatiua Maris. Or, The pollicy of
keeping the Sea.   [page] 187.
   From manuscript. First printed in *PN*, I (1598).
   [It may have been derived from a manuscript then or later in
   Cotton's possession, and perhaps destroyed in 1731. It appears
   also, after Hakluyt's time, to have been quoted by Selden. B.M.,
   Cotton MS, Vitellius E. x, ff. 192–207 (damaged in the 1731 fire),
   is a different version from that used by Hakluyt. See *The libelle
   of Englyshe polycye,* ed. Sir George Warner (Oxford, 1926), pp.
   viii, liv.]

56. A large Charter granted by king Edward the fourth, in the
second yere of his raigne, to the English merchants residing in the
Netherland. [16 April 1462.]   [page] 208.
   From manuscript. First printed in *PN*, I (1598).
   Translated.

57. A perswasion of Robert Thorne merchant of Bristol, and
dwelling long in Siuil in Spaine, to king Henry the eight of noble
memory, to set out and further Discoueries toward the North.   [page] 212.
   Reprinted from *PN* (1589), and *DV* (1582).

58. The discourse of the foresaid Robert Thorne, written to Doctour

Leigh the Kings Ambassadour in Spaine touching that matter.
[page] 214.
Reprinted from *PN* (1589), and *DV* (1582).

59. A briefe treatise of the Emperour of Moscouia his genealogie.
[22 May 1576.] [page] 221.
From 'Magni Moscoviae ducis genealogiae brevis epitome' (probably by Daniel Printz von Buchau), in *Edictum serenissimi Poloniae
regis ad milites* (Cologne, M. Cholinus, 1580), sig. E4v *et seq.*
Identified on p. 164 above.

59a. ¹Epitaphium M. Roberti Thorni, sepulti in Ecclesia Tem-
plariorum Londini. [1519.] [page] 221.
Reprinted from *PN* (1589).

60. The excellent orders and instructions of Sebastian Cabot giuen
to sir Hugh Willoughby and his Fleete in their voyage intended for
Cathay. [9 May 1533.] [page] 226.
Reprinted from *PN* (1589).

61. The names of the twelue Counsellers appointed in sir Hugh
Willoughbies voyage. [page] 230.
Reprinted from *PN* (1589).

62. The letters of king Edward the sixt, written at that time to all
the Kings, Princes, and other Potentates of the Northeast. [14
February 1553.] [page] 230.
Reprinted from *PN* (1589).

63. The names of the Ships, Captains, Mariners, and other officers
of that first worthy enterprise. [page] 232.
Reprinted from *PN* (1589).

64. The othe ministred to the Captaine of the Fleete. [page] 233.
Reprinted from *PN* (1589).

65. The othe ministred to the Masters of the ships. [page] 234.
Reprinted from *PN* (1589).

66. A testimonie of Richard Eden, concerning Clement Adams
his discourse of Richard Chancellers voyage. [page] 242.
Reprinted from *PN* (1589).

¹ Not included in Hakluyt's table of contents.

67. The letters of the Emperour of Russia sent to king Edward the sixt, by Richard Chanceller. [February 1554.]   [page] 255.
  Reprinted from *PN* (1589).

68. The coynes, waights and measures vsed in Russia.   [page] 256.
  [By John Hasse, 1554.]
  Reprinted from *PN* (1589).

69. The letters of King Philip and Queene Mary to Iuan Vasiliuich the Emperor of Russia. [1 April 1555.]   [page] 258.
  From manuscript. First printed in *PN*, I (1598).

70. The Commission giuen to the merchants Agents resiant in Russia.   [page] 259.
  Reprinted from *PN* (1589).

71. The othe ministred to the seruants of the Moscouie company.   [page] 262.
  Reprinted from *PN* (1589).

72. The letter of George Killingworth the first Agent in Russia, written to the Company. [27 November 1557.]   [page] 263.
  Reprinted from *PN* (1589).

73. The first Priuileges graunted by the Emperour of Russia, to the English merchants. [1555.]   [page] 265.
  Reprinted from *PN* (1589).

74. The Charter of the merchants of the Moscouie company granted by Queene Mary. [6 February 1555.]   [page] 267.
  Reprinted from *PN* (1589).

75. Instructions given to the Pursers of the Moscouie voyage. [1556.]
  Reprinted from *PN* (1589).   [page] 273.

76. The strange discourse of Richard Iohnson concerning the Samoeds. [1556.]   [page] 283.
  From manuscript. First printed in *PN*, I (1598).
  [From Muscovy Company archives?]

77. A discourse of the honourable receiuing into England of the first Ambassadour from the Emperour of Russia. [May 1557. Perhaps by Robert Best.]   [page] 285.
  Reprinted from *PN* (1589).

85. Another letter to the aforesaid parties. [5 May 1560.]   [page] 308.
   From manuscript. First printed in *PN*, I (1598).
   [From Lane's personal collections or Muscovy Company archives?]

86. The maner of Iustice by lotts in Russia, written by M. Henry
Lane.   [page] 309.
   From manuscript. First printed in *PN*, I (1598).
   [From Lane's personal collections or Muscovy Company archives?]

87. The description of Russia, with the customes and maners of the
inhabitants. [1557.]   [page] 315. [*recte* 319–323]
   Reprinted from *PN* (1589).

88. Notes and obseruations gathered by Richard Iohnson of the
seuerall wayes from Russia to Cathay ouer-land.   [page] 335.
   Reprinted from *PN* (1589).

89. A letter of Sigismund king of Polonia 1559, vnto the Queenes
most excellent Maiestie. [6 December 1569.]   [page] 337.
   From manuscript. First published in *PN* I (1598).
   Translated.
   [The latter reached Hakluyt from Henry Lane. The correct date is
   6 December 1569. See p. 164 above.]

90. The letters of the Queenes Maiestie written to the Emperour of
Russia, requesting licence and safe-conduct for Anthonie Ienkinson,
to passe through his dominions into Persia. [25 April 1561.]   [page] 338.
   Reprinted from *PN* (1589).

91. The Queenes Maiesties letters to the great Sophie of Persia, sent
by M. Anth. Ienkinson. [25 April 1561.]   [page] 340.
   Reprinted from *PN* (1589).

92. Instructions giuen by the Governours and Assistants of the
Moscouie Company, vnto M. Anthonie Ienkinson [8 May 1561.]
                                                            [page] 341.
   From manuscript. First printed in *PN*, I (1598).
   [From Muscovy Company archives?]

93. The priuileges giuen by Obdoloucan K. of Hircania to the
Company of English merchants trading in Russia, obteined by M.
Anthony Ienkinson.   [page] 352.
   Reprinted from *PN* (1589).

102. The priuileges graunted to the English merchants, at M. Randolfe his sute. [20 June 1569.] [page] 378.
   Reprinted from *PN* (1589).

103. A Commission granted by M. Randolfe for a discouery to the Northeast by sea. [1 August 1568 (1588 in text).] [page] 382.
   Reprinted from *PN* (1589).

104. Instructions giuen to the discouerers for that action. [page] 383.
   A continuation of no. 103 above.

105. Certaine letters in verse, written out of Moscouia, by M. George Turberuile, Secretary to M. Randolfe, touching the state of the Countrey, and maners of the people. [1568.] [page] 384.
   Reprinted from *PN* (1589).

106. Notes concerning the fourth English voyage into Persia. [1568. By Richard Willes.] [page] 392.
   Reprinted from *PN* (1589).

107. Obseruations of the Sophy of Persia, and of the Religion of the Persians. [1568. By Geffrey Ducket.] [page] 397.
   Reprinted from *PN* (1589).

108. A letter of Richard Vscombe to M. Henry Lane touching the burning of the Citie of Mosco by the Crimme Tartar. [5 August 1571.] [page] 402.
   From manuscript. First printed in *PN*, 1 (1598).
   [From Lane's personal collections or Muscovy Company archives?]

109. The Ambassage of M. Anthony Ienkinson from the Queenes Maiestie to the Emperour of Russia, Anno 1571. [26 July 1571–23 July 1572.] [page] 402.
   Reprinted from *PN* (1589).

110. A briefe rehearsall of all the trauiles of M. Anthony Ienkinson. [page] 411.
   Reprinted from *PN* (1589).

111. A letter of James Alday to M. Michael Locke Agent in London for the Moscouie Company touching a trade to be established in Lappia. [1575.] [page] 412.
   From manuscript. First printed in *PN*, 1 (1598).
   [If this came to Hakluyt direct from Lok, it could originally have formed part of his personal collection, or else have come from

Muscovy Company materials in his custody. He could, in the latter case, have been a channel by which certain of these documents reached Hakluyt.]

112. A note of all the necessary instruments and appurtenances belonging to the killing of the Whale. [1575.]   [page] 413.
Reprinted from *PN* (1589).

113. The deposition of William Burrough to certeine Interrogatories mooued vnto him concerning the Narue and Kegor. [23 June 1576.]   [page] 414.
Reprinted from *PN* (1589).

114. The reasons of M. William Burrough to disswade the vse of a trade to the Narue by the way through Sweden.   [page] 416.
Reprinted from *PN* (1589).

115. A remembrance of aduise giuen to the Moscouie merchants, touching a voyage for Cola abouesaid. [1578.]   [page] 416.
Reprinted from *PN* (1589).

116. An Epistle dedicatorie vnto the Queenes most excellent Maiestie written by M. William Burrough.   [page] 417.
[All trace of William Borough's map of Russia has now, it seems, disappeared. It was probably made late in life (he died in 1599), and it is likely that the dedication which Hakluyt printed was from (or intended for) a printed version if, and when, the Queen accepted the dedication. He presumably received it as a manuscript copy from Borough. The epistle is the only record of the map's existence.]

117. The Queenes Maiesties letters to Shaugh Thamas the great Sophy of Persia. [10 June 1579.]   [page] 418.
From manuscript. First printed in *PN*, 1 (1598).
Presumably translated.

118. The Latitudes and Meridian Altitudes of diuers places in Russia, from the North to the South. [By Christopher Borough.]
          [page] 431.
Reprinted from *PN* (1589).
A continuation of no. A 33 above.

119. Directions given by M. Richard Hakluyt Esquire, to Morgan Hubblethorne Dier, sent into Persia. [1579.]   [page] 432.
Reprinted from *PN* (1589).

120. A Commission giuen by sir Rowland Heyward knight, and George Barne Aldermen, and gouernours of the Moscouie Company, to Arthur Pet and Charles Iackman, for the discouery by Sea towards Cathay. [20 May 1580.]   [page] 433.
Reprinted from *PN* (1589).

121. Rules and orders giuen to be obserued by them in that Dis-couery. [By William Borough, 1580.]   [page] 435.
Reprinted from *PN* (1589).

122. Briefe aduises giuen by M. Iohn Dee to that purpose. [1580.]
                                                                [page] 437.
Reprinted from *PN* (1589).

123. Instructions giuen them by Richard Hakluyt Esquire to that purpose also. [1580.]   [pages] 437, 438.
Reprinted from *PN* (1589).

124. The letter of Gerard. Mercator to Richard Hakluyt of Oxford touching that discouery. [28 July 1580.]   [page] 443.
Reprinted from *PN* (1589).

125. Instructions giuen by the Moscouie Company vnto Richard Gibbs, William Biggat, Iohn Backhouse, &c. Masters of their ships. [June 1582.]   [page] 453.
Reprinted from *PN* (1589).

126. The opinion of M. William Burrough, sent to a friend requiring his iudgement for the fittest time of the departure of our ships toward S. Nicolas in Russia. [1582.]   [page] 455.
Reprinted from *PN* (1589).

127. The Queenes Maiesties Commission giuen to sir Ierome Bowes, authorizing him her highnesse Ambassadour with the Emperour of Moscouie. [5 June 1583.]   [page] 455.
Reprinted from *PN* (1589).

128. The Queenes Maiesties letters written to the Emperour by sir Ierome Bowes in his commendation. [19 June 1583.]   [page] 457.
Reprinted from *PN* (1589).

129. The discourse of the Ambassage of sir Ierome Bowes to the aforesaid Emperour. [1583.]   [page] 458.
Reprinted from *PN* (1589).
[Bowes leaves, state 2, see pp. 475–6 below.]

130. The maner of preferring suites in Russia.   [page] 463.
Reprinted from *PN* (1589).

131. A letter of M. Henry Lane to M. William Sanderson merchant
of London, conteyning a briefe discourse of all things passed in our
Northern discoueries for the space of 33. yeeres. [Between 1583 and
1589.]   [page] 464.
Reprinted from *PN* (1589).

132. The most solemne and magnificent Coronation of Pheodor
Iuanowich Emperour of Russia, set downe by M. Ierome Horsey.
[10 June 1584.]   [page] 466.
Reprinted from *PN* (1589).

133. The Priuileges graunted by the newe Emperour, to the English
merchants, and obteined by the foresaid Ierom Horsey. [February
1586–7.]   [page] 470.
Reprinted from *PN* (1589).
[Represented in P.R.O., S.P. Foreign, Russia, S.P. 91/1, ff. 55–8.]

134. The Ambassage of M. Giles Fletcher, Doctor of the Ciuil
lawe, from her Maiestie, to the Emperour of Russia. [1588.]   [page] 473.
Reprinted from *PN* (1589).

135. A notable description of Russia.   [page] 475, &c.
[Giles Fletcher's *Of the Russe common wealth* (1591), S.T.C.
11056, was suppressed not long after its appearance, though a
number of copies have survived. Hakluyt presumably obtained
permission to use such parts of the descriptive matter as he needed
to round off his account of Russia. His action is analysed, though
not clearly understood, in Robert O. Lindsay, 'Richard Hakluyt
and *Of the Russe common wealth*', BSA, *Papers*, LVII (1963),
312–27.]

136. A speciall note gathered by the excellent Venetian Cosmo-
grapher M. Iohn Baptista Ramusius, concerning the Northeast
passage.   [page] 495.
Reprinted from *PN* (1589).
Italian and English.
Interpolated in the extracts from Herberstein no. A. 36, above.

137. The Lord Boris Pheodorowich his letter to the right honourable
William Burghley Lord high Treasurer of England. [July 1591.]
                                                                  [page] 498.

From manuscript. First printed in *PN*, I (1598).
[Extract represented in translation in P.R.O., State Papers, Foreign, Russia, S.P. 91/1, 88. Hakluyt's dating of July 1590 is incorrect.]
Translated.

138. The Queenes Maiesties letter to Pheodor Iuanowich, Emperour of Russia. [14 January 1591/2.]
From manuscript. First printed in *PN*, I (1598).

139. The Queenes Maiesties letters to the Lord Boris Pheodorowich. [14 January 1591/2] [page] 501.
From manuscript. First printed in *PN*, I (1598).

140 The L. Treasurer sir William Cecil his letter to the Lord Boris Pheodorowich. [15 January 1591/2.] [page] 502.
From manuscript. First printed in *PN*, I (1598).

141. A letter of Pheodor Iuanowich to the Queenes Maiestie. [1 January 1592–3]. [page] 502.
From manuscript. First printed in *PN*, I (1598).
[This letter of Fedor Ivanovitch of 1 January 1593, is represented in translations in P.R.O., S.P. Foreign, Russia, S.P. 91/1, 99, and in B.M., Cotton MS, Otho B. VIII, f. 24v. Hakluyt has omitted material critical of Horsey. See p. 165 above.]

142. An other letter to the Queenes most excellent Maiestie from the Lord Boris Pheodorowich. [January 1592.] [page] 503.
From manuscript. First printed in *PN*, I (1598).
[Represented in translation in P.R.O., State Papers, Foreign, Russia, S.P. 91/1, ff. 99–100.]

143. A second letter from the Lord Boris Pheodorowich to the L. William Burghley. [January 1592.] [page] 504.
From manuscript. First printed in *PN*, I (1598).

144. A most gracious letter of Priuileges giuen to the English merchants by Pheodor Iuanowich. [May 1596.] [page] 505.
From manuscript. First printed in *PN*, I (1598).

145. The contents of M. Garlands Commission vnto Thomas Simkinson for the bringing of M. Iohn Dee to the Emperour of Russia his Court. [18 September 1586.] [page] 508.
From manuscript. First printed in *PN*, I (1598).

[Presumably given by John Dee to Hakluyt after his return to England in 1589.]

146. A letter to the right worsh. M. Iohn Dee Esquier, conteyning the summe and effect of M. Garland his message. [17 December 1586.]   [page] 508.
From manuscript. First printed in *PN*, 1 (1598).
[Presumably given by John Dee to Hakluyt with no. 145 above.]

147. A branch of a letter from Iohn Merick touching the death of Pheodor Iuanowich. [14 March 1597.]   [page] 509.
From manuscript. First printed in *PN*, 1 (1598).
[From Muscovy Company archives?]

148. A learned Epistle written vnto the famous Cosmographer M. Gerardus Mercator, concerning the Countreys, Riuers and Seas, towards the Northeast.   [page] 510.
[John Balak to Gerard Mercator 20 February 1581. Already included as no. A. 37 above.]

149. The honourable testimonies of diuers strangers touching the notable discoueries of the English, made in the North-east parts.
                                                                [page] 513.
Reprinted from *PN* (1589).

150. A briefe Commentarie of the true state of Island. [pages] 515. & 550.
From Arngrímr Jónsson (Arngrimus Jonas), *Breuis commentarius de Islandia* (Hafniae, 1593).
[See Purchas, *Pilgrimes*, III (1625), 654. Hakluyt omits two poems which conclude the book and one page of *errata*.]
Latin and English.

151. A letter written by the graue and learned Gudbrandus Thor-lacius, Bishop of Holen in Island, concerning the ancient state of Island and Gronland. [2 July 1595.]   [page] 590.
From manuscript. First printed in *PN*, 1 (1598).
[This letter was given to Hakluyt by its recipient, the Reverend Hugh Branham, incumbent of All Saints, Harwich. He may well have introduced Hakluyt to Jónsson's book, for which Guð-brandur Thorláksson, bishop of Hólar (1542–1627) had written an address to the reader, dated 29 July 1592 (above, p. 307).]

Volume II

[C] *A Catalogue of the English Voyages made by and within the Streight of Gibraltar, to the South and Southeast quarters of the world, conteined in the first part of this second volume.*

Voyages before the Conquest [First numeration]

1. The voyage of Helena the Empresse, daughter of Coelus king of Britain, and mother of Constantine the Great, to Ierusalem. An. 337. pag. 1. 2
   Reprinted from *PN* (1589).

2. The voyage of Constantine the Great, Emperour and king of Britaine, to Greece, Ægypt, Persia, and Asia. Anno 339. pag. 2. 3
   Reprinted from *PN* (1589).

3. The voyage of Pelagius Cambrensis, vnder Maximus king of the Britaines, into Ægypt and Syria, Anno 390. pag. 4
   Reprinted from *PN* (1589).

4. The voyage of certaine Englishmen sent by the French king to Constantinople, vnto Iustinian the Emperour, about the yeere of our Lord 500. pag. 4
   Translated.
   [The passage from *De bello Gothico*, bk. IV appears in Procopius, *History of the wars*, VIII, xx, 6–14 (Loeb Classics, V, 253, 255), but book IV is not to be found in published Latin versions of the sixteenth century. Both Latin and English of the passage in Procopius, *The history of the wars*, translated by Sir Henry Holcroft (1653), differ from Hakluyt's, whose source has not been established.]

5. The memorable voyage of Sighelmus bishop of Shirburne, sent by King Alphred vnto S. Thomas of India, An. 883, confirmed by two testimonies. pag. 5
   From William of Malmesbury, *De gestis regum Anglorum* bk. II, and *De gestis Pontificum Anglorum* bk. II, in Savile, *Rerum Anglicanum scriptores post Bedam* (1596), ff. 24, 141.

6. The voyage of Iohn Erigen, vnder king Alphred, to Athens, in
the yeere of our Lorde 885.   pag. 5. 6
   Reprinted from *PN* (1589).

7. The voyage of Andrew Whiteman, alias Leucander, vnder
Canutus the Dane, to Palestina, Anno 1020.   pag. 6
   Reprinted from *PN* (1589).

8. The voyage of Swanus one of the sonnes of Earle Godwin, vnto
Ierusalem, Anno 1052.   pag. 6
   From William of Malmesbury, *De gestis regum Anglorum*, bk. II,
   in Savile, *Rerum Anglicanum scriptores* (1596), f. 46v.

9. A voyage of three Ambassadours sent in the time of king
Edward the Confessor, vnto Constantinople, and from thence vnto
Ephesus, Anno 1056.   pag. 7
   From William of Malmesbury, *De gestis regum Anglorum*, bk. II,
   in Savile, *Rerum Anglicanum scriptores* (1596), ff. 51–2.

10. The voyage of Alured bishop of Worcester vnto Iersualem,
Anno. 1058.   pag. 8
   From Roger of Hoveden, in Savile, *Rerum Anglicanum scriptores*
   (1596), f. 255.

11. The voyage of Ingulphus, afterward Abbat of Croiland, vnto
Jerusalem, An. 1064.   pag. 8. 9
   From Ingulf, *Descriptio computati per dominum Ingulphum Abbatem
   monasterii Croyland*, in Savile, *Rerum Anglicanum scriptores* (1596),
   f. 514.

Voyages since the Conquest

12. A Voyage made by diuerse of the honourable family of the
Beauchamps, with Robert Curtois the sonne of William the
Conquerour, to Ierusalem, Anno 1096.   pag. 10
   From Holinshed, *Chronicles* (1587), III, 22. [Lumley 1216, 1435.]

13. The voyage of Gutuere an English Lady married vnto Baldwine
brother of Godfrey duke of Bouillion, toward Jersualem, Anno. 1097.
                                                          [pages] 10. 11
   From *Chronicon Hierosolymitanum*, ed. Reiner Reineccius (Helm-
   stadt, 1583), f. 56.

14. The voyage of Edgar the sonne of Edward, which was the sonne
of Edmund surnamed Ironside, brother vnto king Edward the

Confessor (being accompanied with valiant Robert the sonne of
Godwine) to Ierusalem. Anno 1102.   [page] 11
    From William of Malmesbury, *De gestis regum Anglorum*, bk. III,
    in Savile, *Rerum Anglicanum scriptores* (1596), ff. 24, 141.

15. The voyage of Godericus a valiant Englishman, who trauailed
with his ships in an expedition vnto the holy land, Anno 3. Hen. I.
[1102-3.]   [page] 12
    From *Chronicon Hierosolymitanum* (1583), ff. 199-199v.

16. The voyage of Hardine an Englishman, and one of the principall commaunders of 200 sayles of Christians ships, which arriued at
Ioppa, Anno 1102.   [pages] 12. 13
    From *Chronicon Hierosolymitanum* (1583), f. 200.

17. A voyage by sea of Englishmen, Danes, and Flemings, who
arriued at Ioppa in the holy land, the seuenth yeere of Baldwine the
second, king of Ierusalem, and in the 8. yeere of Henry the first, king
of England.   pag. 13, 14, 15
    From *Chronicon Hierosolymitanum* (1583), ff. 221-3.

18. The voyage of Athelard of Bathe to Ægypt and Arabia, in the
yeere of our Lord 1130.   pag. 15. 16
    Reprinted from *PN* (1589).

19. The voyage of William Archbishop of Tyre to Ierusalem and
to the citie of Tyre in Phœnicia, Anno 1130.   [page] 16
    Reprinted from *PN* (1589).

20. The voyage of Robert Ketenensis, vnder king Stephen, to
Dalmatia, Greece, and Asia, Anno 1143.   [page] 16
    Reprinted from *PN* (1589).

21. A voyage of certaine Englishmen vnder the conduct of Lewis
the French king, vnto the holy land, Anno 1147.   [page] 17
    From William of Newburgh, in Commelin, *Rerum Britanni-
    carum scriptores* (Heidelberg, 1587), p. 371.

22. The voyage of Iohn Lacy to Ierusalem, Anno 1173.   [page] 17
    [No source has been found for this item, and it may represent
    some rather ill-digested information passed to Hakluyt by one of
    his correspondents.]

23. The voyage of William Mandeuile Erle of Essex to Ierusalem, Anno 1177. [page] 17
From Holinshed, *Chronicles*, III (1587), 110.

24. The famous voyage of Richard the first, king of England into Asia, for the recouering of Ierusalem out of the hands of the Saracens, Anno 1190. [page] 20
Reprinted from *PN* (1589).

25. The voyage of Baldwine Archbishop of Canterbury vnto Syria and Palæstina, in the yeere 1190. [page] 28
Reprinted from *PN* (1589).

26. The voyage of Richard Surnamed Canonicus, vnder king Richard the first, into Syria, and Palæstina, Anno 1190. [page] 30
Reprinted from *PN* (1589).

27. The voyage of Gulielmus Peregrinus, vnder king Richard the first to Palæstina, Anno 1190. [page] 30
Reprinted from *PN* (1589).

28. The voyage of Hubert Walter bishop of Salisbury, vnder king Richard also, vnto Syria, Anno 1190. [page] 31
Reprinted from *PN* (1589).

29. The voyage of Robert Curson a nobleman of England, and a Cardinall, vnder Hen. the third, to Damiata in Ægypt, Anno 1218. [pages] 31. 32
Reprinted from *PN* (1589).

30. The voyage of Rainulph Earle of Chester, of Saer Quincy Earle of Winchester, of William de Albanie Earle of Arundel, &c, to the holy land, Anno 1218. [page] 32
From Holinshed *Chronicles* (1587), III, 202.

31. The voyage of Henry Bohun, and Saer Quincy to the holy land, in the yeere of our Lord, 1222. [page] 32
From Holinshed, *Chronicles* (1587), III, 202.

32. The voyage of Rainulph Glanuile Earle of Chester to the holy land, and to Damiata in Ægypt. [1218.] [page] 32
Reprinted from *PN* (1589).

33. The voyage of Petrus de Rupibus bishop of Winchester, to Ierusalem, Anno 1231. [page] 33

Matthew Paris, *Angli historia maior* (1571).
Latin and English.

34. The honourable voyage of Richard Earle of Cornwall, brother
to king Hen. the third, accompanied with William Long-espee
Earle of Salisburie, and diuerse other noblemen, into Syria, Anno
1240.   [page] 33
  From Holinshed, *Chronicles* (1587), III, 225.

35. The voyage of William Long-espee, or Long-sword Erle of
Salisburie into Ægypt with Lewis the French king, Anno 1248.
                                                              [page] 33
  Reprinted from *PN* (1589).

36. The voyage of prince Edward the sonne of king Henry the third,
into Syria, An. 1270.   [page] 36
  Reprinted from *PN* (1589).

37. The voyage of Robert Turneham, vnder the said prince Edward,
into Syria, in the yeere of our Lord, 1270.   [pages] 38. 39
  Reprinted from *PN* (1589).

38. The voyage of Frier Beatus Odoricus to Asia minor, Armenia,
Chaldæa, Persia, India, China, and other remote parts, &c. [*c.*
1316–30.]   [pages] 39. 53
  Transcribed and translated by Hakluyt from Lord Lumley's
  manuscript, now B.M., Royal MS 14. C. XIII, ff. 216–24.
  Latin and English.

39. The voyage of Matthew Gurney an English knight, against the
Moores of Alger, to Barbary and to Spaine. [*tempore* Edward III.]   [page] 67
  From Camden, *Britannia* (1594), p. 159.
  Translated.

40. The voyage of Henrie Earle of Derby, after Duke of Hereford,
and lastly Henry the fourth king of England, with an army of
Englishmen, to Tunis in Barbary. [1389–90.]   [page] 69
  In Polydore Vergil, *Anglicae historiae* (Basel, 1570), p. 419
  (Hakluyt's pag. 1389 is a slip). [Lumley 1375 was Basel, 1555
  (and his MS English translation 1380, now B.M., Royal MS 18. C.
  viii–ix)].
  Translated.

41. The trauailes and memorable victories of Iohn Hawkwood Englishman, in diuerse places of Italy, in the reigne of Richard the second. [*Floruit* 1359–94.] [page] 70
From Camden, *Britannia* (1594), pp. 339–40.
Translated.

42. The voyage of Lord Iohn of Holland, Earle of Huntington, brother (by the mother) to K. Richard the second, to Ierusalem, and S. Katherins mount, Anno 1394. [page] 70
In Jean Froissart, *Here beginnith the third and fourth boke of Syr Iohn froissart* (1525), ch. 99, f. 251; R. Holinshed, *Chronicles*, 1 (1587), 473.

43. The voyage of Thomas Lord Mowbrey duke of Norfolke, to Ierusalem, in the yeere of our Lord, 1399. [page] 70
From R. Holinshed, *Chronicles*, III (1587), 1233.

44. The voyage of the bishop of Winchester to Ierusalem, Anno 1417. [page] 71
From Thomas Walsingham, *Historia breuis* (1574), p. 443.
Translated.

45. A voyage intended by king Henry the fourth to the holy land, against the Saracens and Infidels, Anno 1413. [pages] 71. 72
Hakluyt used *The chronicle of Fabian* (1559), p. 388; Polydore Vergil, *Historiae Anglicae* (Basel, 1556), I, 111–12, or another edition; Holinshed, *Chronicles* (1587), III, 540; nothing has been found in Walsingham.

46. A voyage made with two ships called The holy Crosse, and The Matthew Gunson, to the Isles of Candia and Chio, about the yeere 1534. [page] 98
From manuscript. First printed in *PN*, II (1599), i.

47. Another voyage vnto Candia and Chio made by the foresayd ship called The Matthewe Gunson, Anno 1535. [page] 98
From manuscript. First printed in *PN*, II (1589), i.

48. The voyage of the valiant Esquire M. Peter Read to Tunis in Barbarie 1538 [*recte* 1535], recorded in his Epitaph. [page] 99
The inscription on the brass (at the foot of an effigy of a knight in armour) in St Peter Mancroft, Norwich, reads 'Here vnder lyethe yᵉ corps of Peter Rede Esquier who hath worthely serued

not only hys Prynce and cuntrey but allso the Emperor Charles the .5. bothe at the conqueste of Barbaria and at the siege of Tunis as also in other places who had geuen hym by the sayd Emperour for his valiaunt dedes the Order of Barbaria who dyed the 29 of December in the year of oure Lord God 1568.'

49. The voyage of Sir Thomas Chaloner to Alger, with the Emperour Charles the fift, Anno 1541.   [page] 99
    From Thomas Chaloner, *De republica Anglorum instauranda libri decem authore Thomas Chalonero Equite, Anglo.* (1579), sig. *4–4v (the dedication by William Malim, High Master of St Paul's; see p. 179 above).

50. The voyage of M. Roger Bodenham, with the great barke Aucher, to Candia and Chio, Anno 1550.   [page] 99
    From manuscript. First printed in *PN*, II (1599), i.

51. The voyage of M. Iohn Lok to Ierusalem, Anno 1553.   [page] 101
    From manuscript. First printed in *PN*, II (1599), i.
    [Probably obtained from Michael Lok.]

52. The voyage of Iohn Foxe to the Streit of Gibraltar, in a ship called The three halfe-moones, Anno 1563. And his worthy enterprize in deliuering 266 Christians from the captiuitie of the Turkes at Alexandria, Anno 1577.   [pages] 131. 132
    Reprinted from *PN* (1589).

53. The voyage of M. Laurence Aldersey to the cities of Ierusalem, and Tripolis, in the yeere 1581.   [page] 150
    Reprinted from *PN* (1589).

54. The voyage of The Susan of London to Constantinople, wherein M. William Hareborne was sent first Ambassadour vnto Zuldan Murad Can the great Turke. Anno 1582.   [page] 165
    From manuscript. First printed in *PN*, II (1599), i.
    [Possibly given to Hakluyt by Harborne after his return.]

55. The voyage of a ship called The Iesus, to Tripolis in Barbary, Anno 1583. [By Thomas Sanders or Saunders.]   [page] 184
    Reprinted from *PN* (1589).

56. The voyage of M. Henry Austel by Venice to Ragusa, and thence ouer-land to Constantinople: and from thence through Moldauia, Polonia, Silesia, and Germany into England, Anno 1586.   [page] 194

From manuscript. First printed in *PN*, II (1599), i.
[Possibly given by Austell to Hakluyt after his return.]

57. The voyage of Master Cesar Frederick into the east India, and beyonde the Indies, Anno 1563. [page] 213
From Cesare Federici, *The voyage and trauaile of M. Caesar Frederik
...Written at sea in the Hercules of London coming from Turkie the 25.
of March 1588...*
[Translated] out of Italian by T[homas] H[ickocke] (1588).

58. The long, dangerous, and memorable voyage of M. Ralph Fitch marchant of London, by the way of Tripolis in Syria, to Ormuz, to Goa in the East India, to Cambaia, to the riuer of Ganges, to Bengala, to Bacola, to Chonderi, to Pegu, to Siam, &c. begunne in the yeere 1583, and ended in the yeere 1591. [page] 250
Reprinted from *PN* (1589).

59. The voyage of M. Iohn Eldred to Tripolis in Syria by sea, and from thence by land and riuer to Babylon, and Balsara, Anno 1583. [page] 268
Reprinted from *PN* (1589).

60. The voyage of M. Iohn Euesham by sea into Ægypt, Anno 1586.
[page] 281
Reprinted from *PN* (1589).

61. The voyage of M. Laurence Aldersey to the cities of Alexandria and Cairo in Ægypt, Anno 1586. [page] 282
Reprinted from *PN* (1589).

62. The voyage of fiue marchants ships of London into Turkie: and their valiant fight in their returne with 11 gallies and two frigats of the king of Spaine, at Pantalarea within the Streits of Gibraltar, Anno 1586. [page] 285
Reprinted from *PN* (1589).

63. The voyage of Master William Hareborne ouer⸝land from Constantinople to London, Anno 1588. [page] 289
From manuscript. First printed in *PN*, II (1599), i.
[Possibly given to Hakluyt by Harborne after his return.]

64. A description of a voyage to Constantinople and Syria begun the 21 of March, 1593, and ended the ninth of August 1595: [*recte* 1594] wherein is shewed the manner of deliuering the second present,

by M. Edward Barton her Maiesties ambassadour, which was sent
from her Maiestie to Sultan Murad Can, the Emperour of Turkie.

[page] 3[0]3

From manuscript. First printed in *PN*, II (1599), i.
[Sent by Richard Wrag to Rowland Hewish (or Huyshe) of
Sand, Devonshire (with no. D.80, below), on 16 March 1597
[–8?]. Hakluyt may well have obtained it from Hewish.]

[D] *The Ambassages, Letters, Priuileges, Discourses, Aduertisements,
and other obseruations depending vpon the Voyages contayned in the
first part of this second Volume.*

[First numeration]

1. A Testimony, that the Britons were in Italy and Greece, with the
Cimbrians and Gauls, before the incarnation of Christ.   pag. 1
From Camden, *Britannia* (1594), p. 33.

2. A testimony that certain Englishmen were of the guard of the
Emperour of Constantinople, in the time of Iohn the sonne of
Alexius Comnenus.   [page] 17
From Camden, *Britannia* (1594), p. 96.

3. A great supply of money sent to the Holy land by King Henry
the second. [1177.]   [page] 18
From Holinshed, *Chronicles* III (1587), 105.

4. A letter written from Manuel the Emperour of Constantinople,
vnto Henry the second, King of England, Ann. 1177: wherein
mention is made that certaine of king Henries noblemen and subiects
were present with the sayd Emperour in a battel against the Soldan
of Iconium.   [page] 18
From Roger of Hoveden, in Savile, *Rerum Anglicanum scriptores post
Bedam* (1596), ff. 316–17.

5. A note drawn out of a very auncient booke in the custodie of
the right Wor. M. Thomas Tilney Esquire, touching Sir Fredericke
Tilney his ancester, knighted for his valour at Acon in the Holy land,
by king Richard the first.   [page] 29
The book belonged to Sir Philip Tilney of Shelleigh (Shelley),
Suffolk (aged 64 in 1556), whose son, Thomas Tilney of Had-
leigh, Suffolk, allowed Hakluyt to use it.

6. A large contribution to the succour of the holy land made by king
Iohn king of England, Anno 1201.   [page] 30
   From Holinshed, *Chronicles,* III (1587), 164.

7. The comming of Baldwin the Emperour of Constantinople into
England, An. 1247.   [page] 31
   From Holinshed, *Chronicles*, III (1587), 239.

8. A testimony concerning Anthony Beck bishop of Duresme, that
he was elected Patriarke of Ierusalem, and confirmed by Clement the
5, bishop of Rome, Anno 1305.   [page] 39
   Leland is given as the source, but John Leland, *De rebus Britannicis
   collectanea*, ed. Thomas Hearne, I (1770), 334, has merely 'Anno D.
   1305. Antonius de Bek episcopus Dunelmen electus in Patri-
   archam Hierosolymitanum'. The text has not been traced.

9. The coming of Lyon king of Armenia into England, Anno 1386,
to make a treaty of peace betweene Richard the second king of
England, and the French king.   [page] 67
   (Froissart, lib. 3, ch. 56) in *Here beginneth the third and fourthe boke
   of syr Iohn froissart of the cronycles of Englande* (1525), ff. 78v–79r.

10. The comming of the Emperour of Constantinople into England,
to desire the ayde of king Henry the fourth, against the Turkes, Anno
1400.   [page] 70
   From Thomas Walsingham, *Historia breuis* (1574), p. 405.

11. A relation of the siege and taking of the citie of Rhodes, by
Sultan Soliman the great Turke: Wherein honorable mention is
made of diuers valiant English knights, Anno. 1522.   [page] 72
   This translation from a French original by Sir Thomas Dockwra,
   prior of the Knights of St John of Jerusalem in 1524, has not been
   traced. It was probably a manuscript in Hakluyt's hands or to
   which he had access. [The Master of Rhodes wrote to Dockwra
   about the early phase of the seige on 17 June 1522 (*L. & P.
   Henry VIII,* III, no. 2324; B.M., Cotton MS, Otho C. IX, f. 38),
   so that he was in close touch with its progress.]

12. An ambassage from Don Ferdinando, brother to the Emperour
Charles the fift, vnto King Henry the eight, crauing his ayde against
Soliman the great Turke, An. 1527.   [page] 95
   From Holinshed, *Chronicles* (1587), p. 894.

13. The antiquitie of the trade of English marchants vnto the remote
parts of the Leuant seas, Anno 1511, 1512, &c. [page] 96
 Notes collected by Hakluyt from ledgers once belonging to Sir
 William Locke, mercer, Sir William Bowyer, alderman, John
 Gresham, and other London merchants. [Michael Lok may have
 contributed his father's papers.]

14. A letter of Henry the eight, king of England, to Iohn the third
king of Portugale, for a Portugale ship fraighted at Chio, with the
goods of Iohn Gresham, William Lok, and others, and wrongfully
vnladen in Portugale, Anno 1531. [page] 96
 From manuscript. First printed in *PN*, II (1599), i.
 [*L.& P. Henry VIII*, v, 475, gives Hakluyt as the only source for
 this letter.]

15. The maner of the entring of Soliman the great Turke, with his
army, into Alepo in Syria, as hee was marching toward Persia,
against the great Sophi, Anno 1553. [page] 112
 Reprinted from *PN* (1589).

16. A note of the presents that were giuen at the same time in Alepo,
to the Grand Signor, and the names of the presenters. [1553.] [page] 113
 Reprinted from *PN* (1589).

17. The safe conduct granted by Sultan Soliman the great Turke,
to M. Anthony Ienkinson at Alepo in Syria, Anno 1553. [page] 114
 Reprinted from *PN* (1589).

18. A discourse of the trade to Chio written by Gaspar Campion,
in the yeere 1569. [page] 114
 From manuscript. First printed in *PN*, II (1599), i.
 [See no. 19 below.]

19. A letter of the sayd Gaspar Campion, to M. William Winter,
in the yeare 1569. [page] 116
 From manuscript. First printed in *PN*, II (1599), i.
 [Hakluyt may have obtained nos. 18 and 19 from Sir William
 Winter before his death in 1589, or they may have descended to
 him from his elder cousin.]

20. A briefe description of the Isle of Cyprus. [*c.* 1572.] [page] 119
 From William Malim's 'A breefe description of the Iland of
 Cyprus', prefixed to his translation of Count Nestore Martinengo,
 The true report of all the successe of Famagosta (1572), sig. C1–G1.

Hareborne, to bee Her Maiesties Ambassador or Agent in the parts
of Turkie, Anno 1582.   [page] 157
   Reprinted from *PN* (1589). Latin and English.

30. Her Maiesties letter to the great Turke, written in commenda-
tion of M. William Hareborne, when he was sent Ambassador,
Anno 1582.   [page] 158
   Reprinted from *PN* (1589).

31. A letter of the Queenes Maiestie to Alli Bassa, the Turkes high
Admiral, sent by her Ambassador M. William Hareborne, and
deliuered vnto him aboord his Galley in the Arsenal. [20 November
1583.]   [page] 159
   From manuscript. First printed in *PN*, II (1599), i.
   Latin and English.

32. A briefe remembrance of things to bee indeuoured at Constantinople, and at other places in Turkie, touching our Clothing
and Dying, and touching the ample vent of our naturall commodities, &c. written by M. Richard Hakluyt of the middle Temple,
Anno 1582.   [page] 160
   From manuscript. First printed in *PN*, II (1599), I.
   Acquired (probably inherited in 1591) by Hakluyt from his cousin.

33. Certaine other most profitable and wise instructions penned by
the sayd M. Richard Hakluyt, for a principall English Factor at
Constantinople. [1582.]   [page] 161
   From manuscript. First printed in *PN*, II (1599), i.
   [Acquired (or inherited in 1591) by Hakluyt from his cousin.]

34. A letter of Mustafa Chaus to the Queenes Maiestie, Anno 1583.
                                                                        [page] 171
   From manuscript. First printed in *PN*, II (1599), i.

35. A letter of M. William Hareborne, to M. Haruie Millers,
appointing him Consul for the English nation, in Alexandria,
Cairo, & other places of Egypt, in the yeare of our Lord 1583. [page] 171
   From manuscript. First printed in *PN*, II (1599), i.
   [Possibly given by Harborne to Hakluyt after his return.]

36. A Commission giuen by M. William Hareborne the English
Ambassador, to M. Richard Forster, authorizing him Consul of
the English nation, in the partes of Alepo, Damasco, Aman,

Tripolis, Ierusalem, &c. together with a letter of directions to the sayd M. Forster, Ann. 1583.   [page] 172
    From manuscript. First printed in *PN*, II (1599), i.
    [Possibly given by Harborne to Hakluyt after his return.]

37. A letter sent from Alger to M. William Hareborne her Maiesties Ambassador at Constantinople, Anno 1583.   [page] 173
    From manuscript. First printed in *PN*, II (1599), i.
    [Probably given by Harborne to Hakluyt after his return.]

38. A letter of M. Hareborne to Mustafa, chalenging him for his dishonest dealing in translating three of the Grand Signors commandements.   [page] 174
    From manuscript. First printed in *PN*, II (1599), i.
    Latin only.
    [Possibly given by Harborne to Hakluyt after his return.]

39. A Pasport graunted to Thomas Shingleton by the king of Alger, in the yeare 1583.   [page] 174
    Reprinted from *PN* (1589).

40. A letter written in Spanish by Sir Edward Osborne in his Maioraltie, to the king of Alger, on the behalfe of certaine English captiues, An. 1584.   [page] 175
    Reprinted from *PN* (1589).

41. Notes concerning the trades of Alger and Alexandria. [*c.* 1584.]

    Reprinted from *PN* (1589).   [page] 176

42. A letter of M. William Hareborne the English Ambassadour, to M. Edward Barton, Anno 1584.   [page] 177
    From manuscript. First printed in *PN*, II (1599), i.
    [Possibly given by Harborne to Hakluyt after his return.]

43. A commandement obtayned of the Grand Signor by her Maiesties Ambassadour M. William Hareborne, for the quiet passing of her subiects to and from his dominions, sent to the Viceroyes of Alger, Tunis, and Tripolis in Barbary, An. 1584.   [page] 177
    Reprinted from *PN* (1589).

44. A letter of the hon. M. William Hareborne, her Maiesties Ambassadour with the Grand Signor, to M. Tipton, appointing him Consul of the English, in Alger, Tunis, and Tripolis in Barbary, Anno 1585.   [page] 178

From manuscript. First printed in *PN*, II (1599), i.
[Possibly given by Harborne to Hakluyt after his return.]

45. A Catalogue or register of the English ships, goods and
persons wrongfully taken by the Galleys of Alger, with the names of
the English captiues, deliuered to Hassan Bassa the Beglerbeg of
Alger, &c. [*c.* 1580–5?]   [page] 179
From manuscript. First printed in *PN*, II (1599), i.
Latin only.

46. A letter of M. William Hareborne her Maiesties Ambassador
&c. to Assan Aga, Eunuch and treasurer vnto Hassan Bassa king
of Alger: which Assan Aga was sonne to Francis Rowly merchant
of Bristol, and was taken in an English ship called the Swallow.
[28 June 1586.]   [page] 180
From manuscript. First printed in *PN*, II (1599), i.
[Possibly given by Harborne to Hakluyt after his return.]

47. A petition exhibited to the Viceroy of the Turkish empire for
reformation of sundry iniuries offered our nation in Morea, as also for
sundry demaundes needefull for the establishing of the trafficke
in those parts. [*c.* 1585].   [page] 181
From manuscript. First printed in *PN*, II (1599), i.
[Possibly given by Harborne to Hakluyt after his return.]

48. A commandement of the Grand Signor to Patrasso in Morea,
on the behalfe of the English. [1585.]   pag. 181
From manuscript. First printed in *PN*, II (1599), i.
In English.
[It probably came to Hakluyt from William Harborne after his
return from Turkey in December 1588.]

49. The Grand Signors commandement to Chio on the behalfe of
the English merchants. [1585?]   [page] 182
From manuscript. First printed in *PN*, II (1599), i.
Latin only.
[It probably came to Hakluyt from Harborne after his return in
1588.]

50. Two of his commandements sent to Baliabadram and to Egypt,
for the same purpose. [*c.* 1585.]   [page] 182
From manuscript. First printed in *PN*, II (1599), i.
Latin only.

[They probably came to Hakluyt from Harborne after his return in 1588. The original MS of the second is Bodleian Library, MS Turk R (a).]

51. A commandement of the Grand Signor to the Cadi of Alexandria, for the restoring of an English mans goods wrongfully taken by the French Consul. [c. 1585.]   [page] 183
    From manuscript. First printed in PN, II (1599), i.
    In English.
    [It probably came to Hakluyt from Harborne after his return in 1588.]

52. Another commaundement to the Bassa of Alexandria, for the very same purpose. [1586.]   [page] 183
    From manuscript. First printed in PN, II (1599), i.
    In English.
    [It probably came to Hakluyt from Harborne after his return in 1588.]

53. A commandement to the Byes and Cadies of Metelin and Rhodes, and to all the Cadies & Byes in the way to Constantinople, for the courteous and iust vsage of the English merchants. [c. 1585.]
    From manuscript. First printed in PN, II (1599), i.   [page] 183
    In English.
    [It probably came to Hakluyt from Harborne after his return in 1588.]

54. A commandement sent to Alepo concerning the goods of M. William Barret deceased. [May 1586.]   [page] 183
    From manuscript. First printed in PN, II (1599), i.
    In English.
    [It probably came to Hakluyt from Harborne after his return in 1588.]

55. The Queenes letters to the great Turke for the restitution of an English ship called The Iesus, and of the English captiues detained at Tripolis in Barbary, & for certaine other English men which remained prisoners at Alger, Anno 1584.   [page] 191
    Reprinted from PN (1589).
    Latin and English.

56. The great Turkes letters to the king of Tripolis in Barbary,

commanding the restitution of an English ship called The Iesus, with the men and goods &c. Anno 1584.   [page] 192
Reprinted from *PN* (1589).
In English.

57. The letter of M. William Hareborne her Maiesties Ambassadour to Bassa Romadan the Beglerbeg of Tripolis in Barbary, for the restoring of the sayd ship called The Iesus, Anno 1585.   [page] 193
Reprinted from *PN* (1589).
Italian and English.

58. The great Turkes Pasport of safeconduct, for Captaine Austel, and Iacomo Manuchio. [1585.]   [page] 198
From manuscript. First printed in *PN*, II (1599), i.
[It probably came to Hakluyt from Austell after his return to England.]

59. A pasport of the Erle of Leicester, for Thomas Forster gent. traueiling to Constantinople, Anno 1586.   [page] 198
From manuscript. First printed in *PN*, II (1599), i.

60. A description of the yearely voyage or pilgrimage of the Mahu-metans, Turkes and Moores to Mecca in Arabia.   [page] 198
From manuscript. First printed in *PN*, II (1599), i.
[This is a composite. The material on pp. 198-202 has not been located. The sections on pp. 203-13 are represented in a Venetian *Relazione*, B.M., Royal MS 14. A. XV, ff. 41-87.]

61. A letter written from the Queenes Maiestie to Zelabdim Echebar king of Cambaia, and sent by M. Iohn Newbery, Anno 1583.   [page] 245
Reprinted from *PN* (1589).

62. A letter written from her Maiestie to the king of China, in the yeare of our Lord 1583.   [page] 245
Reprinted from *PN* (1589).

63. A letter of M. Iohn Newbery sent from Alepo to M. Richard Hakluyt of Oxford, Ann. 1583.   pag. 245
Reprinted from *PN* (1589).

64. Another letter of the sayd M. Newbery written from Alepo to M. Leonard Poore at London, Anno 1583.   [page] 246
Reprinted from *PN* (1589).

From manuscript. First printed in *PN*, II (1599), i.
Latin and English.

76. A briefe extract specifying the certaine dayly payments answered quarterly in time of peace, by the Grand Signor, out of his treasury, to the officers of his Seraglio or Court, successiuely in degrees. [*c.* 1581.]   [page] 290
Reprinted from *PN* (1589).

77. The chiefe officers of the great Turkes Empire; the number of souldiers attending vpon each of his Beglerbegs; the principal officers in his Seraglio or Court; his yearly reuenues, and his allowances to forren Ambassadours. [*c.* 1581.]   [pages] 292, 293, 294
Reprinted from *PN* (1589).

78. The letters of Sinan Bassa chiefe counsellor to Sultan Murad Can the Grand Signor, An. 1590, to the sacred Maiestie of Elizabeth Queene of England: signifying, that vpon her request, and for her sake especially he granted peace vnto the King of Poland. [12 June 1590.]   [page] 294
From manuscript. First printed in *PN*, II (1599), i.
Latin and English.
[Represented in Latin translation in B.M., Cotton MS, Nero B. XI, ff. 198–9v.]

79. The second letters patents granted by the Queenes Maiestie, to the right wor. company of the English merchants for the Leuant, in the yere of our Lord 1592. [7 January 1592.]   [page] 295
From manuscript. First printed in *PN*, II (1599), i.
In English.
[Enrolled, P.R.O., Patent Rolls, 34 Eliz. part 12, C.66/1391. A copy is in the Harborne papers in Bodleian Library, Tanner MS 77, ff. 18–24, so that Hakluyt could have obtained it from Harborne.]

80. A letter written by the most high and mighty Empresse the wife of the Grand Signor Sultan Murad Can to her most sacred Maiesty of England, Anno 1594. [Received in 1594.]   [page] 311
From manuscript. First printed in *PN*, II (1599), i.
Italian and English.
[This was copied by Richard Wrag – with minor variants – at Constantinople from the Italian version now represented in

P.R.O., State Papers, Foreign, Turkey, S.P. 97/2, ff. 295-6, and is printed by Susan A. Skilliter, 'Three letters from the Ottoman "Sultana" Safiye to Queen Elizabeth I', *Documents from Islamic chanceries*, ed. S. M. Stern (Oxford, 1965), pp. 126-33, with collation and translation. She also prints the Turkish original and refers to another Italian translation sent with it, now B.M., Cotton MS, Nero B. VIII, ff. 61-3 (pp. 120-6). It is probable that Hakluyt received it (with no. C.64 above) from Rowland Hewish (or Huyshe) of Sand, Devonshire (alive in 1620 according to J. L. Vivian, *Visitations of the County of Devon* (1895), p. 495), to whom Wrag had sent a copy.]

[E]   *A briefe Catalogue of the principall English Voyages made without the Straight of Gibraltar to the South and Southeast quarters of the world, contayned in the second part of this second volume immediatly following. Wherein also mention is made of certaine Sea-fights, and other memorable acts performed by the English Nation.*   [Second numeration]

1. The voyage of Macham the first discouerer of the Isle of Madera, in the yeere 1344.
   Reprinted from *PN* (1589).   pag. 1

2. The first voyage to Barbary, Anno 1551. [As in a letter from James Alday to Michael Lok.]
   From manuscript. First printed in *PN*, II (1599), ii.   pag. 7. 8
   [Probably obtained from Michael Lok.]

3. The second voyage to Barbary, Anno 1552. [By James Thomas.]
                                                            pag. 8. 9
   From manuscript. First printed in *PN*, II (1599), ii.
   [Probably obtained from Michael Lok.]

4. The voyage of M. Thomas Windam to Guinea and the kingdom of Benin, Anno 1553.
   Reprinted from *PN* (1589).   pag. 9

5. The voyage of M. John Lok to Guinea, Anno 1554.   [page] 14
   Reprinted from *PN* (1589).

6. The first voyage of Master William Towrson marchant of London to Guinea, in the yeere of our Lord, 1555.   [page] 23
   Reprinted from *PN* (1589).

24. The valiant fight performed in the Streit of Gibraltar by the Centurion of London, against fiue Spanish gallies, An. 1591.

[page] 168

From John Hawes, *The valiant and most laudable fight by the Centurion of London against fiue Spanish gallies* (1591).

25. A true report of the fight about the Isles of the Azores, betweene the Reuenge one of her Maiesties ships, vnder the conduct of Sir Richard Grinuile, and an Armada of the King of Spaine, An. 1591.

[page] 169

From manuscript. It differs from the published version, Sir Walter Ralegh, *A report of the truth of the fight about the iles of Açores* (1591). [Probably obtained from Ralegh.]

26. A voyage of certaine ships of London to the coast of Spaine, and the Azores, Anno 1591. Reported by M. Robert Flick. [page] 176

From manuscript. First printed in *PN*, II (1599), ii. [Probably obtained from Richard Staper.]

27. The voyage of Richard Rainolds and Thomas Dassell to the riuers of Senega and Gambra, neere the coast of Guinea, Anno 1591.

[page] 188

From manuscript. First printed in *PN*, II (1599), ii. [Probably given to Hakluyt by the Dassel family.]

28. The taking of two Spanish ships laden with quicksiluer and with the Popes Bulles, bound for the west Indies, by M. Thomas White in the Amitie of London, An. 1592. [page] 193

From manuscript. First printed in *PN*, II (1599), ii.

29. The taking of the mightie and rich Carak called The Madre de Dios, and of the Santa Clara a Biskaine of 600 tunnes, as likewise the firing of another great Carak called The Santa Cruz, Anno 1592.

[page] 194

From *The sea-mans triumph. Declaring the honorable actions of such gentlemen as were at the taking of the great carrick, lately brought to Dartmouth* (1592). [S.T.C. 22140.]

30. The firing and sinking of the stout and warlike Carak called The Cinquo Chaguas, or The fiue woundes, by three ships of the R.H. the Earle of Cumberland, Anno 1594. [By Captain Nicholas Downton.] [page] 199

From manuscript. First printed in *PN*, II (1599), ii.

[F] *The Ambassages, Letters, Priuileges, Discourses, and other*
necessary matters of circumstance appertaining to the voyages in
the second part of this second volume next ensuing.

[Second numeration]

1. A note concerning the ayde and assistance giuen to king John
the first of Portugale, by certaine English merchants, for the winning
of Ceut in Barbary, Anno 1415.   [pages] 1, 2
Reprinted from *PN* (1589).

2. The Ambassage of Iohn the second king of Portugale to Edward
the 4. king of England, to stay Iohn Tintam, and William Fabian
Englishmen, preparing for a voyage to Guinea, Anno 1481.   pag. 2
Reprinted from *PN* (1589).

3. A briefe note concerning an ancient trade of English marchants
to the Canarie Isles, Anno 1526.
Taken by Hakluyt from a ledger of Nicholas Thorne, probably
seen by him in Bristol.

4. A description of the Canarie Islands, with their strange fruits
and commodities.   [page] 3
From Thomas Nichols, *A pleasant description of the fortunate ilandes*
called the Islands of Canaria...composed by the poore pilgrime (1583).
[See Alejandro Cioranescu, *Thomas Nichols, mercador de azúcar, his-*
panista, y hereje (La Laguna de Tenerife, 1963).]

5. The commodities and wares that are most desired in Guinea,
betwixt Sierra Leona, and the furthest place of the Mina.   [page] 52
Reprinted from *PN* (1589).

6. Certaine articles of remembrance deliuered to M. Iohn Lok,
touching a voyage to Guinea, Anno 1561.   [page] 52
From manuscript. First printed in *PN*, II (1599), ii.
[Probably obtained from Michael Lok.]

7. A letter of M. Iohn Lok to the worshipfull company of marchants
aduenturers of Guinea, Anno 1561.   [page] 53
From manuscript. First printed in *PN*, II (1599), ii.
[Probably obtained from Michael Lok.]

8. The relation of one William Rutter concerning a voyage set out
to Guinea, Anno 1562. Described also in verse by Robert Baker.
[page] 54

From manuscript. First printed in *PN*, II (1599), ii.
[Hakluyt replaced Baker's verse account (*PN* (1589), pp. 130–5)
with this prose narrative. See p. 200 above.]

9. A meeting at Sir William Gerards house for the setting foorth
of a voyage to Guinea, with the Minion of the Queenes, The Iohn
Baptist of London, and the Merline of M. Gonson, Anno 1564.

[page] 55

From manuscript. First printed in *PN*, II (1599), ii.

10. A relation of the successe of the same voyage, taken out of a
voyage of Sir Iohn Haukins to the West Indies.   [page] 56
  Extracted from Sparke's narrative, printed below, III, 500–11
  [No. G 117.]

11. Certaine reports of the mighty kingdome of China deliuered
by Portugales which were there imprisoned.   [page] 68
  From Richard Willes, *The history of trauayle in the West and
  East Indies* (1577), ff. 237–51.
  [This and part of the following item were translated by Willes
  from Galeote Pereira, *Noui auisi delle Indie di Portogallo...Quarta
  parte* (Venice, 1565), pp. 63–87.]

12. A discourse of the Isle of Iapan, and of other Isles in the East
Ocean, &c.   [page] 80
  From Richard Willes, *The history of trauayle in the West and East
  Indies* (1577), ff. 251v–160v.
  [See no. 11 above. Willes took the letter from Luis Froes (ff. 253–
  60), from Petrus Maffeius (Giovanni Pietro Maffei), *Rerum a
  Societate Iesu in Oriente gestarum volumen* (Naples, 1573), ff. 207v–
  14v, but the pieces, 'Of the Ilande Giapon' (ff. 251v–3v) and
  'Of the Isles beyond Giapon' (ff. 260–260v), were his own com-
  position from Jesuit sources.]

13. An excellent description of the kingdome of China, and of the
estate and gouernment thereof.   pag. 88
  From Eduardus de Sande [Duarte Sande], *De missione legatorum
  Iaponensium ad Romanam curiam* (Macao, 1590), colloqium 33,
  pp. 379–99.
  Translated.
  [This book came into Hakluyt's hands from the captured *Madre
  de Deus* in 1592; see p. 305 above. One of the British Museum

copies (G. 6688) has the name 'Edwarde Fletewoode' in an early hand on the title-page.]

14. A briefe relation of the great magnificence and rich trafficke of the kingdom of Pegu, beyond the East India. [Peter of Lisbon, from Cochin, 28 December 1589.]   [page] 102
    From manuscript. First printed in *PN*, II (1599), ii.
    [Apparently an intercepted letter given to Hakluyt by its captors.]

15. Certaine remembrances of a voyage intended to Brasil, and to the riuer of Plate, but miserably ouerthrowen neere Rio grande in Guinea, in the yeere 1583.   [pages] 110, 111
    From manuscript. First printed in *PN*, II (1599), ii.
    [They might appear to be extracts from legal proceedings, possibly in the High Court of Admiralty, after the return of survivors in 1584. They may have been given by Edward Cotton to Hakluyt.]

16. The escape of the Primrose, a ship of London, from before the towne of Bilbao in Biscay, and the taking of the Corrigidor, Anno 1585.   [pages] 112
    From Humphrey Mote, *The Primrose of London, with her valiant aduenture on the Spanish coast* (1585).

17. The king of Spaines Commission for the generall imbargment or arrest of the English &c. Anno 1585.   [page] 114
    From Mote (see no. 16 above.)

18. The Letters patents granted by her Maiestie to certaine noblemen and merchants of London, for a trade to Barbary, Anno. 1585. [July 1585.]   [page] 114
    Reprinted from *PN* (1589).

19. An edict from the Emperour of Marocco in fauour of all Englishmen trading throughout his dominions, Anno 1587. [10/19 March 1588.]   [page] 118
    Reprinted from *PN* (1589).

20. A letter of the sayd emperour written to the Erle of Leicester, in the yeare, 1587. [11/21 August 1588.]   [page] 118
    Reprinted from *PN* (1589).

21. A letter of the Queenes Maiestie written to the emperour of Marocco, in the yere 1587. [20 July 1587.]   [page] 119
    Reprinted from *PN* (1589).

22. A patent graunted to certaine merchants of Exceter, and others of the West parts, and of London, for a trade to the riuers of Senega and Gambra in Guinea, Anno 1588. [3 May 1588.] [page] 123
 Reprinted from *PN* (1589).

23. A relation concerning a voyage set foorth by M. Iohn Newton, and M. Iohn Bird, merchants of London, to the kingdome and citie of Benin, written by Antony Ingram, An. 1588. [page] 129
 Reprinted from *PN* (1589).

24. An aduertisement to king Philip the 2. of Spaine, from Angola, touching the state of the same countrey. An. 1591. [From Baltozar Almeida de Souza 21 May 1591.] [page] 133
 From manuscript. First printed in *PN*, II (1599), ii.
 [Apparently an intercepted letter given to Hakluyt by its captors.]

25. A particular note of the West Indian fleete expected to haue arriued in Spaine, An. 1592 [*recte* 1591], with the number of ships of the same fleete that perished and suffered shipshrack [*sic*] &c. [page] 175
 From manuscript. First printed in *PN*, II (1599), ii.
 [Derived from depositions of captured Spaniards made in England.]

26. A large testimony of Iohn Huighen van Linschoten concerning the worthy exploits atchieued by the right hon. the erle of Cumber‑land, by Sir Martin Frobisher, Sir Richard Grinuile, and diuers other English Captains, about the Isles of the Açores, and vpon the coastes of Spaine, and Portugale, in the yeares 1589, 1590, 1591. [page] 178
 Selected from Jan Huygen van Linschoten, *Discours of voyages into
 yᵉ Easte and West Indies* (1592), pp. 178–97.

27. A relation [sent by Melchior Petoney to Nigil de Moura at Lisbon] concerning the estate of the Island and Castle of Arguin, and touching the rich and secret trade from the inland of Africa thither, written in the yere 1491. [20 January 1591.] [page] 188
 From manuscript. First printed in *PN*, II (1599), ii.
 Translated.
 [Presumably an intercepted letter given to Hakluyt by its captors.]

28. Two briefe relations [sent to Anthony Dassel] concerning the Cities and Prouinces of Tombuto and Gago, and concerning the

exceeding great riches of the sayd Prouinces, and the conquest thereof by the king of Marocco, and of the huge masse of gold, which he yerely receiueth thence for tribute. Written Anno 1594.   [page] 192
 From manuscript. First printed in *PN*, II (1599), ii.
 [Probably given to Hakluyt with no. E.27 above by the Dassel family.]

29. A briefe extract of a patent granted to M. Thomas Gregory of Tanton, and others, for traffick betweene the riuer of Nonnia, and the riuers of Madrabumba and Sierra Leona, on the coast of Guinea, An. 1592. [May 1592.]   [page] 193
 From manuscript (Chancery rolls). First printed in *PN*, II (1599), ii.
 [Enrolled, P.R.O., Patent Roll, 34 Eliz., part 6, C.66/1384.]

30. A report of the casting away of the Tobie, a ship of London, neere Cape Espartel on the coast of Barbary without the Streight of Gibraltar, in the yere of our Lord 1593.   [page] 201
 From manuscript. First printed in *PN*, II (1599), ii.
 [Probably obtained from Richard Staper.]

31. The letters of the Queens Maiestie sent by Laurence Aldersey vnto the Emperour of Ethiopia, Anno 1597.   [page] 203
 From manuscript. First printed in *PN*, II (1599), ii.
 Latin and English.

Volume III

[G] *A general Catalogue diuided, according to the methode obserued in this present volume, into 14. special branches, briefly conteyning all the Voyages, Nauigations, Traffiques, and Discoueries of the English nation, and (where they haue not bene, or not perfectly discouered) of strangers, within the same volume intreated of, which haue been performed to euery part of America hitherto knowen or discouered by any Christian: whereunto are annexed in their due and proper places, all the Patents, discourses, ruttiers, letters, aduertisements, instructions, obseruations, and other particulars incident or belonging to the foresaid Voyages.*

[1] The most ancient voyage and discouery of the West Indies

performed by Madoc the sonne of Owen Guined prince of North Wales, Anno 1170, taken out of the history of Wales &c.   Pag. 1.
   Reprinted from *PN* (1589).

The testimonies and relations immediatly ensuing vpon this voyage.

[2]   The verses of Meredith the sonne of Rhesus making mention of Madoc the sonne of Owen Guined, and of his Nauigation vnto vn⁄knowen lands.   pag. 1.
   Reprinted from *PN* (1589).

[3]   The offer of the discouery of the West Indies by Christopher Columbus to K. Henry the 7. February the 13. Anno 1488; with the Kings acceptance of the said offer.   pag. 2.
   Reprinted from *PN* (1589).

[4]   Another testimony concerning the foresaid offer made by Bartholomew Columbus to K. Henry the seuenth, on the behalfe of his brother Christopher Columbus.   pag. 3. & 4.
   Reprinted from *PN* (1589).

A catalogue of the English voyages vndertaken for the finding of a Northwest passage, to the North parts of America, to Meta incognita, and the backeside of Groenland, as farre as 72. degrees, and 12. minutes.

[5]   The voyage of Sebastian Cabota to the North part of America, for the discouery of a Northwest passage, as farre as 58. degrees of latitude, and from thence back againe all along the coast, till he fell with some part of Florida, anno 1497; confirmed by 6 testimonies:
[5a]   The first taken out of the mappe of Sebastian Cabota cut by Clement Adames;
[5b]   The second vsed by Galeacius Butrigarius the Popes legate, and reported by him;
[5c]   the third out of the preface of Baptista Ramusius before his third volume of Nauigations;
[5d]   The 4. out of the thirde decade of Peter Martyr ab Angleria;
[5e]   The 5. out of the general history of Lopez de Gomara;
[5f]   The 6. out of Fabians chronicle.   pag. 6. 7. 8, and 9.
   Reprinted from *PN* (1589).

[6]   The first voyage of M. Martin Frobisher to the Northwest for the search of a passage to China, anno 1576.   pag. 29. & 57.
   Reprinted from *PN* (1589).

pall notes and obseruations taken in his third and last voyage to the
Northwest.   pag. 115
> From manuscript. First published in *PN*, III (1600).
> [Most probably supplied to Hakluyt by Davis. This specially
> printed pair of leaves was inserted into a normal gathering of six
> leaves, see p. 510 below.]

[26] A report of M. Iohn Dauis concerning his three voyages made
for the discouery of the Northwest passage, taken out of a treatise
of his intituled The worlds hydrographical description.   pag. 119
> From John Davis, *The worldes hydrographical discription* (1595),
> sig. B1v–B5v.
> [Not in S.T.C. Copies in B.M. and Folger Library, Washing-
> ton.]

[27] A testimony of Ortelius for the credit of the history of M.
Nicolas, & M. Antonio Zeni.   p. 128.
> In Ortelius, *Theatrum orbis terrarum* (1570), f. 6. [Lumley 2485
> (1570), 2499 (1575), 2500 (1592).]

*A catalogue of sundry voyages made to Newfoundland, to the isles of Ramea
and the isle of Assumption, otherwise called Natiscotec, as also to the
coasts of Cape Briton and Arambec.*

[28] The voyage of two ships, whereof the one was called The
Dominus vobiscum, set out the 20 of May 1527, for the discouery
of the North parts.   pag. 129
> Reprinted from *PN* (1589).

[29] The voyage of M. Hore, and diuers other gentlemen to Newfoundland, and Cape Briton, in the yere 1536.   pag. 129
> Reprinted from *PN* (1589).

[30] The voyage of Sir Humfrey Gilbert to Newfoundland An.
1583. [By Edward Hayes.]   pag. 143, 165
> Reprinted from *PN* (1589).

[31] The first discouery of the Isle of Ramea, made by [   ]
for Monsieur de la court pre Rauillon & grand pre, with the ship
called The Bonauenture, to kill and make trane-oile of the beasts
called The Morses, with great teeth, Anno 1591.   pag. 189
> From manuscript. First published in *PN*, III (1600).
> [Probably collected by Hakluyt at Bristol.]

carmen (1582), in a somewhat revised edition completed in April 1583. Whether it was published in this form or simply presented as corrected to Hakluyt is not known.

[See Quinn and Cheshire, *Parmenius* (1972), pp. 77–105.]

[40]   Orders agreed vpon by the Captaines and Masters, to bee obserued by the fleete of sir Humfrey Gilbert.   pag. 147
    Portion of no. 30 above.

[41]   A briefe relation of Newfound/land, and the commodities thereof.   pag. 152
    Another portion of no. 30.

[42]   Reckonings of the Master and Masters mate of the Admirall of sir Humfrey Gilbert in their course from cape Rase to cape Briton, and to the Isle of Sablon.   pag. 155
    Another portion of no. 30.

[43]   The maner how the sayd Admirall was lost.   pag. 156
    Another portion of no. 30.

[43]   A letter of the learned Hungarian Stephanus Parmenius Budeius to master Richard Hakluyt the collectour of these voyages.

    Reprinted from *PN* (1589).   pag. 161 & 162

[44]   A relation of Richard Clarke of Weymouth master of the ship called The Delight, which went as Admirall of sir Humfrey Gilberts fleete for the discouerie of Norumbega 1583: written in excuse of the casting away the sayd ship and the men, imputed to his ouersight.   pag. 163
    Reprinted from *PN* (1589).

[45]   A discourse of the necessitie and commoditie of planting English colonies vpon the North partes of America.   pag. 165
    Reprinted from *PN* (1589). By Sir George Peckham.

[47]   A letter of the right honourable sir Francis Walsingham to master Richard Hakluyt then of Christ/church in Oxford, in/couraging him in the studie of Cosmography, and furthering of new discoueries, 1582.   pag. 181
    From manuscript. First printed in *PN*, III (1600).
    [From Hakluyt's personal collection.]

[48]   A letter of the right honourable sir Francis Walsingham to

master Thomas Aldworth marchant, and at that time Mayor of the citie of Bristol, concerning their aduenture in the Westerne discouerie 1582.   pag. 182
> From manuscript. First printed in *PN*, III (1600).
> [Probably given to Hakluyt by Aldworth.]

[49]   A letter written from master Aldworth marchant and mayor of the citie of Bristol, to the right honourable sir Francis Walsingham, concerning a voyage intended for the discouerie of the coast of America lying to the Southwest of cape Briton 1583.   pag. 182
> Reprinted from *PN* (1589).

[50]   A briefe and summarie discourse vpon a voyage intended to the hithermost parts of America, written by master Christopher Carlile 1583.   pag. 182
> Reprinted from *PN* (1589).

[51]   Articles set downe by the committies appointed on the behalfe of the company of the Moscouian marchants, to conferre with master Carlile vpon his intended discouery of the hithermost partes of America.   pag. 188
> Reprinted from *PN* (1589).

[52]   A letter sent to the right honourable sir William Cecil Lord Burghley, Lord high Treasurer of England &c. from master Thomas Iames of Bristol, concerning the discouerie of the Isle of Ramea 1591.
                                                                                       pag. 191
> From manuscript. First printed in *PN*, III (1600).
> [A copy may well have been given by James to Hakluyt, but nos. 31–5 and 52–4 may have formed part of a body of materials col-lected by Hakluyt for Burghley's use as well as for his own collec-tion. See D. B. Quinn, 'England and the St Lawrence 1577–1600', in John Parker, ed., *Merchants and scholars* (Minneapolis, 1965), pp. 121–37.]

[53]   A briefe note of the Morse, and of the vse thereof.   pag. 191
Hakluyt's own note.

[54]   Certaine obseruations touching the countries and places where master Charles Leigh touched in his voyage to cape Briton, and to the Isle of Ramea anno 1597.   pag. 200
> Part of no. 35 above.

[A copy may have been obtained by Hakluyt from Jacques Noël, 1587-8, or else Jean Groute may have supplied it.]

[63]   Part of another letter written by Iaques Noel of Saint Malo to the foresayde M. Iohn Groute student in Paris.   pag. 236
From manuscript. First printed in *PN*, iii (1600).
[Hakluyt is likely to have had this either from Nöel or Groute, 1587-8.]

[64]   An excellent ruttier shewing the course from Belle isle, Carpont, and the Grand bay, vp the riuer of Canada for the space of 230 leagues, obserued by Iohn Alphonse of Xanctoigne, chiefe Pilote to Monsieur Roberual, 1542.   pag. 237
From Jean Alfonse, 'Le cosmographie avec l'espère et régime du soleil et du nord par Jean Fonteneau dit Alfonce de Saintonge.'
[Hakluyt clearly obtained in France a manuscript of this important work, completed 24 May 1544, part of which he translated and printed here, but it has not survived. B.N., ms français 676, ancien fonds (ed. Georges Musset, Paris, 1904), differs in detail from Hakluyt's text.]

[65]   A description of the Saluages in Canada.   pag. 242
Part of no. 58 above.

A catalogue of the voyages and nauigations of the English nation to Virginia, and of the seuerall discoueries thereof, chiefly at the charges of the honourable sir Walter Ralegh knight.

[66]   The first voyage made to the coast of Virginia by M. Philip Amadas, and M. Arthur Barlow, 1584.   pag. 246
Reprinted from *PN* (1589).

[67]   The second voyage made to Virginia by sir Richard Grinuile for sir Walter Ralegh, Anno 1585: at what time the first colonie of English was there left vnder the government of M. Ralfe Lane, now knight.   pag. 251
Reprinted from *PN* (1589).

[68]   The third voyage to Virginia made by a ship sent in the yeere 1586, for the reliefe of the colonie planted in Virginia, at the sole charges of sir Walter Ralegh.   pag. 265
Reprinted from *PN* (1589).

[77]   The names of all the men, women, and children which safely
arriued in Virginia, and remayned to inhabite there Anno 1587.   pag. 287
  Reprinted from *PN* (1589).

[78]   A letter of M. Iohn White to M. Richard Hakluyt written in
February 1593.   pag. 287
  From manuscript. First printed in *PN*, III (1600).
  [Since the narrative (no. 70 above) uses calendar year dating it
  would be legitimate to assume that the letter does also. But it is not
  certain that English style, which would make it 4 February 1594,
  is not being employed.]

A catalogue of certaine voyages to the coast and inland of Florida.

[79]   The voyage of Iohn de Verrazzano a Florentine to the coast
of Florida, sailing from thence Northerly to the latitude of 50. degrees,
Anno 1524.   pag. 295
  Reprinted from *DV* (1582).

[80]   The voyage of captaine Iohn Ribault to Florida, 1562. pag. 308
  Reprinted from *DV* (1582).

[81]   The voiage of captaine René Laudonniere to Florida 1564
where he fortified and inhabited two Summers, and one whole
winter.   pag. 319
  Reprint of Laudonnière, *A notable voyage* (1587).

[82]   A second voyage of captaine Iohn Ribault to Florida 1565.
  A continuation of no. 81.   pag. 349

[83]   The voyage of captaine Dominique Gourgues to Florida 1567.
where he most valiantly, iustly, and sharpely reuenged the bloody
and inhumane massacre committed by the Spaniards vpon his
countreymen, in the yeere 1565.   pag. 356
  A continuation of no. 81.

*Diuers particulars worthy the consideration, intermingled among the voyages
of Florida*

[84]   An Epistle Dedicatorie to sir Walter Ralegh, prefixed by
master Richard Hakluyt before the history of Florida, which he
translated out of French 1587.   pag. 301
  Part of the prefatory material to no. 81.

Printed from 'Relatione Che Mandò Francesco Vasquez di Coronado...quel che successe nel viaggio...', in Ramusio, *Navigationi et viaggi*, III (1556), ff. 359v–63.
Translated.

[94]   The voyage of Frier Augustin Ruis to the 15 prouinces of New Mexico, begun in the yeere 1581.   pag. 383, & 389
   Part of no. 95 following.

[95]   The voyage of Antonio de Espeio from the valley of S. Bartholomew in Nueua Galicia to the foresayd 15 prouinces of New Mexico, begun the 10 of Nouemb. 1582.   pag. 383, & 390
   Reprint of his own edition *El viaie que hizo Antonio de Espeio en el anno de ochenta y tres* (Paris, 1586). [see p. 468 below], with a new translation by himself.

The discourses, letters, &c. depending vpon the former voyages to New Mexico, Cibola and Quiuira

[96]   A Briefe discourse of the famous cosmographer M. Iohn Baptista Ramusius, concerning the three voyages of frier Marco de Niça, Francis Vasquez de Coronado, and that of Fernando Alarchon, &c.   pag. 362
   From 'Discorso Sopra Li Tre Viaggi Subsequenti', in Ramusio, *Navigationi et viaggi*, III (1556), f. 354.
   Translated.

[97]   An extract of a letter of C. Francis Vasquez de Coronado, written from Culiacan the 8 of March 1539, to a secretary of Don Antonio de Mendoça the viceroy of Nueua Espanna.   pag. 362
   From 'Summario Di Lettere Del Capitano Francesco Vasquez di Coronado, scritte ad vn Secretario del...Vicere', in Ramusio, *Navigationi et viaggi*, III (1556), ff. 345–5.
   Translated.

[98]   A letter of the sayd Francis Vasquez de Coronado gouernour of Nueua Galicia, to Don Antonio de Mendoça the viceroy of Nueua Espanna, written from Culiacan the 8 of March, 1539.
                          pag. 363
   A continuation of no. 97.

[99]   A letter written by Don Antonio de Mendoça viceroy of Nueua Espanna to the emperour Charles the fift.   pag. 364

From 'Lettere Scritte dal. .Vice Re', in Ramusio, *Navigationi et viaggi*, III (1556), 355–355v.
Translated.

[100] A testimony of Francis Lopez de Gomara, concerning the strange crook-backed oxen, the great sheepe, and the mighty dogs of Quiuira.   pag. 308 [*recte* 382]
This covers two items in Francisco López de Gómara, *Historia general de las Indias* (Zaragosa, 1552): (a) ch. 214 covering the latter part of Coronado's expedition (continuing no. 93), and (b) from ch. 215 containing the material noted above. [Lumley 1128 was Antwerp 1554.]
Translated.

[101] A letter intercepted of Bartholomew del Cano, written from Mexico the 30 of May 1590, to Francis Hernandez of Siuil, concerning the speedy building of two strong forts in S. Iuan de Vllua, and Vera Cruz, as also touching the notable new and rich discouery of Cibola or New Mexico, 400 leagues Northwest of Mexico.
                                                                                    pag. 396
From manuscript. First printed in *PN*, III (1600).
Translated.
[Given to Hakluyt by its captors, who have not, so far, been identified.]

Certeine voyages made for the discouery of the gulfe of California, and of the sea-coast on the Northwest or backside of America.

[102] The voyage of the right worshipfull knight Francisco de Vlloa, with 3 ships set forth at the charges of the right noble Fernando Cortez, by the coasts of Nueua Galicia, & Culiacan, into the gulfe of California, called El mar vermejo, as also on the backside of Cape California, as far as 30 degrees, begun from Acapulco the 8 of July, 1539.   p. 397
From [Francisco Preciado], 'Relatione Dello Scoprimento Che… va à far l'armata…[di] Francesco di Vlloa', in Ramusio, *Navigationi et viaggi*, III (1556), ff. 339v–54.
Translated.

[103] The voyage and discouery of Fernando Alarchon, made by the order of the R.H. Don Antonio de Mendoça viceroy of New Spaine,

to the very bottome of the gulfe of California, and 85 leagues vp the
riuer of Buena Guia, begun the 9 of May, 1540. pag. 425
From Hernando de Alarcón, 'Relatione Della Navigatione &
scoperta die fece il Capitano Fernando Alarcone,' in Ramusio,
Navigationi et viaggi, III (1556), ff. 363–70v.
Translated.

[104] The voyage and course which sir Francis Drake held from
the hauen of Guatulco, on the backside of Nueua Espanna, to the
Northwest of California, as far as 43 degrees, & from thence backe
againe to 38 degrees, where in a very good harbour he graued his
shippe, entrenched himselfe on land, called the countrey by the name
of Noua Albion, and tooke possession thereof on the behalfe of her
Maiestie. pag. 440
Extracted from *PN* (1589).

[105] The memorable voyage of Francis Gaulle a Spanish captaine
and pilot, vndertaken at the appointment of the viceroy of New
Spaine, from the hauen of Acapulco in the sayd prouince, to the
islands of the Luçones or the Philippinas, vnto the hauen of Manilla,
and from thence to the hauen of Macao in China; and from Macao by
the Lequeos, the isles of Iapan, and other isles to the East of Iapan,
and likewise by the Northwest part of America in 37 degrees and ½
backe againe to Acapulco, begun the 10 of March 1582, & ended
1584. Out of which voyage, besides great probabilities of a North,
Northwest, or Northeast passage, may euidently be gathered, that
the sea betweene Iapan and America is by many hundred leagues
broader, and the land betweene Cape Mendoçino and Cape California, is many hundred leagues narrower, then we finde them to be
in the ordinary maps and relations. pag. 442
From Linschoten's version of Francisco de Gualle journal in
Discours (1598), pp. 411–15.

[106] An extract of a Spanish letter written from Pueblo de los
Angeles in Nueua Espanna in October 1597, touching the discouery
of the rich islands of California, being distant eight dayes sailing
from the maine. pag. 439
From manuscript. First printed in *PN*, III (1600).

A catalogue of diuers voyages made by English men to the famous city of Mexico, and to all or most part of the other principall prouinces, cities, townes, and places thorowout the great and large kingdome of New Spaine, euen as farre as Nicaragna [sic] and Panamá, and from thence to Perú, &c.

A catalogue of the principall English voyages to all the isles called Las Antillas, and to the foure greater islands of Sant Iuan de Puerto rico,

Hispaniola, Iamaica, and Cuba, and Northward thorow the Lucayos: as also along the coasts of Tierra firma, Nombre de dios, Veragua, the Honduras, the coast of Iucatan, to the port of Sant Iuan de Vllua, and the coast of Panuco,&c.

[114]   The voyage of sir Thomas Pert, and Sebastian Cabot in the yere 1516, to Brasil, Santo Domingo, and Sant Iuan de Puerto rico.
pag. 498
Reprinted from *PN* (1589).

[115]   The voyage of Thomas Tison an English man to the West Indies before the yere 1526.   pag. 500
From manuscript. First printed in *PN*, II (1600).
[A somewhat modified version of Hakluyt's notes from Nicholas Thorne's ledger, already given in II (ii), 3 (no. F.3 above).]

[116]   The first voyage of the right worshipfull and valiant knight sir Iohn Hawkins, sometimes treasurer of her Maiesties nauy royall, made to the West Indies in the yere 1562.   pag. 500
Reprinted from *PN* (1589).

[117]   The second voyage made by the R.W. sir Iohn Hawkins knight with the Ieusus of Lubec, one of her Maiesties ships, and the Salomon, and two barks, to the coast of Guinie, & from thence to the isle of Dominica, all along the coast of Tierra firma, & so homewards about the cape of S. Anton vpon the West end of Cuba, & thorow the chanel of Bahama; Begun 1564.   pag. 501
Reprinted from *PN* (1589).

[118]   The third troublesome voyage of the right worshipfull sir Iohn Hawkins, with the Iesus of Lubec, the Minion, and foure other ships, to the parts of Guinea, and the coasts of Tierra firma, and Nueua Espanna, Anno 1567, & 1568.
Reprinted from *PN* (1589).   pag. 521

[119]   The first voyage attempted and set foorth by the valiant and expert captaine M. Francis Drake, with a ship called The Dragon, and another ship & a pinnesse, to Nombre de Dios and Dariene, about the yere 1572.   pag. 525
Reprinted from *PN* (1589).

[120]   The voyage of Iohn Oxnam of Plimmouth to the West India, and ouer the streight of Dariene into the South sea, Anno 1575.
pag. 526
Reprinted from *PN* (1589).

[121] The voyage of M. Andrew Barker of Bristoll with two shippes, the one called The Ragged staffe, and the other The Beare, to the coast of Tierra firma, and the bay of the Honduras in the West Indies, Anno 1576.   pag. 528
From manuscript. First printed in PN, III (1600).
[This was explicitly based on notes taken by Hakluyt from survivors, and from examinations made in the High Court of Admiralty and elsewhere. It might probably suggest that materials from H.C.A. cases were occasionally put in Hakluyt's way, though this is not clearly established.]

[122] The famous expedition of sir Francis Drake to the West Indies, wherein were taken the cities of saint Iago, saint Domingo, Cartagena, with the Fort and towne of saint Augustin in Florida, in the yeers 1585, and 1586.   pag. 534
From Walter Bigges, *A summarie and true discourse of Sir Francis Drakes West Indian voyage* (1589).

[123] The voyage of William Michelson and William Mace of Ratcliffe, master of a ship called The Dog, made to the bay of Mexico, anno 1589.   pag. 557
Reprinted from PN (1589).
[Hastily added in 1589. Hakluyt did not attempt to improve his rather unsatisfactory use of his materials. See Andrews, *English privateering voyages*, pp. 50-1.]

[124] The voyage and valiant fight of The Content, a ship of the right honourable sir George Carey knight, L. Hunsdon, L. Chamberlaine, Captaine of the honourable band of her Maiesties Pensioners, and Gouernour of the Isle of Wight, &c. 1591.

pag. 555 [*recte* 565]
From manuscript. First printed in PN, III (1600).
[Probably given to Hakluyt by Sir George Carey. It may have been written by William King as was no. 126 below. See Andrews, *English privateering voyages*, p. 107.]

[125] The voyage of M. Christopher Newport with a fleete of 3. ships and a Pinnesse to the Isles of Dominica, Saint Iuan de puerto rico, Hispaniola, and to the Bay of the Honduras, begun in Ianuary 1591.   pag. 567
From manuscript. First printed in PN, III (1600).

[126] The voyage of M. William king Captaine (M. Moore,

M. How, & M. Boreman being owners) in the Salomon of 200. tunnes, and the Iane Bonauenture of 40. tunnes, set foorth from Ratcliffe 1592.   pag. 570

From manuscript. First printed in *PN*, III (1600).

[127] The voyage of Henry May one of M. Iames Lancaster his company, in his nauigation to the East Indies 1591, & 1592: who in his returne with M. Lancaster by the yles of Trinidad, Mona, & Hispaniola, was about Cape Tiburon taken into a French ship vnder the conduct of Capitan de la barbotiere, which ship was cast away vpon the yles of Bermuda: where all the company that escaped drowning remained for certain moneths, built themselues a barke, sailed to Newfoundland, and so home 1593.   pag. 573. & 574

From manuscript. First printed in *PN*, III (1600).
[Sir William Foster, *The voyages of Sir James Lancaster* (1940), p. 22, noted that the manuscript passed to Purchas but it has not subsequently reappeared.]

[128] The voyage of sir Robert Duddeley to the yle of Trinidad and the coast of Paria: with his returne homeward by the yles of Granata, Santa Cruz, Sant Iuan de puerto rico, Mona, Zacheo, the sholdes called Abre ojos, and the yle of Bermuda. Anno 1594, & 1595.   pag. 574

From manuscript. First printed in *PN*, III (1600).
[Written by Dudley specifically at Hakluyt's request.]

[129] The voyage of sir Amias Preston and Captaine George Sommers to the West Indies, begun in March 1595: wherein diuers ylands, cities, townes, and forts were part taken and ransomed, and part burned. [By Robert Davie.]   pag. 578

From manuscript. First printed in *PN*, III (1600).
[Probably contributed by one of the leaders of the expedition.]

[130] The last voyage of sir Francis Drake & sir Iohn Hawkins, intended for some special seruices on the ylands and maine of the West Indies, Anno 1595. In which voyage both the foresaide knights died by sicknes.   pag. 583

From manuscript. First printed in *PN*, III (1600).

[131] The voyage of sir Antony Sherley to S. Iago, Dominica, Margarita, along the coast of Tierra firma, to the yle of Iamaica, the

bay of the Honduras, 30. leagues vp Rio dolce, and homeward by
Newfoundland, 1596.   pag. 598
    From manuscript. First printed in *PN*, III (1600).

[132] The voyage of M. William Parker of Plimmouth to Margarita,
Iamaica, Truxillo, Puerto de cauallos, &c. with his surprize of
Campeche, the chiefe towne of Iucatan. An. 1596, 1597.   p. 602
    From manuscript. First printed in *PN*, III (1600).

*The discourses, letters, intelligences, obseruations, and principall ruttiers
belonging to the voyages next before mentioned.*

[133] The opinion of Don Aluaro Baçan marques of Santa Cruz,
and high admirall of Spaine, touching the fleet of sir Francis Drake
lying at the isles of Bayona on the coast of Galicia, written in Lisbon
the 26 of October 1585, after the account of Spaine.   pag. 532
    From manuscript. First printed in *PN*, III (1600).
    Spanish and English.
    [Someone whom Hakluyt knew must have conveyed to him
    ff. 133–8 of what is now B.N., Madrid, MS 9372, which are
    missing and from which he translated his notes (see p. 288 above).]

[134] A resolution of the principall land-captaines, which accom-
panied sir Francis Drake in his memorable voyage to the West
Indies, 1585; what course they thought most expedient to be taken.
Giuen at Cartagena the 17 of February 1585.   pag. 543
    Part of no. 122 above.

[135] A relation of the surueying, new building finishing, making,
and mending of certeine ports, harbours, forts, and cities in the West
Indies: written by Baptista Antonio the king of Spaines surueyour
in those parts 1587.   pag. 548
    From manuscript. First printed in *PN*, III (1600).
    Translated.
    [In Fitzwilliam Museum, Cambridge, Bradfer–Lawrence MS 61,
    ff. 30–9, with a note in the hand of Ralegh, Hakluyt's probable
    source. Not represented in surviving Spanish sources. See Diego
    Angulo Iñiquez, *Bautista Antonelli* (Madrid, 1942), pp. 83–91;
    K. R. Andrews, *The last voyage of Drake and Hawkins* (1972),
    pp. 193–4. Another translation is in Henry E. Huntington
    Library MS EL 1682.]

[136] Twelue Spanish letters written from diuers places of the
islands and of the maine land, aswell of Nueua Espanna, as of

Tierra firma and Perú, intercepted by the ships of the worshipfull M. Iohn Wats, disclosing many secrets touching the aforesayd countreys, and the state of the South sea, and the trade to the Philippinas.

pag. 577 [recte 557]

From manuscript. First printed in *PN*, III (1600).
Translated.
[Probably given to Hakluyt by their captors, or by an official to whom they had been transferred for their intelligence interest. Their dates, ranging from 1 March to 20 November, would suggest they were consigned to Spain early in 1591. The four treasure frigates arrived safely in March. It might appear that these letters were taken either from the advice boat which preceded the fleet (James Sherlok wrote on 5 March 1591 that it had been taken and the captain and master hanged for jettisoning silver and despatches), or else from one of the shallops or boats which accompanied the frigates. Cp. *Cal. S.P., Ire., 1588–92*, p. 387; I. A. Wright, *Further English voyages* (1951), p. lxxxi.]

[137]   The interpretation of certeine words of the language of Trinidad annexed to the voyage of sir Robert Duddeley.   pag. 577
Part of no. 128 above.

[138]   A libell of Spanish lies written by Don Bernaldino delgadillo de * Auellaneda, generall of the king of Spaines armada, concerning some part of the last voyage of sir Francis Drake: together with a confutation thereof by M. Henry Sauile, &c.   pag. 591, & 593.
From Bernaldino Delgadillo de Avellaneda, *A libell of Spanish lies; found at the sacke of Cales with an answere by Henry Savile* (1596).
[S.T.C. 6551.]
Spanish and English.
[* Hakluyt's side-note 'Or, Villa nueua. His treatment of the text is discussed in K. R. Andrews, *The last voyage of Drake and Hawkins* (1972), p. 240.]

[139]   An excellent ruttier for the islands of the West Indies, and for Tierra firma, and Nueua Espanna.   pag. 603
From manuscript. First printed in *PN*, III (1600).
Translated. This corresponds to B.M., Sloane MS 2292, ff. 17–33.

[140]   A principall ruttier conteining most particular directions to saile from Saint Lucar in Andaluzia, by the Canaries, the Antillas,

and the other greater Isles Westward of them, to Saint Iuan de Vllua
in Nueua Espanna. pag. 613
  From manuscript. First printed in *PN*, III (1600).
  Translated.

[141] A declaration of the Capes and Islands aswell of Madera, the
Canaries, and The west Indies, as of the Açores, and the Isles of
Cabo Verde. pag. 624
  From manuscript. First printed in *PN*, III (1600).
  Translated.

[142] A declaration of the longitudes or Westerne and Easterne
distances from Spaine to New Spaine in America, and from thence
backe againe to Spaine. pag. 626
  From manuscript. First printed in *PN*, III (1600).

A catalogue of certaine voyages made for the discovery of the large, rich, and
beautifull empire of Guiana, by sir Walter Ralegh, and others at his charges
and appointment.

[143] The voyage of sir Walter Ralegh himselfe to the Isle of
Trinidad, where he tooke the citie of Saint Iosepho, and Don
Antonio de Berreo the captaine thereof: from whence with a barge
and certaine boates he passed vp the bay of Guanipa, the riuer of
Amana one of the mouths of the great Orenoque, the maine riuer or
Orenoque it selfe, and other riuers, for the space of 400. miles: and
in his returne homeward sacked & burnt the town of Cumaná
1595. pag. 631
  From Sir Walter Ralegh, *The discouerie of the large rich, and bewtiful*
  empyre of Guiana (1596). [Lumley 1520.]

[144] The second voyage to Guiana performed and written in the
yeere 1596. by Laurence Keymis gentleman. pag. 672
  From Lawrence Keymis, *A relation of the second voyage to Guiana*
  (1596).

[145] The 3. voyage set forth by sir Walter Ralegh to Guiana with
a pinnesse called The Wat, begun in the yere 1596, written by M.
Thomas Masham a gentleman of the company. pag. 692
  From manuscript. First printed in *PN*, III (1690).
  [Probably given to Hakluyt by Ralegh.]

From José de Acosta, *Historia natural y moral de las Indias* (Seville, 1590), bk. 2, ch. 6, bk. 3, ch. 20, 25.
Translated.
[Represented in P.R.O., S.P. Dom. Eliz., S.P. 12/235, 43 (see pp. 308–9, above).]

[157] A briefe description of the foresayd riuer of Amazones or Orellana, and of the countries thereabout, as also of the sea of fresh water, taken out of an ancient discourse written by Martin Fernandez de Ençiça. pag. 699

From Martin Fernández de Enciso, *Suma de Geographia* (Seville, 1519) [apparently as translated by John Frampton, *A briefe description of the portes, creekes, bayes, and hauens, of the Weast India* (1578); not in S.T.C.; copy in Henry E. Huntington Library.]

Certaine voyages, nauigations, and traffiques both ancient and of late, to diuers places vpon the coast of Brasill.

[158] The first voyage of M. William Hawkins of Plimmouth, father vnto sir Iohn Hawkins to Brasil Anno 1530. pag. 700
Reprinted from *PN* (1589).

[159] The second voyage of M. William Hawkins to Brasil, 1532.
Reprinted from *PN* (1589). pag. 700

[160] The voyage of M. Robert Reniger & M. Tho. Borey to Brasil, in the yere 1540. pag. 701
It was incorporated in *PN* (1589), E.6, as the information attributed to Anthony Garrard.

[161] The voyage of one Pudsey to Baya in Brasil 1542. pag. 701
First printed in *PN*, III (1600).
[From information contributed to Hakluyt by Edward Cotton of Southampton.]

[162] The voyage of M. Stephan Hare in the Minion of London to Brasil anno 1580. pag. 704
Reprinted from *PN* (1589).

[163] The prosperous voyage of Master Iames Lancaster to the towne of Fernambuck in Brasil, 1594. [By a member of the *Consent's* company.] pag. 708
From manuscript. First printed in *PN*, III (1600).

The letters, discourses, instructions, obseruations, and ruttiers, depending vpon the voyages to Brasil.

[164]   A Letter written to M. Richard Staper by Iohn Whithal from Santos in Brasil, the 26. of Iune, 1578.   pag. 701
 Reprinted from *PN* (1589).

[165]   A letter of the aduenturers for Brasil sent to Iohn Whithal dwelling at Santos, by the Minion of London, dated the 24. of October 1580.   pag. 703
 Reprinted from *PN* (1589).

[166]   An intercepted letter of Francis Suarez to his brother Diego Suarez dwelling in Lisbon, written from the riuer of Ienero in Brasil in Iune 1596. concerning an exceeding rich trade newly begunne betweene that place and Peru by the way of the riuer of Plate, with small barkes of 30. or 40. tunnes.   pag. 706
 From manuscript. First printed in *PN*, III (1600).
 Translated.
 [Probably given to Hakluyt by its captors, who have not been identified.]

[167]   An intercepted letter written from Feliciano Cieça de Carualho the gouernour of Paraiua in the most Northern part of Brasil 1597. to Philip the second King of Spaine, concerning the conquest of Rio grande, &c. [20 August 1597.]   pag. 716
 From manuscript. First printed in *PN*, III (1600).
 Translated.
 [Probably given to Hakluyt by its captors who have not been identified.]

[168]   A speciall note concerning the currents of the sea betweene the Cape of Buena Esperanca, and the coast of Brasilia.   pag. 719
 From manuscript. First printed in *PN*, III (1600).
 [This came to Hakluyt from Sir John Yorke, possibly through his elder cousin. A Brazil voyage was being contemplated *circa* 1551–3 by Cabot, in association with Jean Ribault, but it is not known whether Ribault's association with the French Brazil trade was so extensive as to enable him to be the author referred to.]

[169]   An excellent ruttier describing the course to be kept from

Cabo verde to the coast of Brasil, and all along the said coast from
Fernambuck to the riuer of Plate.   pag. 719
  From manuscript. First printed in *PN*, III (1600).
  Translated.
  [This (with 170 following) is a version of B.M., Sloane 2292,
  ff. 1–9, 10–15 (owned by Thomas Harriot), continued from 139,
  see p. 451 above.]

[170] A ruttier from the riuer of Plate to the Streights of Magellan.

  From manuscript. First printed in *PN*, III (1600).   pag. 724.
  Translated.

A note of two voyages of Englishmen into the Riuer of Plate.

[171] A Voyage of two Englishmen to the riuer of Plate in the
company of Sebastian Cabota, 1527.   pag. 726
  Reprinted from *PN* (1589).

[172] The voyage of M. Iohn Drake after his departure from
M. Fenton, vp the riuer of Plate 1582.   pag. 726
  Reprinted from *PN* (1589).

[173] A Ruttier which declareth the situation of the coast of Brasil
from the yle of Santa Catelina vnto the mouth of the riuer of Plate,
and all along vp within the said riuer, and what armes & mouths it
hath to enter into it, as farre as it is nauigable with small barkes. pag. 728.
  From manuscript. First printed in *PN*, III (1600).
  [This would appear to be a full version of the rutter obtained from
  Lopes Vas in 1586. See pp. 376–7 above.]

*A Catalogue of diuers English voyages, some intended and some performed
to the Streights of Magellan, the South sea, along the coasts of Chili,
Peru, Nicaragua, and Nueua Galicia, to the headland of California, and
to the Northwest thereof as farre as 43. degrees, as likewise to the yles of
the Ladrones, the Philippinas, the Malucos, and the Iauas; and from thence
by the Cape of Buena Esperanza and the yle of Santa Helena (the whole
globe of the earth being circompassed) home againe into England.*

[174] The famous voyage of sir Francis Drake into the South sea,
and therehence about the globe of the whole earth, begunne Anno
1577.
                                     pag. 742
  Reprinted from *PN* (1589).

[175]   The voyage of Nunno de Silua a Portugal Pilot taken by sir Francis Drake at the yles of Cabo Verde, and caried along with him as farre as the hauen of Guatulco vpon the coast of New Spaine: with his confession made to the Viceroy of Mexico of all matters that befell, during the time that he accompanied sir Francis Drake.   pag. 742

From manuscript. First printed in *PN*, III (1600).

Translated. Collated with a translation of the original document in Z. Nuttal, *New light on Drake* (1914), pp. 256–71.

[176]   The voyage of M. Iohn Winter into the South sea by the Streight of Magellan in consort with sir Francis Drake, begun in the yeere 1577. he being the first Christian that euer repassed the said Streight. [By Edward Cliffe.]   pag. 748

From manuscript. First printed in *PN*, III (1600).

[In B.M., Lansdowne MS 100, ff. 17–21v.]

[177]   The voyage of M. Edward Fenton and M. Luke Ward his vice-admirall with 4. ships, intended for China, but performed onely to the coast of Brasil, as farre as 33. degrees of Southerly latitude; begunne in the yeere 1582.   pag. 757

Reprinted from *PN* (1589) [with some cuts].

[178]   The voyage of M. Robert Withrington, and M. Christopher Lister intended for the South sea, with two tal ships set forth at the charges of the right honourable the Earle of Cumberland, but performed onely to the Southerly latitude of 44. degrees, begun Anno 1586. [By John Sarracoll.]   pag. 762 [= 769]

Reprinted from *PN* (1589).

[179]   The prosperous voyage of M. Thomas Candish esquire into the South sea, and so round about the circumference of the whole earth, begun in the yere 1586. and finished 1588. [By Francis Pretty.]
                                                                              pag. 803

From manuscript. First printed in *PN*, III (1600).

[Probably given to Hakluyt by Thomas Cavendish before his departure on his last voyage in 1591. It replaced the narrative by N.H. printed in *PN* (1589).]

[180]   The voyage of the Delight a ship of Bristol one of the consorts of M. Iohn Chidley esquire, and M. Paul Wheele, made to the Streights of Magellan, begun in the yere 1589. [By W. Magoths.]   pag. 840

From manuscript. First printed in *PN*, III (1600).

[181]   The last voyage of M. Thomas Candish intended for the

South sea, the Philippinas, and the coast of China, with three tall ships, and two barks, begun 1591. [By John Jane.] pag. 842
  From manuscript. First printed in *PN*, III (1600).
  [Possibly given to Hakluyt by John Davis as evidence that he did not, as charged by Cavendish, desert him. Later Hakluyt acquired Cavendish's own account (or a copy) which he passed to Purchas, the original being now in the Collection of Paul Mellon.]

The principall obseruations, discourses, instructions, letters, ruttiers, and intelligences belonging to the voyages immediatly going before.

[182] The names of the kings of Iaua, at the time of sir Francis Drakes being there. pag. 742
  Reprinted from *PN* (1589).

[183] Certaine words of the naturall language of Iaua, with the interpretation thereof. pag. 742
  Reprinted from *PN* (1589).

[184] The confession of Nunno de Silua, a Portugall pilot, taken by sir Francis Drake, which he made to the viceroy of Mexico, concerning the proceeding of sir Francis Drake, &c. 1579. pag. 742
  The same as no. 175.

[185] A letter written in the South sea by sir Francis Drake vnto his consort M. Iohn Winter. [page] 748
  Part of no. 175 above.

[186] Instructions giuen by the R.H. the lords of the councell, to M. Edward Fenton esquire, for the order to be obserued in the voyage recommended vnto him for the East Indies and Cathay, April 9. 1582. pag. 754
  Reprinted from *PN* (1589).

[187] A discourse of the West Indies and the South sea, written by Lopez Vaz a Portugall, conteining diuers memorable matters not to be found in any other writers, and continued vnto the yere 1587. pag. 778
  From manuscript. First printed in *PN*, III (1600).
  Translated.
  [An account of English activities in the Spanish empire 1572–87, by Lopes Vas, captured in his possession when he was taken by Cumberland's expedition in the Plate. It most probably came to Hakluyt with the narrative of the voyage, no. 178 above.]

[188]   Certaine rare and speciall notes most properly belonging to the voyage of M. Thomas Candish about the world; concerning the latitudes, soundings, lying of lands, distances of places, the variation of the compasse, and other notable obseruations, diligently taken by M. Thomas Fuller of Ipswich.   pag. 825
   From manuscript. First printed in *PN*, III (1600).
   [Probably obtained from Cavendish before he left on his last voyage in 1591.]

[189]   A letter of M. Thomas Candish to the R.H. the olde Lord Hunsdon, L. Chamberlaine, one of her Maiesties most honourable priuie councell, touching the successe of his voyage rounde about the worlde.   [page] 837
   Reprinted from *PN* (1589).

[190]   Certaine notes or references taken out of a large map of China, brought home by M. Thomas Candish 1588.   [page] 837
   Reprinted from *PN* (1589).

[191]   A petition made in the streight of Magellan by certeine of the company of the Delight of Bristoll, vnto Robert Burnet the Master of the sayd ship, and one of the consorts of M. Chidley the 12 of February 1589.   pag. 840
   Part of no. 181 above.

[192]   The testimoniall of the company of the Desire, a ship of M. Candishes fleet in his last voyage, touching the loosing of their generall, which appeareth to haue bene vtterly against their meanings.
                                                              [page] 845
   Part of no. 181 above.

[193]   The letters of the Queenes most excellent Maiestie, sent in the yere 1596, to the emperour of China, by M. Richard Allot and M. Thomas Bromefield, merchants of London, who were embarked in the fleet, whereof M. Beniamin Wood was generall.   pag. 852
   From manuscript. First printed in *PN*, III (1600).
   Latin and English.

[194]   Three seuerall testimonies concerning the mighty kingdome of Coray, tributary to the king of China, and bordering vpon his Northeast frontiers: and also touching the warres of Quabacondono the monarch of Iapan against China, by the way of Coray.   pag. 854

Translated. In (a) Luis Froes, *Copia di due lettere annue dal Giapone de 1589 & 1590* (Rome, 1593), pp. 122–4; (b) Froes, *Lettera del Giapone degli Anni 1591 et 1592* (Rome, 1595), translated by Ubaldini Bartolini; (c) Organtino [Soldus] Bresciano, *Copia di due lettere scritte de al P. Organtino Bresciano...dal Meaco del Giapone. Al...P. Claudio Acquaviva* (Rome, 1597), translated by G.B. Peruschi, pp. 10–13.
It is not clear which text Hakluyt used.

[195] A briefe note concerning an extreame Northerly prouince of Iapan, called Zuegara, situate 30 dayes iourney from Miacó, & also of a certeine nation of Tartars, called Iezi, inhabiting on the maine to the North of China.   pag. 861
Translated. From Luis Froes, *Re rebus Iaponicis. Historica relatio* (Maguntiae, 1599), pp. 278–9.

[196] Aduertisements touching the ships that goe from Siuil to the Indies of Spaine, together with some sea-orders of the Contractation house of Siuil.   pag. 862
From manuscript. First printed in *PN*, III (1600).
Translated.
[Possibly supplied to Hakluyt by Pedro Diaz. see no. 198.]

[197] The order of the Carena giuen to the ships that goe out of Spaine to the West Indies.   pag. 864.
From manuscript. First printed in *PN*, III (1600).
Translated.
[Possibly supplied to Hakluyt by Pedro Diaz; see no. 198.]

[198] The examination of the Masters and Pilots which saile in the fleets of Spaine to the West Indies, written in Spanish by Pedro Dias a Spanish Pilot.   pag. 864, & 866
From manuscript. First printed in *PN*, III (1600).
Spanish and English.
[Collected by Hakluyt from Pedro Diaz in February 1586 (or February 1587) and translated by him.]

PART FIVE

HAKLUYT'S
BOOKS AND SOURCES

27

The primary Hakluyt bibliography

D. B. QUINN, C. E. ARMSTRONG, and R. A. SKELTON

I

Works compiled, translated or published by Richard Hakluyt

Divers voyages (1582)

1. *Divers voyages* (1582): the printing history.

2. The make-up of the volume.

3. Provisional check-list of surviving copies in Great Britain and U.S.A.

[Revised from D. B. Quinn, *Richard Hakluyt, editor*. A study introductory to the facsimile edition of Richard Hakluyt's *Divers voyages* (1582) to which is added a facsimile of *A shorte and briefe narration of the two navigations to Newe Fraunce* (Amsterdam, 1967), pp. 30–8, 45–6, 48–51. The editor is indebted to Theatrum Orbis Terrarum Ltd. for permission to use the preliminary check-list of copies in Great Britain and the United States from this volume.]

I

Divers voyages, as it emerged in 1582, consisted essentially of three sections which could well have been designed as separate tracts,[1] all directed to putting on record what was available to Englishmen on eastern North America. The first extended from A1 to D4 (D4v being blank), with the Thorne map appended, and ending with 'Finis'. It comprised the Cabot patent of 1496, such items as Hakluyt could get from the English chroniclers and Ramusio on the Cabot and subsequent North American voyages, and the Robert Thorne 'declaration', 'booke' and map of 1527. The second part began with a new signature count – some evidence, though it is not

---

[1] A more detailed analysis will be found in D. B. Quinn, *Richard Hakluyt, editor*, pp. 10–17, 30–2.

conclusive, of an intention to issue the work in separate instalments – and extended from $^2A_1$ to ^2G_3v, again ending with 'Finis' and being followed by a blank leaf. This contained the Verrazzano and Zeno narratives from Ramusio – with Michael Lok's map to go with them – and the Ribault narrative of French Florida which had been published in London in 1563. A final section continued from the end of Ribault ($^2H_1-^2K_4$) with memoranda prepared by the elder Hakluyt in 1578 and 1580 and a list of American commodities. The make-up of the book clearly indicates that it was put together in distinct sections, probably for reasons of haste, but also, it is not improbable, because of changes of mind about what was to be brought out, in what order, and when. We may, therefore, see *Divers voyages* shaping itself from a series of small propaganda tracts with specified purposes into a book which combined all of them. The preliminaries have a more easily analysed history. Hakluyt decided to preface his dedication to Philip Sidney with lists of geographers and travellers. To begin with these would have been designed to occupy recto and verso of the second leaf, but, on acquiring a piece of new information from Antonio de Castillo on a Portuguese voyage after the dedication was set up, Hakluyt got his printer to move the list of geographers to back up the title leaf, enabling him to bring the list of travellers on to the recto of the second leaf (and to revise them more nearly up to date) and so back this up with the new material on the verso.

2

DIVERS | voyages touching the discouerie of | America, *and the Ilands adiacent* | vnto the same, made first of all by our | *Englishmen, and afterward by the French-* | *men and Britons:* | And certaine notes of aduertisements for obserua- | tions, necessarie for such as shall heereafter | make the like attempt, | With two mappes annexed heereunto for the | plainer vnder- standing of the whole | matter. | [ornament] | Imprinted at Lon- | don for Thomas VVoodcocke, | *dwelling in paules Church-yard,* | at the signe of the blacke beare. | 1582.

[ ]², ¶⁴, A–D⁴, *A–G⁴, H², I–K⁴.* Last leaf of preliminaries signed with a printer's flower; third leaf in the second count signed *B₅* for *B₃*. Thorne map to follow D₄ (first count); Lok map after *B₄* (second count).

[S.T.C. 12624] B.M.

DIVERS

voyages touching the difcouerie of
America, *and the Ilands adiacent*
vnto the fame, made firft of all by our
Englifhmen, and afterward by the French-
men and Britons:

And certaine notes of aduertifements for obferua-
tions, neceffarie for fuch as fhall heereafter
make the like attempt,

With two mappes annered heereunto foz the
plainer vnderftanding of the whole
matter.

Imprinted at Lon-
don for Thomas VVoodcocke,
dwelling in paules Church-yard,
at the figne of the blacke beare,

1582,

Fig. 18   Title-page of *Divers voyages* (1582)

A. Great Britain

	Thorne map	Lok map		
LONDON				
1. British Museum I	T	L	On t.p. (trimmed) 'Robertus Hyggons possessor' (16th-century hand). George Chalmers (1841)	Signature: 'Richard Hakluyt' at end of dedication
2. British Museum II	T	L	Thomas Grenville (1847)	
OXFORD				
3. Bodleian Library	—	L	No provenance (acquired between 1674 and 1738)	
4. St John's College	—	—	Edward Middleton; Nathaniel Crynes (1745)	Contemporary limp vellum binding with the 1580 Cartier, gilt rules, central oval Arabesque ornament, stamped on covers 'PS'; spine lettered 'Voyages vnto America' in early hand
CAMBRIDGE				
5. Magdalene College	—	—	Samuel Pepys (1724)	'Magnus ope minorum' on t.p. in contemporary hand
GLASGOW				
6. University Library	T	L	William Hunter (1783)	Bound (18th cent.) with James Rosier on Waymouth voyage (1605)

464

	Thorne map	Lok map		
EDINBURGH				
7. National Library of Scotland	—	—	Advocates Library (acquired between 1787 and 1807)	Incomplete, containing only prelims. and sig. A–D
WILTSHIRE				
8. Longleat (Marquess of Bath)	—	—		Lacks D_{2-4}, E_1

B. *United States*	Thorne map	Lok map		
CALIFORNIA				
9. San Marino, Henry E. Huntington Library	T	—	C. K. Kalbfleisch; M. C. Lefferts; E. Church; Henry E. Huntington	
ILLINOIS				
10. Chicago, Newberry Library	—	—	Edward A. Ayer	Maps in facsimile
MASSACHUSETTS				
11. Cambridge, Harvard University	—	—	R. Heber; Obadiah Rich (1845)	Lacks first A_1, F_3: maps in facsimile

B. *United States* (cont.)

	Thorne map	*Lok map*		
MICHIGAN				
12. Ann Arbor, William L. Clements Library	—	—	G. Chalmers (2nd copy); W. H. Miller; S. R. Christie-Miller; Henry E. Huntington; William L. Clements	
MINNESOTA				
13. Minneapolis, James Ford Bell Coll., University of Minn.	T	L	John Strange; Alexander Dalrymple; James Ford Bell	T.p. in facsimile. Four pages of notes by Dalrymple. Vellum binding (17th century)
NEW JERSEY				
14. Princeton University Library	—	—	John Gott, bishop of Truro; Sotheby's (20 March 1908); Quaritch; Edward N. Crane; Grenville Kane	Maps in facsimile
NEW YORK				
15. New York Public Library	—	—	British Museum (exchanged 1849); James Lenox	Maps in facsimile
16. Pierpont Morgan Library, New York	—	—	Henry C. Murphy; Theodore Irwin; Pierpont Morgan (1900)	G4–K4 lacking

466

	Thorne map	Lok map	
PENNSYLVANIA			
17. Free Library of Philadelphia	T	—	Inscribed: 'Liber Aedmundi Brudnell' militis/empt' termino pasce/1582 die Maīj/1582/'. Contemporary limp vellum
			Sir Edmund Brudenell; H. F. Du Puy; William D. Breaker; Rosenbach Company; William E. Elkins
RHODE ISLAND			
18. Providence, John Carter Brown Library, I	—	L	Thorne map in facsimile: first D3, D4 repaired
			Mondidier (Dec. 1851); Henry Stevens; John Carter Brown
19. Providence, John Carter Brown Library, II	T	—	Incomplete; A–G^4 (from one copy), H^2, I^4, K^3 (from another)
			Lathrop C. Harper; John Carter Brown Library 1929
VIRGINIA			
20. Upperville, Paul Mellon	—	—	Maps and twelve leaves in facsimile. Inscribed 'Christo. Fulthorpe' and 'pretium 2d.'
			Sotheby's (5 May 1942) H. C. L. Morris; W. H. Robinson; Paul Mellon

EL VIAIE QVE | HIZO ANTONIO DE | ESPEIO EN EL ANNO DE | ochenta y tres: el qual con sus compan- | eros descubrieron vna tierra en que | hallarõ quinze Prouincias todas llenas | de pueblos, y de casas de quatro y cinco | altos, a quien pusieron por nõbre nueuo | Mexico, por parecerse en muchas cosas | al vieio Esta ála parte del Norte, y se | cree que por ella y por poblado, se pue- | de venir hasta llegar a la tierra que lla- | man del Labrador, de quien diximos | mas largemente adelante. | [Ornament.] Impressa a Madrid, anno de 1586. Y de | nueuo en Paris el mesmo anno, a la | costa de Richardo Hakluyt. | M. D. LXXXVI.

Collation a–d⁴.

[Not in Atkinson.] B.M. (unique copy: inscribed 'Ioannes Dee: A° 1590. Ianuarij 24. Ex dono Thomae Hariot, Amici mei').

EL VIAIE QVE

HIZO ANTONIO DE

ESPEIO EN EL ANNO DE
ochenta y tres: el qual con sus compan-
neros descubrieron vna tierra en que
hallarō quinze Prouincias todas llenas
de pueblos, y de casas de quatro y cinco
altos, a quien pusieron por nóbre nueuo
Mexico, por parecerse en muchas cosas
al viejo. Esta àla parte del Norte, y se
cree que por ella, y por poblado, se pue-
de venir hasta llegar a la tierra que lla-
man del Labrador, de quien diximos
mas largamente adelante.

Impressa en Madrid, anno de 1586. Y de
nueuo en Paris el mesmo anno, a la
costa de Richardo Hakluyt.

M. D. LXXXVI.

Fig. 19   Title-page of Antonio de Espejo, *El viaie* (1586)

A NOTABLE HISTORIE | containing foure voyages made by | certayne French Captaynes vnto FLORIDA: | Wherein the great riches and fruiteful⁄ nes | of the countrey with the maners of the people hitherto con⁄ | cealed are brought to light, written all, sauing the last | by *Monsieur Laudonniere,* who remained there | himselfe as the French Kings Lieuetenant | a yere and a quarter: | *Newly translated out of French into English by R.H.* | In the end is added a large table for the | better finding out the principall matters con⁄ tayned | *in this worke.* | [ornament] | AT LONDON, | Imprinted by Thomas Dawson 1587.

Collation: [ ]⁴, A–R⁴.

[S.T.C. 15316] B.M.

A NOTABLE HISTORIE

containing foure voyages made by

certayne French Captaynes vnto FLORIDA:

VVherein the great riches and fruitefulnes
of the countrey with the maners of the people hitherto con-
cealed are brought to light, written all, sauing the last,
by *Monsieur Laudonniere*, who remained there
himselfe as the French Kings Lieuetenant
a yere and a quarter:

Newly translated out of French into English by R. H.

In the end is added a large table for the
better finding out the principall matters contayned
in this worke.

AT LONDON,
Imprinted by Thomas Dawson 1587.

Fig. 20   Title-page of René de Laudonnière, *A notable historie* (1587)

DE | ORBE NOVO | PETRI MARTYRIS AN⁄ | GLERII MEDIOLANENSIS, PRO⁄ | tonotarij, & Caroli quinti Senatoris | Decades octo, diligenti temporum ob⁄ | seruatione, & vtilissimis annotationibus | illustratae, suóque nitori restitutæ, | *Labore & industria* RICHARDI HAKLVYTI | *Oxoni⁄ ensis Angli.* | Additus est in vsum lectoris accuratus | totius operis index. | [Ornament] PARISIIS, | Apud GVILLELMVM AVVRAY, via D. | Ioannis Bellouacensis, sub insigni | Bellerophontis coronati. | M.D. LXXXVII. | [Rule] | *Cum priuilegio Regis.*

Collation: a⁸, A–Rr⁸.

B.M. (Richard Harvey's copy with his notes), C.45.b.10 (with map).

DE
ORBE NOVO
PETRI MARTYRIS AN-
GLERII MEDIOLANENSIS, PRO-
tonotarij , & Caroli quinti Senatoris
Decades octo, diligenti temporum ob-
feruatione, & vtilissimis annotationibus
illuftratæ, fuóque nitori reftitutæ,

Labore & induftria RICHARDI HAKLVYTI
Oxoniensis Angli.
Additus eft in vfum lectoris accuratus
totius operis index.

PARISIIS,
Apud GVILLELMVM AVVRAY, via D.
Ioannis Bellouacenfis , fub infigni
Bellerophontis coronati.
M. D. LXXXVII.
────────────────
Cum priuilegio Regis.

Fig. 21   Title-page of Pietro Martiro d'Anghiera, *De orbe nouo...decades* (1587)

The principall navigations (1589)

1. *The principall navigations* (1589): printing history.

2. The make-up of the volume.

3. Provisional check-list of surviving copies.

[Extracted and revised from the introduction, by D. B. Quinn and R. A. Skelton, to the facsimile edition of *Principall navigations* (1589) (2 vols., Hakluyt Society, 1965), 1, xxii–iv, liii–lx.]

I

The printing history of the book[1] probably opens at the beginning of 1589. It is likely that when Richard Hakluyt returned to England from France late in 1588 he had ready, or almost ready, the first sections of his first part, the medieval material including the Mandeville. Thereafter he appears to have fed his material systematically to the printer and there is no sign of any hitch in the composition of the book down to p. 792 (sig. Bbbb 6), though no analysis of the typographical variants has yet been made by which this statement can be fully tested. Thereafter, for the remaining pages of the text (793–825) the material is in the nature of an appendix, being additional matter which became available too late for it to be inserted in its proper place. One of these documents gives some help in dating the progress of the book. The brief note on the voyage of the *Dog* in 1589 was based on letters from William Mace to Edward Wilkinson of Tower Hill, London, after the return of the ship to Plymouth on 10 September 1589[2]. The letters would have taken some little time to reach Hakluyt and be abstracted by him and printed, so that they could scarcely have been ready before October, but perhaps, since they do not appear in either contents list or index, they were not set up until a month or more later. How long the index took to compile cannot easily be computed, but it is much more extensive for the earlier part of the book than the later. The dedication was dated 17 November, though whether the date was added before or after the setting remains conjectural, but the preliminaries, title-page, contents' lists (which assimilated almost all the late-coming documents), dedication and address to the reader could presumably have been printed off by the end of the calendar year, along with the index, which

---

[1] Rewritten from the introduction by D. B. Quinn and R. A. Skelton, to the facsimile edition of *Principall navigations*, pp. xxii–iv.

[2] *PN* (1589), 817.

again assimilated almost all the late-coming elements. Without any external evidence to help us, it would be safe to say that if *Principall navigations* did not appear in December 1589, it was probably ready in January 1590. If there were further delays, and the book did not appear until February or March, we could reasonably expect that the dating on the title-page would have been changed to conform with the practice that major books normally bore the dating of the calendar year.[1]

At some point after the book was complete and printed off two events took place which were to alter the form of surviving copies. In the first place permission was received to print an account of Drake's circumnavigation. Hakluyt had indeed begun to prepare such an account but withdrew it so as not to prejudice a collection of Drake's voyages which was in preparation.[2] Permission now came to insert it, not improbably from Drake himself. Accordingly Hakluyt, or one of his assistants, pared down the available materials to a length of some 10,000 words (there being internal evidence of some reduction in scale), had them printed on the same paper and in the same type as the rest of the book, and sent them out with most of the copies sold. It would appear that some few copies were issued without the Drake leaves, and that then a certain number were issued with the Drake leaves and without any other changes.[3] At that point a further alteration took place: the leaves containing Sir Jerome Bowes' report of his Russian embassy in 1583–4 were cancelled. It was evidently thought that Bowes had put himself in rather an undignified light by some of his comments and that in any event there were statements in the report which might prejudice the Muscovy Company in its future dealings with the Tsar. It seems likely that the initiative came from the Muscovy Company as it was to do in the case of Giles Fletcher's book *Of the Russe common wealth*, published in 1591, the chapter headings of which Hakluyt managed to include from a manuscript version.[4] In any event, a more discreet and shorter

[1] See W. W. Greg. *Some aspects and problems of London printing between 1550 and 1650* (1956), pp. 82–3.

[2] Sig. *4v.

[3] See W. H. Kerr, 'The treatment of Drake's circumnavigation in Hakluyt's "Voyages", 1589', BSA, *Papers* XXXIV (1940), 287–8, and p. 480 below.

[4] Robert O. Lindsay, 'Richard Hakluyt and *Of the Russe Common Wealth*', BSA, *Papers,* LVII (1963), 312–27, gives a full account of Hakluyt's dealings with Fletcher in 1589 and in his second edition. His criticisms of Hakluyt's handling of the matter are almost wholly erroneous since he assumes that Hakluyt was free to print what he wished (which he was not) and that, if he printed any of Fletcher, he was obliged to print all (which again is baseless):

version of Bowes' narrative was prepared: 'printed this second time, according to the true copie I receiued of a gentleman that went on the same voyage, for the correction of the errours in the former impression,' as Hakluyt says.[1] This replaced the 'Bowes leaves, first state', and, with the added Drake leaves, was the normal form in which the remainder of the edition was issued. It might appear that surviving copies containing both states of the Bowes leaves are sophisticated ones since none were found in a contemporary binding which had remained intact, though this cannot be regarded as fully established. About one copy in three of the surviving examples contains the map.

Of the 130 copies listed there are probably a few duplications amongst the booksellers' and auction copies, but as the check-list is not an exhaustive one, it might seem that this number roughly represents the scale of survival. If the total number of copies printed was about 1,000, which was usual, we can estimate that it was apparently exhausted by 1597, because by then Hakluyt was able to think seriously of the second edition which he began to publish in 1598. The total number of copies surviving is high, but not, it would seem, excessive: the comparable figure for sets of the second edition is in the region of 200. The degree of sophistication which many of the surviving copies have undergone suggests that the book was read vigorously and that a good number of copies suffered in the process, to provide material for cannibalization in their turn.

No variety in paper, type-fount, and make-up of pages in the book as originally prepared, and no divergence in these respects in the Drake leaves and the second state of the Bowes leaves, have been observed. The paper is a 'pot' watermark, commonly used by the Queen's printer. A detailed analysis of the typographical variants, using modern techniques, has still to be made. Contemporary prices ranging, in five instances, from 9s (probably unbound as this gives a normal price of $\frac{1}{2}d$ a sheet) to 10s and 11s 11d (both presumably bound), have been recorded.[2]

> indeed it is probable that Hakluyt, in printing what he did, sailed as close to suppression as he dared. Nor does Mr Lindsay show any detailed appreciation of what could or could not be said about Russia without creating diplomatic or commercial crises between the two countries.

[1] P. 491. Purchas defended himself for making further cuts in Fletcher (*Pilgrimes*, III (1625), 413) by saying, 'I haue in some places contracted, in others mollified the biting or more bitter stile which the Authour vseth of the Russian Gouern-ment; that I might doe good at home, without harme abroad.'

[2] See Quinn and Skelton, introduction, p. xxiv, n. 6, and pp. 482, 484, 486–8 below.

2

THE PRINCIPALL | NAVIGATIONS, VOIA⁄ | GES AND DISCOVERIES OF THE | English nation, made by Sea or ouer Land, | ... | *Imprinted at London by* GEORGE BISHOP | and RALPH NEWBERIE, Deputies to | CHRISTOPHER BARKER, Printer to the | Queenes most excellent Maiestie. | *1589.*

Small folio. (A tall copy measures $11\frac{1}{4} \times 8$ inches.)

Signatures (with Bowes leaves in State I and without Drake leaves: see below):*⁸, A–T⁶, V–X⁴ (X4 blank), Aa–Yy⁶, Aaa–Yyy⁶, Aaaa–Eeee⁶, Ffff⁴(Ffff4 blank).

Page numeration:

*1–8	Unnumbered
A1r–Yy6r	1–505
Aaa1r–Eeee4v	506–825
Eeee5r–Ffff4v	Unnumbered

The following pages are blank, without page numbers, and were disre⁄ garded in the page⁄numeration: X4r, X4v, Yy6v. From sig. Aaa1r (p. 506) to the end, even page⁄numbers are on the recto, odd ones on the verso. The map is usually bound in before sig. A1.

The following errors in page⁄numeration, a number of which were corrected in the course of printing, are found in various copies.

93 for 39	211 for 215
59 for 51	466 for 463
52 for 64	463 for 466
89 for 90	*494* for *499* (Bowes leaves, State I)
90 for 91	*494* for *499* (Bowes leaves, State II)
150 for 138	559 for 593
151 for 139	798 for 779

Bowes leaves, State I (eight leaves): sig. Xx5r–Yy6r, paginated 491–505. (See collation above.)

Bowes leaves, State II (six leaves): sig. Yy1r–6r, paginated 491–501 (sig. Yy6v blank and without page number; p. 494 misnumbered as 499, p. 499 as 494). Note that where the leaves are in State II, the page numbering jumps from 501 to 506.

Drake leaves (six leaves): the first three signed Mmm4–6, the last three (conjugates) without signatures; all without page numeration. This additional 6-leaf gathering is inserted in the centre of the original signature Mmm, the two together making a gathering of 12 leaves.

[S.T.C. 12625]

3

For the provisional check-list printed below neither completeness nor the character of a 'census' is claimed. Its foundation is the list by W. H. Kerr in BSA *Papers*, XXXIV (1940), pp. 300–2, on which we have tried to build by circularizing national and academic libraries and of the principal collectors and booksellers. An attempt has been made, from collation of the information assembled, to form a general impression (first) of the degree of survival and (second) of the evidential value of extant copies, by identifying those which, retaining their original form and constitution, may be taken into account in a bibliographical reconstruction of the printing history of the volume.

It is plain that extensive sophistication has been practised with the object of completing imperfect, or supposedly imperfect, copies. Any copy which has appeared in the book-market and passed into a library since the eighteenth century, or which has been rebound in modern times, may be open to suspicion on these grounds. The inferior or incomplete copies which have been broken up to supply deficiencies in others must be very numerous, perhaps almost half as many as those recorded in the check-list, from which fragmentary copies known to be, or to have been, in the pos-session of booksellers are omitted. In the list we have employed conventional symbols to distinguish those copies which positive evidence (provenance and history, early binding, physical congruity of contents) or strong presump-tion suggests to be in their original condition from those whose history or make-up contains elements pointing to possible sophistication, such as modern rebinding or the presence of leaves (not necessarily the Drake or Bowes leaves) from another copy. The presence of the Bowes leaves in both states has been taken as evidence of sophistication, but insertion of the map alone in a copy which lacked it has not. A few copies (e.g. nos. 46, 68) in which the Drake or Bowes leaves have plainly been supplied are reported to be in contemporary or near-contemporary binding, which cannot therefore be considered in isolation as evidence of original condition. Among copies for which we have no evidence one way or the other, and for which no indicative symbol is given in the check-list, there may of course be a number in the original condition.

Analysis of the unsophisticated, or 'pure', copies in our list, a good many

THE PRINCIPALL
NAVIGATIONS, VOIA-
GES AND DISCOVERIES OF THE
English nation, made by Sea or ouer Land,

to the most remote and farthest distant Quarters of
the earth at any time within the compasse
of these 1500. yeeres: Deuided into three
seuerall parts, according to the positions of the Regions wherunto they were directed.

The first, conteining the personall trauels of the English vnto *Iudæa, Syria, A-rabia,* the riuer *Euphrates, Babylon, Balsara,* the *Persian* Gulfe, *Ormuz, Chaul, Goa, India,* and many Islands adioyning to the South parts of *Asia* : toge-ther with the like vnto *Egypt,* the chiefest ports and places of *Africa* with-in and without the Streight of *Gibraltar,* and about the famous Promon-torie of *Buona Esperança.*

The second, comprehending the worthy discoueries of the English towards the North and Northeast by Sea, as of *Lapland, Scrikfinia, Corelia,* the Baie of *S. Nicholas,* the Isles of *Colgoieue, Vaigats,* and *Noua Zembla* toward the great riuer *Ob,* with the mightie Empire of *Russia,* the *Caspian* Sea, *Georgia, Armenia, Media, Persia, Boghar* in *Bactria,* & diuers kingdoms of *Tartaria.*

The third and last, including the English valiant attempts in searching al-most all the corners of the vaste and new world of *America,* from 73. de-grees of Northerly latitude Southward, to *Meta Incognita, Newfoundland,* the maine of *Virginia,* the point of *Florida,* the Baie of *Mexico,* all the In-land of *Noua Hispania,* the coast of *Terra firma, Brasill,* the riuer of *Plate,* to the Streight of *Magellan:* and through it, and from it in the South Sea to *Chili, Peru, Xalisco,* the Gulfe of *California, Noua Albion* vpon the backside of *Canada,* further then euer any Christian hitherto hath pierced.

Whereunto is added the last most renowmed English Nauigation,
round about the whole Globe of the Earth.

By *Richard Hakluyt* Master of *Artes, and Student sometime*
of Christ-church in Oxford.

Imprinted at London by GEORGE BISHOP
and RALPH NEWBERIE, Deputies to
CHRISTOPHER BARKER, Printer to the
Queenes most excellent Maiestie.

1589.

Fig. 22   Title-page of *Principall navigations* (1589)

479

of which were unknown to W. H. Kerr, lends partial support to his conclusion that copies of the volume were sold in three successive states (or 'issues'):

	Bowes leaves		Drake leaves
	First state	Second state	
State I	Yes	No	No
II	Yes	No	Yes
III	No	Yes	Yes

Of thirty-six copies, the contents of which we have good reason to believe to be in their original condition, there are six of State I, three of State II, twenty-six of State III, and one (no. 12) with the Bowes leaves in the second state but no Drake leaves. State II is, however, represented by fifteen copies which may be in original condition, though positive evidence is wanting.

The fact that the map is absent from a number of copies (e.g. those in the Oxford libraries) which have certainly been undisturbed since the sixteenth or early seventeenth centuries suggests that its engraving was not completed when the book was first put on sale. Evidence of the original price is provided by five copies (nos. 40, 78, 21, 75, 102). The copy in the collection of Mr Robert H. Taylor (no. 64) seems to be that presented by Hakluyt to Philippe Desportes, from whom it passed to J. A. de Thou.

Twelve errors in the numbering of individual pages have been noted; most of these were corrected in the course of printing the book. Since corrected pages, in various combinations, are found in copies in all three states, no inference on the sequence of printing or on the differentiation of 'issues' can be drawn from them.

We list 130 copies of which about 120 is the net figure (allowing for duplication in trade copies). This is a good survival rate but not an exceptional one. As our search (in 1962 and again in 1971) has been reasonably comprehensive we might put the total survival figure around our maximum, approximately 130.

The information on the great majority of copies in the Check-list is based on the reports supplied by librarians, collectors and booksellers; and we take this opportunity of expressing our cordial thanks to all those who have generously helped us in this way. Our serial number for each copy is (where appropriate) followed by Kerr's number, in brackets, and preceded by * (i.e. copy believed to be in the original condition), or † (copy believed to have been sophisticated). The location of the copy is followed by four columns giving the following information:

(a) presence of the Bowes leaves in the first state (B1) or second state (B2);

(b) presence of the Drake leaves (D);

(c) presence of the map; our records on this point, which has no particular bibliographical significance, are incomplete and do not extend to all copies (O);

(d) summary information on the history and special features of the copy.

Abbreviations used: bg, binding; ctp., contemporary; bt, bought; beq., beqeathed; pres., presented; inscr., owner's inscription; bkpl., bookplate; p/o., previous owner(s); impf., imperfect; P.L., public library; U.L., university library; C.L., college library.

Great Britain

London

†1 (1)	British Museum, I	B 1	B 2	D	—	Inscr. Edward Keighley 1655
2 (2)	British Museum, II	—	B 2	D	O	Grenville copy
3 (3)	University College L.	—	B 2	D	O	
4	London U.L.	—	B 2	D	O	Sterling Lib.
5	Admiralty L. (N.H.L.)	—	B 2	D	O	Inscr. by Dr Samuel Johnson
†6	R. Geogr. Society	—	—	D	—	Impf.
7	Cruising Association	—	B 2	D	O	Inscr. Anthony Dennis; Sarah Strange; Walter Gerard

Oxford

*8 (4)	Bodleian, I	B 1	—	—	—	Ashmole copy. Bg 17th cent.
*9 (5)	Bodleian, II	—	B 2	D	—	Douce copy. Bg near ctp.
*10	All Souls C.L.	—	B 2	D	—	Pres. by Dudley Digges
*11	Christ Church C.L.	—	B 2	—	—	Inscr. Ralfe Cuyton 1594, Robert Burton (bt 1599), Robert Burton 1622, Wm Burton. Beq. by Robert Burton 1640. Bg near ctp.
*12	New C.L.	B 1	—	—	—	Pres. by Thomas Martyn (d. 1597). Bg ctp.

*13	Wadham C.L.	—	B 2	D	—	Beq. by Gilbert Drake (d. 1629). Five earlier owners'(?) names. Bg near ctp.
*14	Worcester C.L.	—	B 2	D	—	Inscr. Sir Wm Clarke (d. 1666)

Cambridge

†15 (6)	Cambridge U.L., I	B 1	B 2	D	O	Young copy. B 2 inserted
*16 (7)	Cambridge U.L., II	—	B 2	D	—	
*17 (8)	Cambridge U.L., III	—	B 2	D	—	
*18	Christ's C.L.	—	B 2	D	—	Impf.
*19	Pembroke C.L.	—	B 2	D	—	Bg 17th cent.
*20	Trinity C.L.	—	B 2	D	—	Rouse Coll.

Durham

*21	Durham U.L.	B 1	—	—	—	Beq. by M. J. Routh. Inscr. (16th cent.) Thomas Scott, 10s.; Henry Bagshaw. Impf.

Liverpool

†22	Liverpool U.L.	—	—	—	—	Impf.

Sheffield

*23	Sheffield P.L.	—	B 2	D	—	Inscr. Tho. Arthington, Da. Dysard

Ireland

Co. Tipperary, Cashel

*24	Cashel Diocesan L.	—	B 2	D	—	18th cent. Inscr. Patk. FitzSymonds. Impf.

Finland

Helsinki

*25	Helsinki U.L., I	B 1	—	—	—	Nordenskiöld Coll. Inscr. I.H. to D.S. 1753, B. Smith 1829, A. E. Nordenskiöld (bt Barcelona 1881). Impf.
*26	Helsinki U.L., II	B 1	—	—	—	Nordenskiöld Coll. Inscr. C. Wellbeloved, York. Impf .

U.S.S.R.
Leningrad

26a	Leningrad, L. of Academy of Sciences	—	B 2	D	—	In Academy L. Cat. 1742.
26b	Leningrad, Saltykov-Shchedrin P.L.	—	B 2	D	—	Inscr. James Bacon, Gulielmus Martin

South Africa

27	Johannesburg P.L.	B 1	—	D	—	

Australia
Melbourne

28	State L. of Victoria	B 1	—	D	O	

Sydney

†29	P.L. of N.S. Wales, I	B 1	B 2	D	O	Mitchell Lib. p/o David Scott Mitchell
30	P.L. of N.S. Wales, II	—	B 2	D	—	Mitchell Lib.
31	P.L. of N.S. Wales III	—	B 2	—	O	Dixson Lib. Inscr. Mary Leigh (16th–17th cent.?)

New Zealand
Wellington

†32	Turnbull L.	—	—	—	O	Inscr. Th. Watkins 1800. Bkpl. W. H. Duignan. Impf.

Canada
Ottawa

33	Pub. Archives of Canada	—	—	—	—	

Toronto

34 (9)	Toronto P.L.	—	B 2	D	—	S.L.M. Barlow copy

Montreal

35	McGill U.L.	—	B 2	D	—	Redpath Lib. Impf. 17th cent. bg.

Halifax, N.S.

35a	Provincial Archives	—	B 1	—	—	Lacks tp.

Victoria, B.C.

36	Provincial Library	—	B 2	D	O	

U.S.A.

California

37 (10)	Calif. Hist. Soc.	B 1	—	D	—	H. R. Wagner copy. Inscr. Hydrog. Office 46
†38 (12)	Huntington Lib., I	B 1	—	D	O	Church copy (no. 139). Drake leaves inserted between p. 649 and p. 653. Inscr. John Sturges 1672
39 (11)	Huntington Lib., II	B 1	B 2	D	O	Church copy (no. 139A). B 1 inserted
*40 (13)	Huntington Lib., III	—	B 2	D		Bridgewater copy. Cancel stubs after p. 491. Inscr. 'Thomas Egertons Lincolns 9 σ'
†41 (14)	Pomona C.L.	B 1	B 2	D	—	Huth copy. B 2 inserted

Connecticut

42 (15)	Hartford, Watkinson L.	—	B 2	D	—	
43 (16)	New Haven, Yale U.L., I	B 1	—	D	—	Bg ctp.?
43a	New Haven, Yale U.L., II	B 1	—	D	O	The Henry C. Taylor copy, no. 75 below
44 (17)	Southport, Pequot L.	B 1	—	D	—	

Delaware

45	Wilmington, Pierre S. Du Pont	—	B 2	D	O	

Illinois

†46 (18)	Chicago, Newberry L.	B 1	—	D	O	Ayer Coll. Drake leaves inserted. Bg ctp.

Indiana

47	Bloomington, Indiana U.L.	B 1	—	D	O	Lilly Lib.

Iowa

48 (19)	Iowa City, Iowa U.L.	—	—	D	—	Talbot Lib. Impf.

Maine

49 (2)	Brunswick, Bowdoin C.L.	—	—	—	—	Impf.

Maryland

50	Baltimore, Johns Hopkins U.L., I	B 1	—	D	O	Garrett Lib. Bkpl. Sir Edward Hales
51	Baltimore, Johns Hopkins U.L., II	—	—	—	—	Garret Lib. Bkpl. Wm. H. Bradish. Impf.

Massachusetts

†52 (21)	Boston P.L.	—	B 2	—	—	S.L.M. Barlow copy
53 (22)	Cambridge, Harvard C.L., I	—	B 2	D	—	
54	Cambridge, Harvard C.L., II	B 1	—	D	—	Bkpl. Gordon Abbott
55	Cambridge, Harvard C.L., III	B 1	—	D	—	
55a	Cambridge, Harvard C.L., IV	B 1	—	D	—	William S Spaulding copy: map in facsimile
*56 (23)	Williams Coll., Chapin L.	—	B 2	D	—	Bg ctp.
*57 (24)	Worcester, Amer. Antiq. Soc.	—	B 2	D	—	Bg ctp. Impf.

Michigan

*58 (25)	Ann Arbor, Clements L.	B 1	—	—	O	Bkpl. E. S. and H. Lloyd
*59 (48)	Detroit P.L.	—	B 2	D	O	Bg ctp.

Minnesota

*60	Minneapolis, Minnesota U.L.	—	B 2	D	O	Bell Coll. Herman LeRoy Edgar copy. Bg ctp.

New Hampshire

61	Hanover, Dartmouth C.L.	—	B 2	D	—	

New Jersey

62	Morristown, Thos. W. Streeter	B 1	—	D	O	
†63	Princeton U.L.	B 1	B 2	D	—	P/o Bishop Gott, Edward N. Crane, Grenville Kane

*64	Princeton, Robert H. Taylor	—	B 2	D	O	Inscr. 'Dono Auctoris', 'Desportes', 'Ex Augustissima Bibliotheca Thuana'. Bkpl. J. C. MacCoy, Sir H. Hope-Edwardes
64a	West Orange, Charles E. Armstrong	—	—	D	—	Bowes leaves & map in facsimile

New York

*65 (26)	Albany, State Lib.	—	B 2	D	—	Joseph Harford copy
66 (27)	New York, Hispanic Soc., I	—	B 2	—	—	A. M. Huntington copy. Impf.
*67 (28)	New York, Hispanic Soc., II	—	B 2	D	—	A. M. Huntington copy. Bkpl. Constantine John Phipps. Bg near ctp.? Impf.
†68 (30)	New York, N.Y. Hist. Soc.	—	B 2	D	—	Buckingham Smith copy. Drake leaves inserted. Bg ctp.
†69 (29)	New York, Pierpont Morgan L.	B 1	B 2	D	—	Drake leaves inserted
70 (32)	New York P.L., I	—	B 2	D	—	Lenox copy
*71 (33)	New York P.L., II	—	B 2	D	—	Lenox copy
†72 (34)	New York P.L., III	B 1	B 2	D	—	B 1 inserted
73	New York P.L., IV	B 1	—	D	O	Arents copy. Impf.
74 (31)	Poughkeepsie, Vassar C.L.	—	B 2	D	—	Brinley copy
75	New York, Henry C. Taylor (see 43 above)	B 1	—	D	O	Inscr. (16th cent.) Bt. from Christopher Payne 10s. P/o Herschel V. Jones
75a	New York, Frank S. Streeter	B 1	—	D	O	
75b	New York, Henry Bradley Martin	—	B 2	D	O	The Penrose copy, no. 78 below

North Carolina

76	Chapel Hill, N. N. Carolina U.L.	—	B 2	D	O	Inscr. Wm Thomas, London

Pennsylvania

77 (35)	Bethelehem, Lehigh U.L.	—	B 2	D	—	
78	Devon Hill, Boies Penrose (see no. 75b above)	—	B 2	D	O	Inscr. 'Ed. Wyatt, 1590 xis. xid.', 'Wm Bligh...Carnedon in Cornwall'. Bg ctp.
79	Philadelphia, Free Lib.	—	B 2	D	—	William Elkins Coll. Bkpl. John Hart, Dublin 1757
80	Philadelphia, Hist. Soc. Penna.	B 1	—	D	O	Frederick Kirkland copy. Inscr. (early 17th cent.) J.R.
81 (36)	Philadelphia Library Coy, I	—	B 2	D	—	
82 (37)	Philadelphia Library Coy, II	B 1	—	D	—	
83	Philadelphia, Rosenberg Foundation	—	B 2	D	O	Britwell-Huntington-Phelan copy

Rhode Island

83a	Newport, Naval War College	—	B 2	D	—	
84 (38)	Providence, J. C. Brown Lib., I	B 1	—	—	—	
85 (39)	Providence, J. C. Brown Lib., II	B 1	—	D	—	B 2 as separate
86 (40)	Providence, Albert E. Lownes	—	B 2	D		

Virginia

| †87 (43) | Charlottesville, Virginia U.L., I | B 1 | B 2 | D | O | Tracy W. McGregor copy. Inscr. (17th cent.) James Salt, Thomas Stone (18th cent.) Ralph Every |

†88 (44)	Charlottesville, Virginia U.L., II	—	B 2	D	—	Tracy W. McGregor copy.¹ Bkpl. Edw. Rose Tonno
88a	Richmond, Virginia Historical S.	—	B 2	D	O	
†89	Upperville, Paul Mellon	B 1	B 2	D	O	Bg ctp.

Washington, D.C.

90 (41)	L.C., I	—	B 2	D	—	Inscr. Thos. Bowes
91 (42)	L.C., II	—	B 2	D	—	Thacher copy
92 (43)	Folger Lib., I	B 1	—	—	—	Menzies (1878)—Sewall Lib. 1896
93 (44)	Folger Lib., II	B 1	—	D	O	Ingoldsby-Harmsworth copy
†94 (45)	Folger Lib., III	B 1	B 2	D	—	B 1 inserted

Wisconsin

95	Madison, Wisconsin U.L.	—	B 2	D	O	P/o Chester Thordarson. Bkpl. E. of Mexborough

Booksellers

Held in 1962

*96	Maggs, I	—	B 2	D	—	Cancel stubs, pp. 487–501. Bg ctp.
†97	Maggs, II	B 1	B 2	D	O	
*98	Maggs, III	—	B 2	D	—	Bg ctp.? Impf.
*99	Maggs, IV	—	B 2	D	—	Signet Lib. copy
*100	Maggs, V	—	B 2	D	—	Bg ctp.?
*101	Maggs, VI	B 1	—	D	O	
*102	Broadhurst (Southport)	B 1	—	D	—	Weld-Blundell copy. Inscr. 'precium x s'; 'Robertus Blundell'. Bg ctp.

Unlocated. (Some perhaps are identical with copies held in libraries, 1962.)

103 (49)	Quaritch, I	—	B 2	D	—	
104 (50)	Quaritch, II	—	—	D	—	
†105	Quaritch, III (1960)	B 1	—	D	O	
106 (52)	Hodgson, I (1932)	—	?	D	M²	

¹ This contains a copy of the 1599 Wright map, State 1.
² This contained a copy of the 1599 Wright map, State unknown.

107 (53)	Hodgson, II (1933)	B 1	—	D	—
108 (54)	Scribner (1938)	B 1	—	D	—
109 (55)	Goodspeed (1938)	—	B 2	D	—
110	Stevens, I (1940)	—	—	D	O
111	Stevens, II (1940)	—	—	D	O
112	Grafton (1951)				

Other unlocated copy

| 113 | Lumley Library–Old Royal Library 1610–British Museum 1757– probably sold as duplicate 1805(?) | | | | |

Additional Trade Copies, 1964–73

114	Parke–Bernet, (9 November 1943, lot 166)	B 1	B 2	D	O	
115	Sotheby's (18 November 1963, lot 86)	B 1	—	D	O	Cunliffe copy
116	Stevens (Rare Americana, 34 (1965))	—	B 2	D	O	
117	Parke–Bernet (29 October 1966, lot 28)	B 1	—	D	O	Streeter copy
118	Sotheby's (11 December 1967, lot 103)	B 1	—	D	—	Bowes leaves impf
119	Parke–Bernet (20 October 1970, lot 13)	B 1	—	D	O	
120	Stevens (Americana 74, no. 259)	—	B 2	D	—	Map in facsimile
121	Stevens (Americana 78, no. 406)	—	B 2	D	O	Map and t.p. inserted. State III

The principal navigations (1598–1600)

1. *The principal navigations* (1598–1600): printing history.
2. The make-up of the volumes.
3. Provisional check-list of surviving copies.

By Charles E. Armstrong, D. B. Quinn and R. A. Skelton

Section 1 is based on Charles E. Armstrong's paper, 'The "Voyage to Cadiz" in the second edition of Hakluyt's "Voyages",' BSA *Papers*, XLIX (1955), 254–62. This has been substantially revised in the light of further information and of the additional copies surveyed by C. E. Armstrong and D. B. Quinn in 1970–3. They are indebted to a number of libraries and individuals for the material on which their conclusions are based. We are particularly grateful to Mr A. N. L. Munby, King's College, Cambridge, Dr J. P. W. Gaskell, Mr Derek Nuttall and Mr J. S. G. Simmons, for their help.

Section 2 was begun by R. A. Skelton but had not been taken very far at the time of his death; it has been completed by D. B. Quinn, with help from C. E. Armstrong.

Section 3 is based on the survey included in the 1955 paper, continued so far as proved practicable in 1970–1. It is, we believe, substantially complete for the British Isles and North America, though circumstances did not permit the extensive circularization which would have brought us a better sample under our 'other locations' heading. Australia, New Zealand and South Africa are probably adequately covered; continental Europe much less well, the remainder of the world not at all. We accumulated many debts to librarians who have been most helpful in answering our enquiries. A few of them, like Mr Paul Morgan at Oxford, brought a whole flotilla of additional copies to our notice. The additional copies were added by C. E. Armstrong and D. B. Quinn working together. Late additions to the lists for 1589 and 1598–1600 were made possible through the courtesy of the Librarians of the Department of Rare Books and Manuscripts, Library of the Academy of Sciences of the U.S.S.R., Leningrad, and of the State Saltykov–Shchedrin Public Library, Leningrad.

I

Late in 1598 (or possibly in the opening days of the year 1599) the first volume of Hakluyt's enlarged edition of his *Principal navigations* appeared in London. The dedication was dated 7 October 1598, but it appears unlikely that the book was available before the end of the year. The volume consisted in the main of voyages to the north and north-west, but it contained near the end an account of the victory over the Armada in 1588 and concluded with a laudatory account of the Cadiz expedition of 1596, with much emphasis on the part the earl of Essex had played in the affair. Moreover, the 'famous victorie' was mentioned on the title-page, the 'honorable voyage' in the dedicatory epistle, 'the renoumed Erle of Essex' in the address to the reader, and the item was included in the table of contents. Probably unintentionally, the volume was excellent publicity for the earl.

Essex returned without leave from Ireland on 28 September 1599, which disgraced him with the Queen. By that time *Principal navigations* was in circulation and it is probable that a copy had already been presented to Queen Elizabeth. Instructions were evidently given for the removal of the title-page and its replacement by one which made no mention of the Cadiz voyage, and also for the excision of the offending leaves from the book, the latter being easily done since they were at the end of the volume. Other references including the table of contents were not interfered with. How much success this operation had will be indicated later. Meantime the second volume of the work had come from the press, its dedication dated 7 October 1599. It was published along with the re-issued and modified first volume either towards the end of the calendar year 1599 or at the beginning of 1600. The two volumes stitched together made a thick but not unmanageable book of 1175 pages: it is in this form that the majority of those copies which survive are found.

Including the original issue, the title-page is represented by five distinct states:

1. 1598, the original issue, line 8 reading 'these 1500. yeeres'.
2. 1599, the second, modified issue, line 7 reading 'these 1600 yeres'.
3. 1599, a revision of two, line 7 reading 'these 1600 yeares'.
4. Dated '1600' and with the reading 'Rivers' on line 14.
5. Reprint of State 1 *c.* 1794.

The original issue (State 1) contained the reference to 'the famous victorie atchieued at the citie of *Cadiz, 1596*'. Mr Derek Nuttall suggests that the revised title-page (State 2) was printed while the original type was still standing, and that 'several lines are not just set up in the same type face, but are the actual line (complete with defective letters) which had been kept standing. Other lines have been altered from standing type and consist partly of type used in State 1 and partly of newly set type of the same fount

(e.g. line 11, "The first Volume", line 20, "*VVhereunto is annexed*").'
States 2 and 3 were evidently printed in succession and both referred to
volumes I and II together, though volume II had its separate title‑page,
dated 1599 and with the spelling 'HACKLVYT.' State 3 is very rare
and only six copies are known. Mr Nuttall writes 'this is a completely
reset page. Many of the types are identical founts to those used in State 2,
but are definitely not from lines left standing.[1] State 4 had been taken at its
face value but problems concerning it have arisen and are discussed below.
State 5 is readily identifiable from its type which does not attempt a facsimile,
and examples have the date 1794 in the watermark, which indicates it was
made about this time. It may be worth mentioning that a facsimile reprint
of State I was made about 1900, and it may be that some copies reported
to us as State I are provided with it as a replacement.

When Dr A. N. L. Munby was reporting the copy in King's College
Library, Cambridge (no. 38 in the list below), he raised the question
of whether or not its State 4 title page was a contemporary setting. At a
later stage he reported 'I have now looked at the title‑page carefully
together with Dr J. P. W. Gaskell. It is his opinion that the title‑page
is mostly printed in a Dutch type of late‑seventeenth century origin,
but probably in a mixture sold to a British printer early in the eighteenth
century. Taking all the indications together we would guess that the title‑
page was printed in England probably *c.* 1730–40. It may well have
been made to perfect the volume when it entered the library of the
owner of the book‑plate dated 1744...In our view it was a one‑off
operation.' On the last point it may be indicated that there are other copies
in existence, namely at the William L. Clements Library (no. 149) and
the New York Public Library (no. 179), in the latter case State 5 is also
present.

[1] C. E. Armstrong in 1955 saw a photocopy of the title‑page of a copy then on
sale by Quaritch (no. 91), the location of which is unknown. Torn on the
right‑hand margin, it had been repaired and some letters added by hand to com‑
plete lines, so that it proved useless as an example of State 3, but it had
the initial 'THE' apparently printed from a block instead of from type
inside a border, so that it could be classed as a variant of State 3. It appeared
thus:

Fig. 23   Extract from title‑page of *Principal navigations*, I (1599). State 3 (no. 91)

On the type and its dating there is also a difference of opinion. Mr Nuttall writes 'This is certainly a new setting, although several lines have been reset in the same founts as were used on State 3. The type used for the first three lines are new types, and, although I have not been able to identify them with certainty, they are almost sure to be types cut and cast *c.* 1600, whereas the type used for "PRINCIPAL NAVL" in all previous states is the two-line double pica, or Canon Roman cut by François Guyot *c.* 1542. The matrices for this type are still preserved at Antwerp. John Day, the famous 16th-century printer, made good use of this type, especially around 1570. It is of interest that Day had a new set of capitals cut *c.* 1574 but retained the use of the lower case, and these new capitals were very similar (but not identical) to the type used for the main line on State 4. The real clue to the dating of State 4 is the double pica italic on line 5 "English Nation." This may appear different from the same wording on States 2 and 3, but it is a recasting (hence slight differences in the alignment, especially in the capital E) of the same typeface. The swash N has been replaced by the normal capital. This type was in use in Plantin's office in Antwerp in 1616 and may well have been supplied in the form of "strikes" to an English letter-founder who cast the types used by George Bishop. As far as I can ascertain, this particular italic type was not used much later than 1620, and by the end of the 17th century it would be completely out of use, being by then almost two centuries old. There could be a remote possibility that a printer might have had matrices for this type stored away for a hundred years or more – but the chance seems too great. Apart from this unlikely occurrence, I am also fairly certain that the type used in the line "BY RICHARD HAKLVYT" contains the same small capitals as were used on all the other versions, including State 1.'

There is, clearly, a considerable area of disagreement about the State 4 title-page, and if it is not contemporary some pains were taken to make it look convincing. It should be remarked that the mistake of printing 'Rivers' (line 14) is an unlikely one to be made in 1600 and an easy slip in the eighteenth century when practice had changed. The ornament, too, is not in R. B. McKerrow, *Printers' and publishers' devices in England and Scotland, 1585–1640* (1913), which is a little surprising in the case of a printer so prominent as George Bishop, nor has it so far been identified later. Finally, we might note that the period 1720–40 is the period when Oldys was planning a new edition of Hakluyt and could possibly have been experimenting with a type facsimile. It must be stressed that no attempt to resolve these problems can be made this time, but it may prove useful that the issues have at least been raised.

If we analyse the 186 institutional and private copies reported (a certain number of which are imperfect) we have:

Title-page		'Voyage to Cadiz'	
State 1 70	(38 per cent)	State A 89	(48 per cent)
State 2 93		State B 38	
State 3 5	87 (52 per cent)	State C 8	52 (28 per cent)
State 4 3		State D 6	
State 5 2		Lacking 45	(24 per cent)
Lacking 13			

If we take the two categories separately we see that two copies in five retain the original, uncensored title-page of 1598, whereas one copy in two has the cancel title-page in either State 2 or State 3. For the 'Voyage' we have something less than one in two retaining the censored 'Voyage' leaves of 1598, and one copy in four lacking them, while nearly one in three has had them replaced by one of the three eighteenth-century reprints. Here the survival of so many examples of the uncensored leaves in State A is the somewhat surprising feature to be found.

The combinations of the different states of the title-page and of the 'Voyage' are potentially very numerous. The two natural ones would be, of course, that of the original title-page and the original 'Voyage' and that of the cancel title-page and the deleted 'Voyage'. The figures are:

State 1 plus State A 43 (17 per cent)
State 2 and 3 with no 'Voyage' 18 (10 per cent)

In addition 32 copies (17 per cent) with State 2 and 3 and no 'Voyage' were perfected with one of the three eighteenth-century reprints, so that Some 30 per cent of the surviving copies were before 1720 in State 2 or 3 without the 'Voyage' leaves. What is less to be expected is that 40 copies (22 per cent) contain the cancelled title-page (State 2 and 3) with the original 'Voyage' leaves. This might indicate that the cancel title-page was added to copies from which the 'Voyage' was not deleted or that sets of leaves, excised in 1599, were retained and re-attached to copies which had the new title-page. Of course, since so much sophistication has taken place with copies of this edition since the early eighteenth century, it would be unwise to be dogmatic about any of these combinations.

What might seem to be a surprising number of the copies which survive contain the 'Voyage to Cadiz' in its original form, including a number with the title-page in its second or third states, that is after the suppression – though it is not clear how many of these may have been sophisticated at a much later date. Nevertheless there were many copies which lacked the Cadiz leaves. Just as, since they were at the end of volume I, it was easy to remove them without damage to the make-up of the book, so it was simple to replace them by a reprint. According to William Oldys, writing in 1737,[1] 'about the middle of the late King's reign' [i.e. about 1720], the leaves were reprinted in an eighteenth-century 'gothic' type. The original page 607 had 53 lines of text in eight paragraphs: in the reprint this became 52 lines in seven paragraphs, ending on p. 620 without a tailpiece. This is by far the most prevalent of the 'Voyage' leaves reprints. A further reprint appeared towards the end of the eighteenth century, which may have been produced by the printer of State 5 of the title-page. It is printed in smaller type, with 63 lines to p. 607, and ends on p. 617, which has been mis-numbered '417', with a new tailpiece. Some copies show watermark dates of 1790 and 1794, linking it very closely, in time at least, with State 5 of the title-page. Yet again, about 1850, Henry Stevens of Vermont, who was energetically sophisticating early items of *Americana* got John Harris to bring out an excellent type-facsimile of the original 'Voyage' on old paper: close examination is necessary to reveal its nature and it is probable that not all examples have been detected in surviving sets.

The 'Voyage to Cadiz' is, therefore, to be found in four States:

A. The original printing of 1598 (53 lines on p. 607)
B. The 52 line reprint (p. 607) of *c.* 1720.
C. The 63 line reprint (p. 607) of *c.* 1794.
D. The 53 line type-facsimile reprint of *c.* 1850.

Another matter of importance is the question of the presence or absence of the world map, with the construction of which the name of Edward Wright has been associated. It was intended to appear in the second volume and so theoretically should have been included in all the sets sold in 1599–1600 and later. The map was also, it seems, sold separately. It survives in two issues:

State 1, which has a single cartouche in the lower part of the map, located in the South Atlantic.
State 2, which has a second cartouche, containing an inscription relating to Sir Francis Drake, located in the South Pacific.

Only 19 maps have been reported in the 186 copies (6 in State 1 and 13 in State 2) in institutional and private libraries, while a few have had facsimiles added, either from that made for the Hakluyt Society and edited

---

[1] *The British Librarian*, no. 3 (1737), p. 158.

by C. H. Coote in 1880, or from one made about 1900. This covers only some 11 per cent of the copies. No attempt has been made to list separate copies of the map.[1] The low survival rate may reflect the attractions of the map itself. It was one of the most interesting and detailed maps of the world available at the time, certainly the only English one of any appreciable merit. This could account for its removal from many copies for independent use. A double-page map too is very vulnerable to wear in use in a book and many copies could have lost their maps in course of time. At the same time the survival rate is sufficiently low to raise the possibility that not all copies were equipped with the map, either because it was made available after many sets had already been sold (which would mean that its date might be later than 1599), or because it was an optional extra supplied at additional cost. In these respects as well as others the 1599 world map deserves further detailed study.

It has seemed unwise to take the trade copies into account on this occasion, though it could be done for the 1954–5 across-the-board survey. The additional trade copies represent the floating population of copies, some of which have come to rest in institutional or private collections or are on their way to do so, and amongst which there is much duplication.

As has been indicated already very many of the sets which survive have volumes I and II bound together and certainly those which emerged from the censorship operation in 1599 are in this form, but again so much rebinding has taken place that dogmatism on numbers would be unwise.

In the course of the surveys reports on the dimensions of 140 copies were obtained. These were:

Inches	Copies
$10\frac{1}{4}$ to $10\frac{3}{8}$	1
$10\frac{1}{2}$ to $10\frac{5}{8}$	6
$10\frac{3}{4}$ to $10\frac{7}{8}$	14
11 to $11\frac{1}{8}$	37
$11\frac{1}{4}$ to $11\frac{3}{8}$	43
$11\frac{1}{2}$ to $11\frac{5}{8}$	28
$11\frac{3}{4}$ to $11\frac{7}{8}$	3
12 to $12\frac{1}{8}$	4
$12\frac{1}{4}$ to $12\frac{3}{8}$	1
$12\frac{1}{2}$ to $12\frac{5}{8}$	3

[1] Two more are known in copies of the 1589 edition. We can suggest that, with separate copies, a total of between 25 and 30 may exist.

The average surviving copy is about $11\frac{1}{4}$ inches tall, but the original was undoubtedly taller than this. Dibden reported 'copies are usually cropt. I never saw it uncut'.[1]

[1] T. F. Dibden, *The library companion* (1824), p. 378.

2

Volume I *State* I THE | PRINCIPAL NAVI⁄ | GATIONS, VOIAGES, | TRAF⁄
FIQVES AND DISCO⁄ | ueries of the English Nation, made by Sea | or
ouer⁄land, to the remote and farthest di⁄ | stant quarters of the Earth, at any
time within | the compasse of these 1500. yeeres: Deuided | into three
seuerall Volumes, according to the | positions of the Regions, whereunto |
they were directed. |

This first Volume containing the woorthy Discoueries, | &c. of the English
toward the North and Northeast by sea, | as of *Lapland, Scriksinia, Corelia,*
the Baie of S. *Nicolas*, the Isles of *Col⁄* | *goieue, Vaigatz*, and *Noua Zembla*,
toward the great riuer *Ob*, | with the mighty Empire of *Russia*, the *Caspian*
sea, *Geor⁄* | *gia, Armenia, Media, Persia, Boghar* in *Bactria*, | and diuers king⁄
doms of *Tartaria*: |

Together with many notable monuments and testimo⁄ | nies of the ancient
forren trades, and of the warrelike and | other shipping of this realme of
England in former ages. |

Whereunto is annexed also a briefe Commentarie of the true | state of *Island*, and
of the Northren Seas and | lands situate that way. |

And lastly, the memorable defeate of the Spanish huge | *Armada, Anno 1588.* and
the famous victorie | atchieued at the citie of *Cadiz, 1596.* | are described. |

By RICHARD HAKLVYT *Master of* | Artes, and sometime Student of Christ⁄ |
Church in Oxford. |

[Ornament]

[Printer's flower] Imprinted at London by GEORGE | BISHOP, RALPH
NEWBERIE | and ROBERT BARKER. | 1598.

B.M.

THE

PRINCIPAL NAVI-
GATIONS, VOIAGES,
TRAFFIQVES AND DISCO-
ueries of the Englifh Nation, made by Sea
or ouer-land , to the remote and fartheft di-
ftant quarters of the Earth, at any time within
the compaffe of thefe 1500. yeeres: Deuided
into three feuerall Volumes, according to the
pofitions of the Regions, whereunto
they were directed.

This firft Volume containing the woorthy Difcoueries,
&c. of the Englifh toward the North and Northeaft by fea,
as of *Lapland*, *Scrikfinia*, *Corelia*, the Baie of S. *Nicolas*, the Ifles of *Colgoieue*, *Vaigatz*, and *Noua Zembla*, toward the great riuer *Ob*,
with the mighty Empire of *Ruffia*, the *Cafpian* fea, *Georgia*, *Armenia*, *Media*, *Perfia*, *Boghar* in *Bactria*,
and diuers kingdoms of *Tartaria*:

Together with many notable monuments and teftimo-
nies of the ancient forren trades, and of the warrelike and
other fhipping of this realme of *England* in former ages.

*VVhereunto is annexed alfo a briefe Commentarie of the true
ftate of Ifland*, and of the Northren Seas and
lands fituate that way.

*And laftly, the memorable defeate of the Spanifh huge
Armada, Anno 1588. and the famous victorie*
atchieued at the citie of *Caliz, 1596.*
are defcribed.

By RICHARD HAKLVYT *Mafter of*
Artes, and fometime Student of Chrift-
Church in Oxford.

❧ Imprinted at London by GEORGE
BISHOP, RALPH NEWBERIE
and ROBERT BARKER.
1598.

Fig. 24 Title-page of *Principal navigations*, 1 (1598). State 1

State II THE | PRINCIPAL NAVI⁄ | GATIONS, VOYAGES, | TRAFFIQVES AND DISCOVE⁄ | ries of the *English Nation*, made by Sea or ouer⁄ | land, to the remote and farthest distant quarters of the | Earth, at any time within the compasse of these 1600 yeres: | Diuided into three seuerall Volumes, according to the | positions of the Regions, whereunto they | were directed. |

The first Volume containeth the worthy Discoueries, | &c. of the *English* toward the North and Northeast by Sea, as of | *Lapland, Scriksinia, Corelia,* the Baie of *S. Nicolas,* the Isles of *Colgoieue, Vaigatz,* | and *Noua Zembla,* toward the great Riuer *Ob,* with the mighty Empire of *Russia,* | the *Caspian* Sea, *Georgia, Armenia, Media, Persia, Boghar* in *Bactria,* | and diuers kingdomes of *Tartaria:* |

Together with many notable monuments and testimonies | of the ancient forren trades, and of the warrelike and other | shipping of this Realme of *England* in former ages. |

Whereunto is annexed a briefe Commentary of the true state of Island, | and of the Nort ren Seas and lands situate that way: As also the | memorable defeat of the *Spanish* huge *Armada,* Anno 1588. |

[Paragraph mark] The second Volume comprehendeth the principall | Nauigations, Voyages, Traffiques, and discoueries of the *English* | Nation made by Sea or ouer⁄land, to the South and South⁄east | parts of the World, as well within as without the Streight of | *Gibraltar,* at any time within the compasse of these 1600. | yeres: Diuided into two seueral parts, &c. |

[Paragraph mark] By RICHARD HAKLVYT Preacher, and sometime Stu⁄ | dent of Christ⁄Church in Oxford. |

[Ornament]

[Printer's flower] Imprinted at London by *George Bishop,* | *Ralph Newberie,* and *Robert Barker.* | ANNO 1599.

B.M.

THE

PRINCIPAL NAVI-
GATIONS, VOYAGES,
TRAFFIQVES AND DISCOVE-
ries of the *English Nation*, made by Sea or ouer-
land, to the remote and fartheſt diſtant quarters of the
Earth, at any time within the compaſſe of theſe 1600 yeres:
Diuided into three ſeuerall Volumes, according to the
poſitions of the Regions, whereunto they
were directed.

The firſt Volume containeth the worthy Diſcoueries,
&c. of the *Engliſh* toward the North and Northeaſt by Sea, as of
Lapland, Scrikfinia, Corelia, the Baie of *S. Nicolas,* the Iſles of *Colgoieue, Vaigatz,*
and *Noua Zembla,* toward the great Riuer *Ob,* with the mighty Empire of *Ruſſia,*
the *Caſpian* Sea, *Georgia, Armenia, Media, Perſia, Boghar* in *Batlria,*
and diuers kingdomes of *Tartaria:*

Together with many notable monuments and teſtimonies
of the ancient forren trades, and of the warrelike and other
ſhipping of this Realme of *England* in former ages.

VVhereunto is annexed a briefe Commentary of the true ſtate of Iſland,
and of the Northren Seas and lands ſituate that way: As alſo the
memorable defeat of the *Spaniſh* huge *Armada,* Anno 1588.

¶ The ſecond Volume comprehendeth the principall
Nauigations, Voyages, Traffiques, and diſcoueries of the *Engliſh*
Nation made by Sea or ouer-land, to the South and South-eaſt
parts of the World, as well within as without the Streight of
Gibralter, at any time within the compaſſe of theſe 1600.
yeres: Diuided into two ſeuerall parts, &c.

¶ By RICHARD HAKLVYT Preacher, and ſometime Student of Chriſt-Church in Oxford.

¶ Imprinted at London by *George Biſhop,*
Ralph Newberie, and *Robert Barker.*
ANNO 1599.

Fig. 25   Title-page of *Principal navigations,* I (1599). State 2

State III THE | PRINCIPAL NAVI⁄ | GATIONS, VOYAGES, | TRAFFIQVES AND DISCOVE | ries of the *English Nation,* made by Sea, or ouer⁄ | land, to the remote and farthest distant quarters of the | Earth, at any time within the compasse of these 1600. yeares: | Diuided into three seuerall Volumes, according to the | positions of the Regions whereunto they | were directed. |

The first Volume containeth the worthy Discoue⁄ | ries, &c. of the English toward the North and Northeast by Sea, as of | *Lapland, Scriksinia, Corelia,* the Baie of *S. Nicholas,* the Isles of *Colgoieue, Viagatz,* | and *Noua Zembla,* toward the great Riuer *Ob,* with the mightie Empire of *Russia,* | the *Caspian* Sea, *Georgia, Armenia, Media, Persia, Boghar* in *Bactria,* | and diuers King⁄ domes of *Tartaria:* |

Together with many notable monuments and testimonies of the antient | forren trades, and of the warrelike and other shipping of this | Realme of England in former ages. |

Whereunto is annexed a briefe Comentarie of the true state of Island, | and of the Northren Seas and lands situate that way: As also the me⁄ | morable defeat of the *Spanish* huge *Armada,* Anno 1588. |

[Printer's flower] *The second Volume comprehendeth the principall Na⁄* | uigations, Voiages, Traffiques, and discoueries of the *English* Nation, made | by Sea or ouer⁄land, to the South and South⁄east parts of the World, | as well within as without the Streight of *Gibraltar,* at any time | within the compasse of these 1600 yeres: Diui⁄ | ded into two seuerall parts, &c. |

By RICHARD HAKLVYT Preacher, and sometime Student | of Christ⁄ Church in Oxford. |

[Ornament: variant from State 2] |

[Printer's flower] *Imprinted at London by* George Bishop, | Ralph Newberie, and Robert Barker. | ANNO. 1599.

Virginia Historical Society.

THE

PRINCIPAL NAVI-
GATIONS, VOYAGES,
TRAFFIQVES AND DISCOVE-
ries of the *English Nation*, made by Sea, or ouer-
land, to the remote and farthest distant quarters of the
Earth, at any time within the compasse of these 1600 yeares:
Diuided into three seuerall Volumes, according to the
positions of the Regions, whereunto they
were directed.

The first Volume containeth the worthy Discoue-
ries,&c. of the English toward the North and Northeast by Sea, as of
Lapland, Scrikfinia, Corelia, the Baie of *S. Nicholas,* the Isles of *Colgoieue Vaigatz,*
and *Noua Zembla,* toward the great Riuer *Ob,* with the mightie Empire of *Russia,*
the *Caspian* Sea, *Georgia, Armenia, Media, Persia, Boghar* in *Bactria,*
and diuers Kingdomes of *Tartaria:*

Together with many notable monuments and testimonies of the antient
forren trades, and of the warrelike and other shipping of this
Realme of England in former ages.

Wherunto is annexed a briefe Comentarie of the true state of Island,
and of the Northren Seas and lands situate that way: As also the memorable defeat of the *Spanish* huge *Armada,* Anno 1 5 8 8.

The second Volume comprehendeth the principall Na-
uigations, Voiages, Traffiques, and discoueries of the *English* Nation, made
by Sea or ouer-land, to the South and South-east parts of the World,
as well within as without the Streight of *Gibraltar,* at any time
within the compasse of these 1600 ycres: Diui-
ded into two seuerall parts, &c.

By RICHARD HAKLVYT Preacher, and sometime Student
of Christ-Church in Oxford.

Imprinted at London by George Bishop,
Ralph Newberie, and Robert Barker.
ANNO. 1599.

Fig. 26   Title-page of *Principal navigations,* 1 (1599). State 3

State IV THE | PRINCIPAL NAVI⁄ | GATIONS, VOYAGES, | TRAFFIQVES
AND DISCOVE | ries of the *English Nation*,...within the compasse of these
1600 yeres:...
The first Volume...toward the great River *Ob*...Boghar...Together
with many notable monuments and testimonies | ...*Whereunto is annexed
a briefe Commentary of the true state of* Island, | ...

[Paragraph mark] The second Volume comprehendeth the principall |
Nauigations,...

[Paragraph mark] By RICHARD HAKLVYT Preacher, and sometime´ Stu⁄ |
dent...

[Ornament] |

Imprinted at London by *George Bishop,* | *Ralph Newberie,* and *Robert
Barker.* | ANNO 1600.

King's College, Cambridge.

THE
PRINCIPAL NAVI-
GATIONS, VOYAGES,
TRAFFIQVES AND DISCOVE-
ries of the *English Nation*, made by Sea or ouer-
land, to the remote and fartheſt diſtant quarters of the
Earth, at any time within the compaſſe of theſe 1600 yeres:
Diuided into three ſeuerall Volumes, according to the
poſitions of the Regions, whereunto they
were directed.

The firſt Volume containeth the worthy Diſcoueries,
&c. of the *English* toward the North and Northeaſt by Sea, as of
Lapland, Scrikfinia, Corelia, the Baie of *S. Nicolas,* the Iſles of *Colgoieue, Vaigatz,*
and *Noua Zembla,* toward the great River *Ob,* with the mighty Empire of *Ruſſia,*
the *Caſpian* Sea, *Georgia, Armenia, Media, Perſia, Boghar* in *Bactria,*
and diuers kingdomes of *Tartaria.*

Together with many notable monuments and teſtimonies
of the ancient forren trades, and of the warrelike and other
ſhipping of this Realme of *England* in former ages.

Whereunto is annexed a briefe Commentary of the true ſtate of Iſland,
and of the Northren Seas and lands ſituate that way: As alſo the
memorable defeat of the *Spaniſh* huge *Armada,* Anno 1588.

¶ The ſecond Volume comprehendeth the principall
Nauigations, Voyages, Traffiques, and diſcoueries of the *Engliſh*
Nation made by Sea or ouer-land, to the South and South-eaſt
parts of the World, as well within as without the Streight of
Gibraltar, at any time within the compaſſe of theſe 1600.
yeres: Diuided into two ſeueral parts, &c.

¶ By RICHARD HAKLVYT Preacher, and ſometime Student of Chriſt-Church in Oxford.

Imprinted at London by *George Biſhop,*
Ralph Newberie, and *Robert Barker.*
ANNO 1600.

Fig. 27   Substitute title-page of *Principal navigations,* I (1600). State 4

Volume II THE | SECOND VOLVME | OF THE PRINCIPAL NA⁄ | VIGATIONS, VOYAGES, TRAF⁄ | fiques and Discoueries of the *English Nation*,...within the compasse of these 1600. yeres...Diuided into two seuerall parts:...

[Paragraph mark] By Richard HACKLVYT Preacher, and sometime Stu⁄ | dent...

[Printer's flower] Imprinted at London by *George Bishop*, | *Ralph* | *Newbery*, and *Robert Barker*. | ANNO 1599.

B.M.

THE
SECOND VOLVME

OF THE PRINCIPAL NA-
VIGATIONS, VOYAGES, TRAF-
fiques and Difcoueries of the *English Nation*, made by
Sea or ouer-land, to the South and South-eaft parts of the
World, at any time within the compaffe of thefe 1600. yeres:
Diuided into two feuerall parts :

Whereof the firft containeth the perfonall trauels, &c.
of the *English*, through and within the Streight of *Gibraltar*, to *Al-
ger*, *Tunis*, and *Tripolis* in *Barbary*, to *Alexandria* and *Cairo* in *AEgypt*, to the Ifles
of *Sicilia*, *Zante*, *Candia*, *Rhodus*, *Cyprus*, and *Chio*, to the Citie of *Conftantinople*, to diuers parts
of *Afia minor*, to *Syria* and *Armenia*, to *Ierufalem*, and other places in *Iudea*; As alfo to *A-
rabia*, downe the Riuer of *Euphrates*, to *Babylon* and *Balfara*, and fo through the *Per-
fian* gulph to *Ormuz*, *Chaul*, *Goa*, and to many Iflands adioyning vpon the
South parts of *Afia*; And likewife from *Goa* to *Cambaia*, and to all the
dominions of *Zelabdim Echebar* the great *Mogor*, to the mighty
Riuer of *Ganges*, to *Bengala*, *Aracan*, *Bacola*, and *Chonderi*, to *Pegu*, to *Iamahai* in the kingdome of *Siam*, and almoft to the very fron-
tiers of *China*.

The fecond comprehendeth the Voyages, Trafficks, &c.
of the *English Nation*, made without the Streight of *Gibral-
tar*, to the Iflands of the *Açores*, of *Porto Santo*, *Madera*, and the *Canaries*,
to the kingdomes of *Barbary*, to the Ifles of *Capo Verde*, to the Riuers of *Senega*, *Gambra*, *Madrabumba*, and *Sierra Leona*, to the coaft of *Guinea* and *Benin*, to the Ifles
of *S. Thomé* and *Santa Helena*, to the parts about the Cape of *Buona Efpe-
ranza*, to *Quitangone* neere *Mozambique*, to the Ifles of *Comoro* and
Zanzibar, to the citie of *Goa*, beyond *Cape Comori*, to the Ifles
of *Nicubar*, *Gomes Polo*, and *Pulo Pinaom*, to the
maine land of *Malacca*, and to the kingdome of *Iunfalaon*.

¶ By RICHARD HACKLVYT Preacher, and fometime Student of Chrift-Church in Oxford.

 Imprinted at London by *George Bishop*,
Ralph Newbery, and *Robert Barker*.
ANNO 1599.

Fig. 28   Title-page of *Principal navigations*, II (1599)

Volume III THE | THIRD AND LAST | VOLVME OF THE VOY⸴ | AGES, NAVIGATIONS, TRAF⸴ | fiques, and Discoueries of the *English Nation,*...

Collected by RICHARD HAKLVYT *Preacher, and sometimes* | student...

[Printer's flower] Imprinted at London by *George Bishop, Ralfe* | *Newberie,* and ROBERT BARKER. | ANNO DOM. 1600.

B.M.

THE

THIRD AND LAST
VOLVME OF THE VOY-
AGES, NAVIGATIONS, TRAF-
fiques, and Difcoueries of the *Englifh Nation*, and in
fome few places, where they haue not been, of ftrangers, performed within and before the time of thefe hundred yeeres, to all
parts of the *Newfound* world of *America*, or the *Weft Indies*, from 73.
degrees of Northerly to 57. of Southerly latitude:

As namely to *Engronland, Meta Incognita, Eftotiland,*
Terra de Labrador, Newfoundland, vp *The grand bay,* the gulfe of *S.Lau-*
rence, and the Riuer of *Canada* to *Hochelaga* and *Saguenay,* along the coaft of *Aram-*
bec, to the fhores and maines of *Virginia* and *Florida,* and on the Weft or backfide of them
both, to the rich and pleafant countries of *Nueua Bifcaya, Cibola, Tiguex, Cicuic,*
Quiuira, to the 15. prouinces of the kingdome of *New Mexico,* to the
bottome of the gulfe of *California,* and vp the
Riuer of *Buena Guia:*

And likewife to all the yles both fmall and great lying before the
cape of *Florida, The bay* of *Mexico,* and *Tierra firma,* to the coafts and Inlands
of *Newe Spaine, Tierra firma,* and *Guiana,* vp the mighty Riuers of *Orenoque,*
Deffekebe, and *Maranuon,* to euery part of the coaft of *Brafil,* to the Riuer of *Plate,*
through the Streights of *Magellan* forward and backward, and to the
South of the faid Streights as farre as 57. degrees:

And from thence on the backfide of *America,* along the coaftes, harbours,
and capes of *Chili, Peru, Nicaragua, Nueua Efpanna, Nueua Galicia, Culiacan,*
California, Noua Albion, and more Northerly as farre as 43. degrees:

Together with the two renowmed, and profperous voyages of Sir *Francis Drake*
and M. *Thomas Candifh* round about the circumference of the whole earth, and
diuers other voyages intended and fet forth for that courfe.

Collected by RICHARD HAKLVYT *Preacher, and fometimes*
ftudent of Chrift-Church in Oxford.

¶ Imprinted at London by *George Bifhop, Ralfe*
Newberie, and ROBERT BARKER.

ANNO DOM. 1600.

Fig. 29   Title-page of *Principal navigations,* III (1600)

Collation

Vol. I: *⁶ **⁶ A–Eee⁶ Fff⁴.

Sig. A1r–Fff4r are paginated 1–619. 'A briefe and true report of the Honor‑able voyage vnto Cadiz, 1596...', when present, sig. Eee4r–Fff4r, pp. 607–19: Fff4v [p. 620] blank.

Vol. II: *⁸ A–Cc⁶ Aaa–Rrr⁶.

Sig. A1r–Cc6v (the first part), paginated 1–312; A1r–Rrr6v (the second part), 1–204.

The Map, if present, is normally found at the beginning of Vol. II, before signature A1.

Vol. III: (*A*)⁸ A–I⁶ K⁸ L–Cccc⁶.

Sig. A1r–Cccc6v are paginated 1–868. The extra pair of leaves in sig. K is made up of the ruled and tabulated 'Traverse‑Booke' of John Davis' third voyage in 1587 (III, 115–18), interpolated in the middle of the gathering.

The following errors in page‑numeration, a number of which were corrected in the course of printing, are found in various copies:

Vol. I

46 for 49	204 for 206
57 for 75	276 for 278
87 for 73	593 for 493
57 for 75	486 for 510
294 for 194	487 for 511
169 for 196	459 for 559
168 for 198	608 for 605
203 for 205	605 for 608

Vol. II (1st series)

126 for 114	243 for 249
127 for 115	252 for 254

Vol. II (2nd series)

318 for 6	32 for 20
319 for 7	333 for 21
326 for 14	335 for 23
328 for 16	4 for 64
29 for 17	110 for 111
330 for 18	143 or 145 for 155
331 for 19	

Vol. III

101 for 99	534 for 550
104 for 106	680 for 608
259 for 359	671 for 617

3

The attempt made in 1970–3 to bring the survey of copies up to date has considerably expanded the number of entries, but the tabulation which follows cannot be claimed (some of the reasons have been indicated above) as more than a provisional list. The list includes 246 entries, of which 186 are institutional and private library sets, representing either 185 or 186 copies, but some are defective to the extent of lacking one or more volumes. Of these 75 are in the British Isles and 96 in the United States, with only 14 elsewhere. The first two groups are probably reasonably complete except for a few copies in private libraries in the British Isles and an appreci‑ably larger number in those of the United States. It may be that there are between 15 and 20 more copies in these areas. The 14 copies elsewhere are probably a serious underestimate: the true figure is likely to be more in the region of 30. The trade copies fall into three groups: (a) those located by C. E. Armstrong in 1954–5 which were then in booksellers' hands in England or the United States, (b) those which have appeared at auction in London and New York, 1956–71, of which a few may have appeared more than once, and (c) a small selection from booksellers' catalogues and from stocks located in 1970–3. While these comprise 58 copies, those in group (a) have already gone to swell the list of those in institutional or private hands; most of those which appeared at auction have gone from there either to permanent homes, to booksellers' stocks or to their catalogues. A number of copies clearly appear at least twice in the list. It would be unwise to say that this group taken as a whole would add more than about 25 copies net to the total. This would give us our firm total of 186 plus about 25 + 20 which we guess must exist in addition, to produce a survival total of about 230. Even if this is an overestimate it is certain that 200 copies exist. With a print of 1,000, which was the maximum authorized by the Stationers' Company, this would mean a 20 per cent survival rate, which would be high. But it would not be excessive for a work in more than one volume which was for the most part safeguarded in libraries from the beginning. If a further complete survey brought the total of surviving copies into the range 230–50, it might be desirable to consider whether more than 1,000 copies were printed in the first place. It must be emphasized, however, that no close study of the composition of the book has so far been attempted. Until this is done and a complete survey is also carried out, it will not be possible to point to more definitive conclusions.

	Title-page state	Voyage state	Map state
The British Isles			
England			
London			
1.a. Admiralty Library I[1] (N.H.L.)	2	A	—
2.a. Admiralty Library II (N.H.L.)	2	—	—
3.a. British Museum I (C.212 d.2)	1	A	1
4.a. British Museum II (G 6605–6)	2	A	2
5.a. British Museum III (683.h.5–6)	1	B	2
6.a. British Museum IV (984.g.1–2)	2	B	—
7.a. British Museum V (Maps C.8.a. 12)[2]	2	B	—
8.b. Dulwich College Library	2	—	—
9.b. Guildhall Library	1	C	—
10.b. Lambeth Palace Library	1	A	—
11.a. London Library	2	—	—
12.a. Middle Temple Library	1	A	—
13.a. Royal Geographical Society Library	2	B	—
14.b. Science Museum Library	2	—	—
Oxford			
15.a. Bodleian Library, I (Douce H.238–9)	1	A	—
16.a. Bodleian Library, II (Savile X.12)[3]	1	A	—
17.a. Bodleian Library, III (H.8.15, 16 Art.)	2	A	2
18.b. Bodleian Library, IV (Radcliffe Science L.)	2	B	—
19.b. Balliol College Library	5	B	—
20.b. Christ Church Library	2	B	—
21.b. Christ Church Library (Evelyn Deposit)	2	A	—
22.b. English Faculty Library	2	—	—
23.b. Exeter College Library	2	—	—
24.b. Hertford College Library	3	B	—
25.b. Magdalen College Library	1	—	—
26.b. New College Library	2	—	—
27.b. Oriel College Library	2	—	—

[1] Which may be identical with no. 202 below.
[2] Somewhat defective.
[3] Vol. I only: 'Liber Henrici Sauil' on t.p.

	Title-page state	Voyage state	Map state
Oxford (cont.)			
28.b. The Queen's College Library	2	—	—
29.b. St Edmund Hall Library	2	A	—
30.b. St John's College Library	1	A	—
31.b. Trinity College Library	1	—	—
32.b. Worcester College Library	—	B	—
Cambridge			
33.a. University Library I	2	—	—
34.a. University Library II	—	A	—
35.b. Christ's College Library[1]	—	—	—
36.b. Emmanuel College Library	1	—	—
37.b. King's College Library I	1	B	—
38.b. King's College Library II	4	B	—
39.b. Magdalene College, Pepys Library	2	A	—
40.b. Pembroke College Library[2]	1	—	—
41.b. Queen's College Library	2	—	—
42.b. St John's College Library I	1	—	—
43.b. St John's College Library II	2	B	—
44.b. Sidney Sussex College Library	2	A	—
Other English locations			
45.b. Banbury, Wardington Manor (Lord Wardington)	2	A	—
46.a. Birmingham Public Library	2	B	—
47.b. Blackburn Public Library	1	—	—
47(1).b. Chatsworth House (Duke of Devonshire), I	2	A	2
47(2).b. Chatsworth House (Henry Cavendish copy, sold Christie's, 18 November 1970), II	2	A	—
48.a. Cheltenham, E. Van Dam	1	—	—
49.b. Durham University Library	1	—	—
50.b. Durham, Ushaw College Library	2	A	—
51.b. Gloucester Cathedral Library[3]	—	—	—
52.b. Hereford Cathedral Library	2	—	—
53.b. Hertfordshire, Hatfield House[4]	1	A	—

[1] Imperfect.　　　[2] Vols. I–II only.　　　[3] Vol. III only.

[4] Vol. I only: 'The second Volume of Navigacion' (that dedicated to Sir Robert Cecil) was in the library but is now missing (Library Catalogue 1614. Cecil MS 165/1).

	Title-page state	Voyage state	Map state
Other English locations (cont.)			
54.b. Leeds University, Brotherton Library	2	A	—
55.b. Lincoln Cathedral Library[1]	—	—	—
56.a. Manchester, John Rylands Library	I	A	—
57.b. Manchester, Chetham's Library	2	—	—
58.b. Newcastle-on-Tyne Public Library[2]	—	—	—
59.b. Norwich Public Library[3]	—	—	—
60.b. Peterborough Cathedral Library	—	—	—
61.b. Sheffield University Library	I	—	—
62.b. Windsor, Eton College Library	3	A	2
Ireland			
63.a. Dublin, Trinity College Library I	I	A	—
64.a. Dublin, Trinity College Library II	I	—	—
65.a. Dublin, Trinity College Library III	2	B	—
66.b. Dublin, National Library of Ireland[4]	—	—	—
67.b. Dublin, Marsh's Library	I	A	—
68.b. Cashel Diocesan Library[5]	2	—	—
Scotland			
69.b. Edinburgh, National Library of Scotland I	2	A	—
70.b. Edinburgh, National Library of Scotland II	2	A	—
71.a. Edinburgh, Edinburgh University Library	2	A	—
72.a. Glasgow University Library	I	A	—
73.b. Glasgow, Public Library	I	C	—
Auction and booksellers' copies: Great Britain			
74.c. Christie's. 6 December 1967, 138	I	?	—
75.a.c. Francis Edwards I	2	B	—
76.c. Francis Edwards II (925 (1969), 55)	2	—	—
77.a.c. Maggs I	I	A	—
78.a.a. Maggs II	I	B	—
79.a.c. Maggs III	I	—	—
80.a.c. Maggs IV	2	B	—
81.a.c. Maggs V	2	B	—
82.a.c. Maggs VI	4	—	—
83.a.c. Maggs VII	5	C	—
84.c. Maggs VIII	I	B	—
85.c. Maggs IX	2	C	—

[1] Vols. I–II only. [2] Imperfect. [3] Imperfect.
[4] Imperfect. [5] 'Voyage' in MS.

	Title-page state	Voyage state	Map state
Auction and booksellers' copies: Great Britain *(cont.)*			
86.c. Maggs x	2	—	—
87.c. Maggs xi	2	B	—
88.a.c. Quaritch i	1	—	—
89.a.c. Quaritch ii	2	A	—
90.a.c. Quaritch iii	2	—	—
91.a.c. Quaritch iv	3	—	—
92.a.c. Henry Stevens, Son & Stiles i	1	A	—
93.a.c. Henry Stevens, Son & Stiles ii	1	A	—
94.a.c. Henry Stevens, Son & Stiles iii	2	A	—
95.c. Henry Stevens, Son and Stiles (Americana, n.s. 59, 42)	2	B	—
96.c. Henry Stevens, Son & Stiles (Americana, 70, 201)	1	A	—
97.c. Henry Stevens, Son & Stiles (Americana, 74, 259)	2	B	—
98.c. Sotheby's, 27 March 1956, 322	1	?	—
99.c. Sotheby's, 5 March 1957, 361	2	A	—
100.c. Sotheby's, 10 November 1959, 208	2	B	—
101.c. Sotheby's, 13 February 1961, 109	2	B	—
102.c. Sotheby's, 5 June 1961, 121	2	A	—
103.c. Sotheby's, 17 October 1961, 121	2	A	—
104.c. Sotheby's, 27 July 1964, 88	1	B	—
105.c. Sotheby's, 21 December 1965, 510	2	B	—
106.c. Sotheby's, 2 May 1966, 14	2	A	—
107.c. Sotheby's, 8 April 1968, 100	2	?	—
108.c. Sotheby's, 17 February 1969, 58	2	?	—
109.c. Sotheby's, 21 June 1971, 38 (Hodgsons' Rooms)	2	?	—
110.c. Sotheby's, 5 October 1971, 205	2	A	—
111.c. Sotheby's, 20 December 1971, 245	1	—	—
112.c. Thomas Crowe, Norwich, Cat., 133 (1971), 16	1	A	—
112(i) c. John Grant, Edinburgh	2	B	—
112(ii) c. Heffer (Cat. 48 (1973), 831	1	—	—

North America

United States

California

	Title-page state	Voyage state	Map state
113.b. Berkeley, University of California	1	—	—
114.a. Claremont, Pomona College Library	1	D	—

	Title-page state	Voyage state	Map state
California (cont.)			
115.a. Los Angeles Public Library	1	A	—
116.b. Oakland, Mills College Library[1]	2	A	—
117.a. San Marino, Henry E. Huntington Library I	2	A	2
118.a. San Marino, Henry E. Huntington Library II	2	—	1
District of Columbia			
119.a. Washington, Folger Shakespeare Library	1	A	—
120.a. Washington, Library of Congress I	1	C	—
121.a. Washington, Library of Congress II	2	B	—
Connecticut			
122.a. New Haven, Yale University I	1	A	—
123.a. New Haven, Yale University II	2	B	—
124.b. New Haven, Yale University III[2]	1	A	—
125.b. Southport, Pequot Library	5	A	—
Delaware			
126.b. Wilmington, Pierre DuPont	2	A	—
Florida			
127.b. Tallahassee, Florida State University[3]	2	C	—
Georgia			
128.b. Macon, Wesleyan College	2	A	—
129.b. Savannah, Georgia Historical Society	2	—	—
Illinois			
130.a. Chicago, Newberry Library I	1	A	2
131.a. Chicago, Newberry Library II	2	D	—
132.a. Urbana, University of Illinois I	1	—	—
133.a. Urbana, University of Illinois II	2	B	—
Indiana			
134.a. Bloomington, University of Indiana, Lilly Library I	1	A	1
135.a. Bloomington, University of Indiana, Lilly Library II	1	B	—

[1] Map in facsimile.

[2] Formerly in the possession of Henry C. Taylor, of New York, deceased.

[3] Map in facsimile.

	Title-page state	Voyage state	Map state
Kentucky			
136.b. Lexington, University of Kentucky	2	B	—
Louisiana			
137.b. New Orleans, Tulane University	2	C	—
Maryland			
138.a. Baltimore, John Work Garrett Library	1	A	—
139.a. Baltimore, Walters Gallery of Art	1	B	—
Massachusetts			
140.a. Boston Public Library	2	D	—
141.a. Cambridge, Harvard University I	1	A	—
142.a. Cambridge, Harvard University II	2	A	—
143.a. Cambridge, Harvard University III	2	A	—
144.a. Cambridge, Harvard University IV	2	A	—
145.a. Cambridge, Harvard University V	2	B	—
146.b. Cambridge, Harvard University VI[1]	2	A	—
147.a. Williamstown, Williams College, Chapin Library	1	A	—
Michigan			
148.a. Ann Arbor, William L. Clements Library I	2	A	1
149.a. Ann Arbor, William L. Clements Library II	4	B	—
Minnesota			
150.a. Minneapolis, University of Minnesota Library	2	D	—
New Hampshire			
151.a. Hanover, Dartmouth College Library	1	A	—
New Jersey			
152.a. Newark Public Library	2	B	—
153.b. New Brunswick, Theological Seminary, Gardner A. Sage Library	2	—	—
154.a. Princeton University I	2	A	1
155.a. Princeton University II	2	A	2
156.a. Princeton, Robert H. Taylor	1	A	—
157.a. West Orange, Charles E. Armstrong	1	A	—

[1] Map in facsimile.

	Title-page state	Voyage state	Map state
New York			
158.a. Albany, New York State Library	1	A	—
159.a. Brooklyn Public Library	—	—	—
160.a. Ithaca, Cornell University Library I	1	B	—
161.a. Ithaca, Cornell University Library II	2	C	—
162.a. Ithaca, Cornell University Library III	2	—	—
163.a. New York, American Geographical Society	1	B	—
164.a. New York, Columbia University Library I	1	A	—
165.a. New York, Columbia University Library II	2	A	—
166.a. New York, Columbia University Library III	2	D	—
167.a. New York, C. Warren Force	1	A	—
168.b. New York, Frank Streeter	2	A	—
169.a. New York, New York Historical Society I	1	A	—
170.a. New York, New York Historical Society II	2	B	—
171.a. New York, New York Historical Society III	—	C	—
172.a. New York, New York Public Library I	1	A	—
173.a. New York, New York Public Library II	1	—	—
174.a. New York, New York Public Library III	2	A	—
175.a. New York, New York Public Library IV	2	A	—
176.a. New York, New York Public Library V	2	A	—
177.a. New York, New York Public Library VI	2	B	—
178.a. New York, New York Public Library VII	2	C	2
179.a. New York, New York Public Library VIII[1]	4	B	—
180.a. New York, Pierpont Morgan Library I	1	A	—
181.a. New York, Pierpont Morgan Library II	2	A	—
182.a. New York, Carl H. Pforzheimer Library	1	A	—
183.b. New York, Henry Bradley Martin	1	A	—
North Carolina			
184.a. Durham, Duke University Library	2	A	—
185.b. Winston Salem, Wake Forest University Library[2]	1	D	—

[1] This copy, in a late eighteenth- or early nineteenth-century binding has a State 5 title-page bound in front of the State 4 title-page. The latter has no watermark.
[2] Map in facsimile.

	Title-page state	Voyage state	Map state
Ohio			
186.a. Cincinnati Public Library	1	A	—
Pennsylvania			
187.a. Bethelehem, LeHigh University	2	A	—
188.b. Devon, Boies Penrose	2	A	—
189.b. Meadsville, Allegheny College Library[1]	2	B	—
190.a. Philadelphia Public Library	1	A	2
Rhode Island			
191.b. Newport, Naval War College Library I	2	B	2
192.b. Newport, Naval War College Library II	2	B	—
193.a. Providence, John Carter Brown Library I	1	A	2
194.a. Providence, John Carter Brown Library II	1	A	—
195.a. Providence, John Carter Brown Library III	2	B	—
Texas			
196.a. Austin, University of Texas Library	1	A	—
Virginia			
197.a. Charlottesville, University of Virginia I	1	A	2
198.a. Charlottesville, University of Virginia II[2]	2	A	—
199.b. Newport News, Mariners' Museum	2	A	—
200.b. Richmond, Virginia Historical Society	3	A	—
201.b. Upperville, Paul Mellon I	1	A	—
202.b. Upperville, Paul Mellon II[3]	2	A	—
203.a. Williamsburg, College of William and Mary	1	B	—
Wisconsin			
204.a. Madison, University of Wisconsin, Olin Library	1	A	—
Auction and booksellers' copies: United States			
205.a.c. Argosy Bookstores, New York	—	A	—
206.a.c. G. A. Baker Gallery, New York	1	A	—
207.a.c. Wright, Howes, New York I	1	A	—
208.a.c. Wright, Howes, New York II	2	B	—
209.a.c. Wright, Howes, New York III	2	B	—
210.a.c. Lathrop, Harper, Inc., New York	1	A	—

[1] Map in facsimile.
[2] Map in facsimile. The State A 'Voyage' is present but is not bound into the volume.   [3] Apparently identical with no. 1 above.

	Title-page state	Voyage state	Map state
Auction and booksellers' copies: United States *(cont)*.			
211.a.c. Mendoza Book Company, New York	2	D	—
212.a.c. P. Stammer, formerly New York	2	B	—
213.a.c. Parke, Bernet, Inc. New York, November 1943, 167[1]	1	A	—
214.c. Parke, Bernet, Inc. New York, 28 October 1958, 151	1	A	—
215.c. Parke, Bernet, Inc. New York, 24 November 1959, 143	1	A	—
216.c. Parke, Bernet, Inc. New York, 8 November 1962, 69	1	A	—
217.a. Swann Auction Galleries, New York, 1954	—	B	—
218.c. Swann Auction Galleries, New York, 4 December 1958, 1220	2	A	—
219.c. Swann Auction Galleries, New York, 23 January 1969, 174	1	—	—
220.c. Swann Auction Galleries, New York, 6 February 1969, 104	1	A	—
221.c. Seven Gables Bookshop, New York, November 1971	1	—	—
Canada			
222.a. British Columbia, Provincial Archives, Victoria, 1	1	A	—
223.a. British Columbia, Provincial Archives, Victoria 11[2]	2	A	—
224.b. Newfoundland, Memorial University, St John's[3]	2	A	—
225.b. Nova Scotia, Provincial Archives, Halifax[4]	—	—	—
226.a. Ontario, Parliamentary Library, Ottawa	2	A	—
Other locations			
France			
227.a. Paris, Bibliothèque Nationale, 1	1	—	—
228.a. Paris, Bibliothèque Nationale, 11	2	—	—
229.b. Strasbourg, Bibliothèque Nationale et Universitaire	3	A	—

[1] Library of Col. E. H. R. Green.   [2] Map in facsimile.
[3] R A. Skelton's copy: somewhat imperfect.   [4] Title-page in MS.

	Title-page state	Voyage state	Map state
Norway			
230.b. Oslo, Universitetsbiblioteket	3	—	—
South Africa			
231.b. Johannesburg, University of the Witwatersrand	2	B	—
U.S.S.R.			
232.b. Leningrad, Saltykov-Shchedrin Public Library	—	A	—
233.b. Leningrad, Library of Academy of Sciences	2	A	—
Australia			
234.b. Melbourne, Victoria State Library	2	B	—
235.b. Sydney, New South Wales Library I	1	—	—
236.b. Sydney, New South Wales Library II (Dixson L.)	1	A	1
237.b. Sydney, New South Wales Library III (Mitchell L.)	2	B	—
238.b. Sydney, New South Wales Library IV (Mitchell L.)	1	B	—
239.b. Sydney, New South Wales Library V[1] (Mitchell L.)	2	—	—
New Zealand			
240.b. Wellington, Turnbull Library[2]	1	A	—

Unlocated copy

241   Lumley 1436 'Richarde Hacluites bookes of the navigations and travailes of English men. anglice. vol: 3'. This was in the Old Royal Library in the British Museum and appears in the 1761 manuscript catalogue of that date in the B.M. but was subsequently disposed of as a duplicate. The set appeared in Stevens' catalogues (*Rare Americana*, 16 and 24), described as 'the Lumley copy, the name being faintly visible on two of the titles', with B.M. sale duplicate stamp 1787 on the reverse of the titles, with State I of the title-page and State A of the 'Voyage'. No indication of its present whereabouts has been found. A separate Lumley copy of volume II (1599), in a Prince Henry binding, which was never in the B.M., was in the Carton Library, County Kildare, and in 1933 was bought for the Bodleian (Don. C. 25).

[1] Vols. I–II only.   [1] Map in facsimile.

[Galvão, Antonio.] THE | DISCOVERIES | of the World from their | first originall vnto the | *yeere of our Lord* | 1555. | Briefly written in the Por- | tugall tongue by ANTONIE | GALVANO, *Gouernour of* | Ternate, the chiefe Island | of the *Malucos*: | Corrected, quoted, and now | *published in English by* Richard | Hakluyt, *sometimes student* | of Christchurch in | *Oxford.* | *LONDINI,* | Impensis G. Bishop. | 1601.

Collation: A–O⁴.

[S.T.C. 11543] B.M.

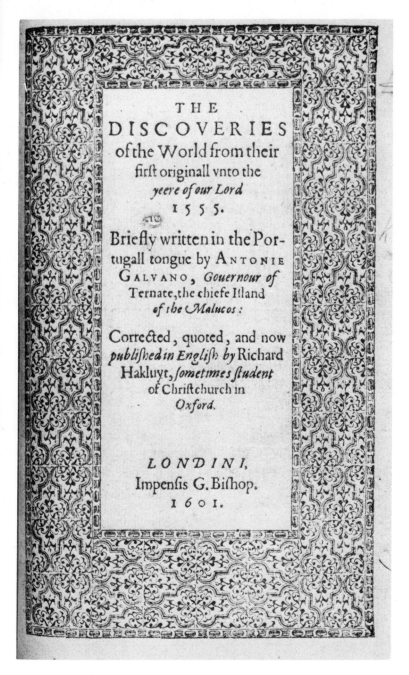

THE
DISCOVERIES
of the World from their
firſt originall vnto the
yeere of our Lord
1 5 5 5.

Briefly written in the Portugall tongue by ANTONIE
GALVANO, *Gouernour of*
Ternate, the chiefe Iſland
of the Malucos:

Corrected, quoted, and now
publiſhed in Engliſh by Richard
Hakluyt, *ſometimes ſtudent*
of Chriſtchurch in
Oxford.

LONDINI,
Impenſis G. Biſhop.
1 6 0 1.

Fig. 30 Title-page of Antonio Galvão, *The discoueries of the world* (1601)

[A Gentleman of Elvas.] VIRGINIA | richly valued, | *By the description of the maine land of* | *Florida,* her next neighbour: | Out of the foure yeeres continuall trauell and discouerie, | for aboue one thousand miles East and West, of | *Don Ferdinando de Soto,* and sixe hundred | able men in his companie. | *Wherein are truly obserued the riches and fertilitie of those parts,* | *abounding with things necessarie, pleasant, and profitable* | *for the life of man*: *with the natures and dispo-* | *sitions of the Inhabitants.* | Written by a Portugall gentleman of *Eluas,* emploied in | all the action, and translated out of Portugese | by RICHARD HAKLUYT. | [ornament] | *AT LONDON* | Printed by FELIX KYNGSTON for *Matthew Lownes,* | and are to be sold at the signe of the Bishops | head in Pauls Churchyard. | 1609.

Collation: A–Z⁴, Aa²

[S.T.C. 22938] B.M.

VIRGINIA
richly valued,

By the description of the maine land of Florida, her next neighbour:

Out of the foure yeeres continuall trauell and difcouerie, for aboue one thoufand miles Eaft and Weft, of *Don Ferdinando de Soto,* and fixe hundred able men in his companie.

Wherin are truly obferued the riches and fertilitie of thofe parts, abounding with things neceffarie, pleafant and profitable for the life of man: with the natures and difpofitions of the Inhabitants.

Written by a Portugall gentleman of *Eluas,* emploied in all the action, and tranflated out of Portugefe by RICHARD HAKLVYT.

AT LONDON
Printed by FELIX KYNGSTON for *Matthew Lownes,* and are to be fold at the figne of the Bifhops head in Pauls Churchyard.
1609.

Fig. 31   Title-page of Gentleman of Elvas, *Virginia richly valued* (1609)

[A Gentleman of Elvas.] THE | WORTHYE | AND FAMOVS HIS⁄ | *TORY,* *OF THE TRAVAILES,* | Discouery, & Conquest, of that great | Continent of *Terra Florida*, being liuely | Paraleld, with that of our now Inha⁄ | bited *VIRGINIA.* | As also | The Comodities of the said Country, | With diuers excellent and rich Mynes, of Golde, | Siluer, and other Mettals, &c. which cannot but | giue vs a great and exceeding hope of our | *VIRGINIA,* being so neere | of one Continent. | Accomplished and effected, by that worthy | Generall and Captaine, *Don Ferdinaudo* [*sic*] | *de Soto,* and his six hundreth Spaniards | his followers. | [ornament] | LONDON | *Printed for* Mathew Lownes, *dwelling* | in Paules Church⁄yard, at the Signe of | the Bishops head. 1611.

Another issue with a new title⁄page only.

[S.T.C. 22939] B.M.

THE
WORTHYE
AND FAMOVS HIS-
TORY, OF THE TRAVAILES,
Difcouery, & Conqueſt, of that great
Continent of *Terra Florida*, being liuely
Paraleld, with that of our now Inha-
bited *VIRGINIA.*

As alſo
The Comodities of the ſaid Country,
With diuers excellent and rich Mynes, of Golde,
Siluer, and other Mettals, &c. which cannot but
giue vs a great and exceeding hope of our
VIRGINIA, being ſo neere
of one Continent.

Accompliſhed and effected, by that worthy
Generall and Captaine, *Don Ferdinaudo
de Soto*, and fix hundreth Spaniards
his followers.

LONDON
Printed for Mathew Lownes, *dwelling*
in Paules Church-yard, at the Signe of
the Biſhops head. 1611.

Fig. 32 Title-page of Gentleman of Elvas, *The worthye and famous history...of
Terra Florida* (1611)

II

Works in which Hakluyt's influence is known or acknowledged

[Cartier, Jacques] A shorte and briefe narration of the two nauigations and discoueries to the northwest partes called Newe Fraunce.

H. Bynneman, 1580.

Collation: A–B², C–M⁴

[S.T.C. 4699] B.M.

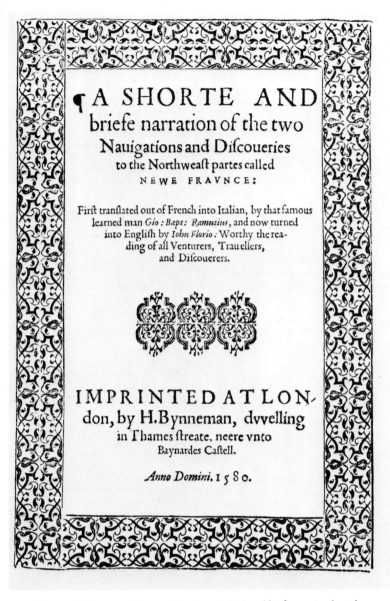

¶A SHORTE AND
briefe narration of the two
Nauigations and Discoueries
to the Northweaſt partes called
NEWE FRAVNCE:

Firſt tranſlated out of French into Italian, by that famous
learned man *Gio : Bapt: Ramutius*, and now turned
into Engliſh by *Iohn Florio* : Worthy the reading of all Venturers, Trauellers,
and Diſcouerers.

IMPRINTED AT LON-
don, by H. Bynneman, dvvelling
in Thames ſtreate, neere vnto
Baynardes Caſtell.

Anno Domini. 1 5 8 o.

Fig. 33   Title-page of Jacques Cartier, *A shorte and briefe narration* (1580)

Pigafetta, Marco Antonio. Itinerario di Marc'Antonio Pigafetta gentil' huomo Vicentino.

Londra, Appresso Giouanni Wolfio Inghilese. 1585.

Collation: A–T⁴

[S.T.C. 19914] B.M.

ITINERARIO
DI MARCANTONIO
Pigafetta gentil'huomo Vicentino,

All'Illustrissimo Signore Eduardo Seymer
Conte d'Hertford &c.

FIDELE · POVR

A · LAMY · · · IAMAIS

LONDRA
Appresso Giouanni Wolfio Inghilese.
1585.

Fig. 34   Title-page of M. A. Pigafetta, *Itinerario* (1585)

René de Laudonnière. L'histoire notable de la Floride.

Paris, Guillaume Auuray, 1586.

Collation: a⁸. A–P⁸, Q⁴ (E3 is signed R3)

[Atkinson, no. 321] B.M.

[It is arguable that this should be included in the previous section since Hakluyt obtained the MS on loan and arranged that it should be published (see pp. 288, 292 above), but since he left Martin Basanier to bring it out and to sign the dedication, it would seem that he did not wish his own association in its production to be explicit.]

L'HISTOIRE

NOTABLE DE LA FLORIDE SITVEE ES INDES

Occidentales, contenant les trois voyages faits en icelle par certains Capitaines & Pilotes François, deſcrits par le Capitaine Laudonniere, qui y a commandé l'eſpace d'vn an trois moys : à laquelle a eſté adiouſté vn quatrieſme voyage fait par le Capitaine Gourgues.

Miſe en lumiere par M. B ASANIER, *gentil-homme François Mathematicien.*

IEAN MAVRICE.

A PARIS,
Chez Guillaume Auuray, ruë ſainct Iean de Beauuais, au Bellerophon couronné.

M. D. LXXXVII.

AVEC PRIVILEGE DV ROY.

Fig. 35 Title-page of René de Laudonnière, *L'histoire notable de la Floride*

Espejo, Antonio de. Histoire des terres nouuellement descouuertes...
nommees le nouueau Mexico.

Traduict de l'Espagnol...par M. Basanier.

Paris, vefue [*sic*] Nicolas Roffet, 1586.

Collation: A–F⁴

[Atkinson, supplément, no. 318A] New York Public Library

HISTOIRE DES
TERRES NOVVELLEMENT

DESCOVVERTES, AVSQVELLES
a esté ja trouué quinze belles Prouinces remplies de villes & villages:
ausquelles Prouinces il se trouue
grandes commoditez, & abondance
de diuerses especes metalliques : les-
quelles terres ont esté descouuertes
par Antonio de Espeio & nommees
le nouueau Mexico.

*Traduict de l'Espagnol en langue françoise,
par M. Basanier gentil-homme François.*

A PARIS,
Chez la vefue Nicolas Roffet, fur le pont Sainct
Michel, à la Roze blanche.
M. D. LXXXVI.
AVEC PRIVILEGE DV ROY.

Fig. 36 Title-page of A. de Espejo, *Histoire des terres nouuellement descouuertes*
(1586). N.Y.P.L.

González de Mendoza, Juan. The historie of the great and mightie king⸝dome of China.

Translated out of Spanish by R. Parke.

I. Wolfe for Edward White, 1588.

Collation: ¶⁴, A–Z⁸, Aa–Bb⁸, Cc⁶

[S.T.C. 12003] B.M.

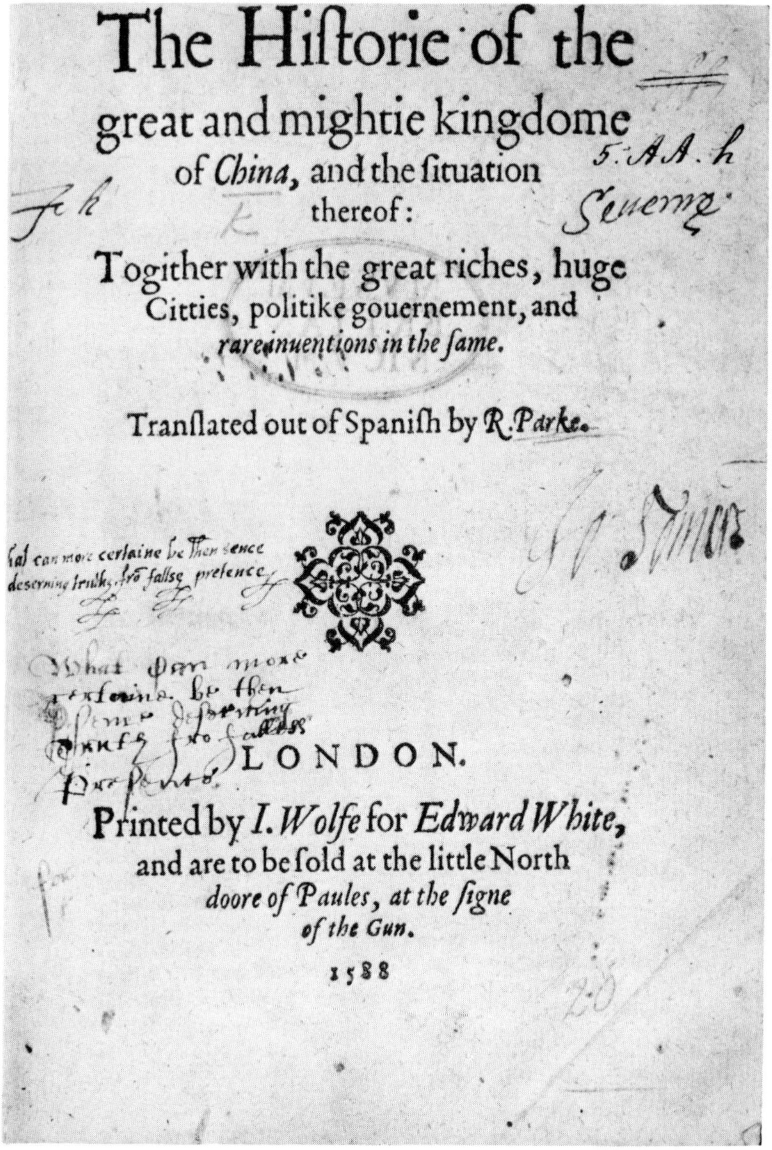

The Hiſtorie of the

great and mightie kingdome
of *China*, and the ſituation
thereof:

Togither with the great riches, huge
Citties, politike gouernement, and
rare inuentions in the ſame.

Tranſlated out of Spaniſh by *R. Parke.*

LONDON.

Printed by *I. Wolfe* for *Edward White,*
and are to be ſold at the little North
doore of *Paules*, at the ſigne
of the Gun.

1588

Fig. 37   Title-page of J. González de Mendoza, *The historie of the great and mightie
kingdome of China* (1588)

Meierus, Albertus. Certaine briefe, and speciall instructions for gentlemen merchants, students, souldiers, marriners, &c. Employed in seruices abrode.

Iohn Wolfe, 1589.

Collation: A–C⁴, D⁴

[S.T.C. 17784] B.M.

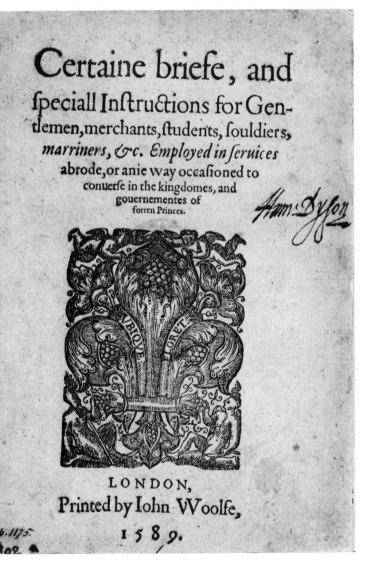

Certaine briefe, and

ſpeciall Inſtructions for Gentlemen, merchants, ſtudents, ſouldiers, marriners, &c. *Employed in ſeruices* abrode, or anie way occaſioned to conuerſe in the kingdomes, and gouernementes of forren Princes.

Ham: Dyſon

UBIQVE · FLORET·

LONDON,
Printed by Iohn VVoolfe,
1 5 8 9.

Wf. p. 1175.
Ch. 202.

Fig. 38   Title-page of A. Meïerus, *Certaine briefe, and speciall instructions* (1589)

Bry, Theodor de. America. Part i
Frankfurt, Johannes Wechel for Theodor de Bry, 1590.
Latin. B.M.

Bry, Theodor de. America. Part i
Frankfurt, Johannes Wechel for Theodor de Bry, 1590.
English. B.M.

Bry, Theodor de. America. Part i
Frankfurt, Johannes Wechel for Theodor de Bry, 1590.
French. B.M.

Bry, Theodor de. America. Part i
Frankfurt, Johannes Wechel for Theodor de Bry, 1590.
German. B.M.

Fig. 39   Title-page of T. de Bry, *America*, part i (1590), English

Bry, Theodor de. America. Part ii.
Frankfurt, Johannes Wechel for Theodor de Bry, 1591.
Latin. B.M.

Bry, Theodor de. America. Part ii.
Frankfurt, Johannes Wechel for Theodor de Bry, 1591.
German. B.M.

BREVIS NARRATIO
EORVM QVÆ IN FLORIDA AMERICÆ PROVICIA
Gallis acciderunt, secunda in illam Nauigatione, du
ce Renato de Laudōniere classis Præfectō
Anno M D LxIIII.

QVAE EST SECVNDA PARS AMERICAE.

Additæ figuræ & Incolarum eicones ibidem ad viuū expressæ
breuis item Declaratio Religionis, rituum, viuendique
ratione ipsorum.

Auctore
Iacobo le Moyne, cui cognomen de Morgues, Laudōnierum
in ea Nauigatione sequuto.
Nunc primum Gallico sermone à Theodoro de Bry Leodiensi
in lucem edita: latio verò donata a C.C.A.

Cum gratia & priuil. Cæf. Maiest. ad quadriennium.

FRANCOFORTI AD MOENVM
Typis Ioānis Wecheli, Sumtibus verò Theodori
de Bry ANNO M D XCI.
Venales reperiūtur in officina Sigismundi Feirabendij

Fig. 40   Title-page of T. de Bry, *America*, part ii (1591), Latin

543

Lopes, Duarte. A report of the kingdome of Congo, a region of Africa...
Drawen out of the writinges and discourses of Odoardo Lopez a Portingall, by Philippo Pigafetta.

Translated by Abraham Hartwell.

Iohn Wolfe, 1597.

Collation: *⁴, *⁴, **¹, A–Z⁴, Aa–Ee⁴: two maps, ten illustrations (including two duplicates).

The book contains a second title-page, *A reporte*, at A2. As this has
been used to replace the primary title-page in some copies, both are given.

[S.T.C. 16805] B.M.

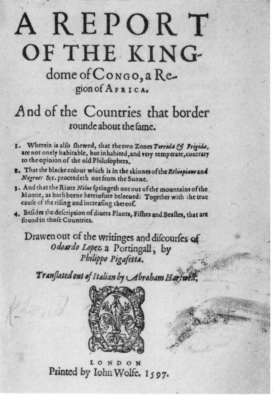

A REPORT
OF THE KING-
dome of CONGO, a Re-
gion of AFRICA.

And of the Countries that border
rounde about the same.

1. Wherein is also shewed, that the two Zones *Torrida & Frigida*,
are not onely habitable, but inhabited, and very temperate, contrary
to the opinion of the old Philosophers.

2. That the blacke colour which is in the skinnes of the *Ethiopians* and
Negroes &c. proceedeth not from the Sunne.

3. And that the Riuer *Nilus* springeth not out of the mountains of the
Moone, as hath beene heretofore beleeued: Together with the true
cause of the rising and increasing thereof.

4. Besides the description of diuers Plants, Fishes and Beastes, that are
found in those Countries.

Drawen out of the writings and discourses of
Odoardo Lopez a Portingall, by
Philippo Pigafetta.

Translated out of Italian by Abraham Hartwell.

LONDON
Printed by Iohn Wolfe. 1597.

Fig. 41   First title-page of D. Lopes, *A report of the kingdom of Congo* (1597)

544

A REPORTE
OF THE KING-
dome of CONGO, a Re-
gion of AFRICA.

And of the Countries that border
rounde about the same.

1. Wherein is also shewed that the two Zones, Torrida & Frigida, are not onely habitable, but inhabited, and very temperate, contrary to the opinion of the olde Philosophers.

2. That the blacke colour which is in the skinnes of the *Ethiopians* & *Negroes* &c. proceedeth not from the Sunne.

3. And that the Riuer *Nilus* springeth not out of the mountains of the Moone, as hath beene heretofore beleeued: Together with the true cause of the rysing and increase thereof.

4. Besides the description of diuers plantes, Fishes and Beastes, that are founde in those Countries.

Drawen out of the writinges and discourses of
Odoardo Lopes a Portingall, by
Philippo Pigafetta.

Translated out of Italian by Abraham Hartwell.

LONDON
Printed by Iohn Wolfe. 1597.

Fig. 42 Second title-page of Lopes, *A report of the kingdom of Congo*

Linschoten, Jan Huygen van. Iohn Huighen van Linschoten. his discours of voyages into yᵉ East & West Indies.

Translated by William Philip.

Iohn Wolfe, 1598.

Collation: A⁴, B–Q⁶, R⁸, *S², S–Z⁶, Aa⁶, Bb–Cc⁴, Dd–Pp⁶, Q⁸: maps in text, three folding plates, thirteen folding maps.

[S.T.C. 15691] B.M.

Fig. 43   Title-page of J. H. van Linschoten, *His discours of voyages* (1598)

Leo Africanus, Johannes. A geographical historie of Africa.

Translated by Iohn Pory.

George Bishop, 1600.

Collation: [ ]^4. a–e^6, A–O^6, Q–Z^6, Aa–Nn^6: one map.

[S.T.C. 15481] B.M.

A GEOGRAPHICAL
HISTORIE of AFRICA,
Written in Arabicke and Italian
by I O H N L E O a More, borne
in Granada, and brought vp
in Barbarie.

*Wherein he hath at large deſcribed, not onely the qualities, ſituations, and true
diſtances of the regions, cities, townes, mountaines, riuers, and other places
throughout all the north and principall partes of Africa; but alſo the
deſcents and families of their kings, the cauſes and euents of their warres,
with their manners, cuſtomes, religions, and ciuile gouernment, and
many other memorable matters : gathered partly out of his owne diligent obſeruations, and partly out of the ancient records and Chronicles
of the Arabians and Mores.*

Before which, out of the beſt ancient and moderne writers, is prefixed a generall
deſcription of Africa, and alſo a particular treatiſe of all the maine lands
and Iſles vndeſcribed by *Iohn Leo.*

*And after the ſame is annexed a relation of the great Princes, and the manifold religions
in that part of the world.*

Tranſlated and collected by I O H N P O R Y, lately
of Goneuill and Caius College
in Cambridge.

LONDINI,
Impenſis Georg. Biſhop.
1 6 0 0

Fig. 44   Title-page of J. Leo Africanus, *A geographical historie of Africa* (1600)

Neck, Jacob Corneliszoon van. The iournall, or dayly register, contayning a true manifestation, and historical declaration of the voyage...vnder the conduct of Iacob Corneliszen Neck...which sayled from Amsterdam the first day of March, 1598.

Translated by William Walker.

For Cuthbert Burby and Iohn Flasket, 1601.

Collation: ¶², A²⁻⁴, B–Q⁴

[S.T.C. 18417] B.M.

THE
IOVRNALL, OR DAY-
ly Regifter,

CONTAYNING A TRVE
manifeftation, and Hiftoricall declaration of the
voyage, accomplifhed by eight fhippes of Amfterdam, vnder
the conduct ot *Iacob Corneliszen Neck* Admirall, & *Wybrandt*
van Warwick Vice-Admirall, which fayled from Amfterdam *the firft day of March,*
1598.

SHEWING THE COVRSE THEY
kept, and what other notable matters happened
vnto them in the fayd voyage.

Imprinted at London for Cuthbert Burby & Iohn Flafket:
And are to be fold at the Royall Exchange, & at the figne
of the blacke beare in Paules Church-yard.
1601.

Fig. 45 Title-page of C. van Neck, *The iournall, or dayly register* (1601)

Veer, Gerrit de. The true and pt erfecdescription of three voyages...per-
formed...by the ships of Holland and Zeland.

Translated by William Phillip.

T. Pauier, 1609.

Collation: A², B–U⁴, X⁴

[S.T.C. 24628] B.M.

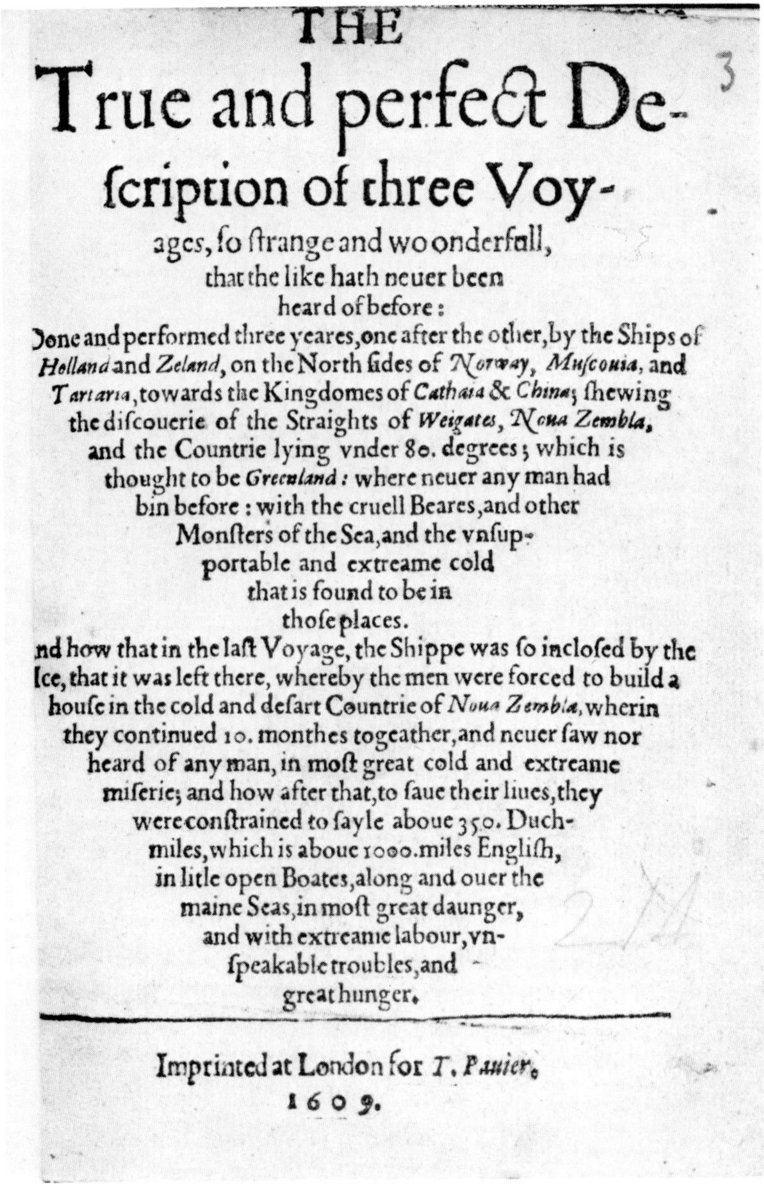

THE
True and perfect De-
scription of three Voy-
ages, so strange and woonderfull,
that the like hath neuer been
heard of before :

Done and performed three yeares, one after the other, by the Ships of
Holland and *Zeland*, on the North sides of *Norway*, *Muscouia*, and
Tartaria, towards the Kingdomes of *Cathaia* & *China*; shewing
the discouerie of the Straights of *Weigates*, *Noua Zembla*,
and the Countrie lying vnder 80. degrees ; which is
thought to be *Greenland* : where neuer any man had
bin before : with the cruell Beares, and other
Monsters of the Sea, and the vnsup-
portable and extreame cold
that is found to be in
those places.

And how that in the last Voyage, the Shippe was so inclosed by the
Ice, that it was left there, whereby the men were forced to build a
house in the cold and desart Countrie of *Noua Zembla*, wherin
they continued 10. monthes togeather, and neuer saw nor
heard of any man, in most great cold and extreame
miserie; and how after that, to saue their liues, they
were constrained to sayle aboue 350. Duch-
miles, which is aboue 1000. miles English,
in litle open Boates, along and ouer the
maine Seas, in most great daunger,
and with extreame labour, vn-
speakable troubles, and
great hunger.

Imprinted at London for *T. Pauier.*
1609.

Fig. 46   Title-page of Gerrit de Veer, *The true and perfect description of three...*
voyages...performed...by the ships of Holland and Zeland (1609)

553

Lescarbot, Marc. Noua Francia: or the description of that part of New France, which is one continent with Virginia...Translated out of French into English by P[ierre] E[rondelle].

For George Bishop, 1609.

Collation [ ]², ¶¶–¶¶¶⁴, A–Z⁴, Aa–Pp⁴, Qq². 1 map

[S.T.C. 15491] B.M.

NOVA FRANCIA:
Or the
DESCRIPTION
OF THAT PART OF
NEVV FRANCE,
which is one continent with
VIRGINIA.

Deſcribed in the three late Voyages and Plantation made by
Monſieur de Monts, Monſieur du Pont-Graué, and
Monſieur de Poutrincourt, into the countries
called by the French men *La Cadie,*
lying to the Southweſt of
Cape Breton.

Together with an excellent ſeuerall Treatie of all the commodities
of the ſaid countries, and maners of the naturall
inhabitants of the ſame.

Tranſlated out of French into Engliſh by
P. Erondelle

LONDINI,
Impenſis GEORGII BISHOP.
1609.

Fig. 47   Title-page of M. Lescarbot, *Noua Francia* (1609)

555

Lescarbot, Marc. Noua Francia or the description of that part of New France, which is one continent with Virginia...Translated out of French into English by P[ierre] E[rondelle].

For Andrew Hebb [*c.* 1625].

Another issue with a new title-page only.

[S.T.C. 15492] N.Y.P.L.

NOVA FRANCIA

Or the

DESCRIPTION
OF THAT PART OF
N E vv F R A N C E,

which is one continent with
VIRGINIA.

Defcribed in the three late Voyages and Plantation
made by *Monfieur de Monts, Monfieur du Pont-Graué*, and
Monfieur de Poutrincourt, into the countries called
by the French-men *La Cadie*, ly-
ing to the Southweft of
Cape Breton.

Together with an excellent feuerall Treatie of all the commodities
of the faid countries, and maners of the naturall
inhabitants of the fame.

Tranflated out of French into English by
P. E.

LONDON,

Printed for *Andrew Hebb*, and are to be fold at the figne
of the Bell in *Pauls* Church-yard.

[1625]

Fig. 48   Title-page of M. Lescarbot, *Noua Francia* [*c.* 1625.] N.Y.P.L.

Anghiera, Pietro Martire d'. De nouo orbe, or The historie of the west Indies...Comprised in eight decades...Whereof three haue beene formerly translated into English, by R. Eden, whereunto the other fiue, are newly added by...M Lok Gent.

For Thomas Adams, 1612.

Collation: A–Z^8, Aa–Ss^8

[S.T.C. 650] B.M.

De Nouo Orbe,
OR
THE HISTORIE OF
the weſt *Indies*, Contayning the actes
and aduentures of the Spanyardes, *which haue*
conquered and peopled thoſe Countries,
inriched with varietie of pleaſant re-
lation of the Manners, Ceremonies,
Lawes, Gouernments, and
Warres of the Indians.

Compriſed in eight Decades.

Written by *Peter Martyr a Millanoiſe of Angleria,* Cheife
Secretary to the Emperour *Charles* the fift,
and of his Priuie Councell.

Whereof three, haue beene formerly tranſlated into Engliſh, by *R. Eden,* whereunto the other
fiue, are newly added by the Induſtrie, and
painefull Trauaile of *M. Lok* Gent.

In the handes of the Lord are all the corners of
the earth. Pſal. 95.

LONDON
Printed for *Thomas Adams.*
1612.

Fig. 49   Title-page of P. Martiro d'Anghiera, *De orbe nouo* (1612)

Anghiera, Pietro Martire d'. The historie of the West-Indies...Published in Latin by M^r. Hakluyt, and translated into English by M. Lok. Gent.

For Andrew Hebb [*c.* 1625].

Another issue with a new title-page only.

[S.T.C. 651] B.M.

W. Herbert *1773.*

THE
HISTORIE OF
THE WEST-INDIES,

Containing the Actes and Aduentures
of the Spaniards, which haue conquered
and peopled thofe Countries, inriched with varietie of pleafant relation of the Manners,
Ceremonies, Lawes, Gouernments,
and Warres of the
INDIANS.

Publifhed in Latin by M^r. *Hakluyt,*
and tranflated into Englifh by M.*Lok*.Gent.

In the hands of the Lord are all the corners of
the earth. Pfal. 95.

R. Anglorum (P.M.)

LONDON,
Printed for *Andrew Hebb*, and are to be fold at the figne
of the Bell in *Pauls* Church-yard.

Fig. 50 Title-page of P. Martiro d'Anghiera, *The historie of the West-Indies*
[*c.* 1625]

Anghiera, Pietro Martire d'. The famous historie of the Indies...Set forth first by Mr Hackluyt, and now published by L.M. [*sic*] Gent.

The second edition.

For Michael Sparke, 1628.

Another issue with a new title-page only.

[S.T.C. 652] N.Y.P.L.

THE
FAMOVS
HISTORIE OF
THE INDIES:

Declaring the aduentures of
the SPANIARDS, which haue conque-
red thefe Countries, with varietie of Relations
of the Religions, Lawes, Gouernments, Manners,
Ceremonies, Cuftomes, Rites, Warres,
and Funerals of that People.

Comprifed into fundry Decads.

Set forth firft by Mr *Hackluyt*, and now publifhed by *L. M.* Gent.

The fecond Edition.

LONDON:
Printed for *Michael Sparke* dwelling at the figne
of the blue Bible in Green-Arbor. 1628.

Fig. 51   Title-page of P. M. d'Anghiera, *The famous historie of the Indies* (1628)
N.Y.P.L.

Samuel Purchas. Purchas his pilgrimage. Or relations of the world and the religions obserued in all ages and places discouered, from the creation vnto this present...The second edition, much enlarged.

London, William Stanley for Henrie Fetherstone, 1614.

Collation: ¶⁶, A⁸, B–Z⁶, Aa–Zz⁶, Aaa–Zzz⁶, Aaaa–Kkkk⁶

[S.T.C. 20506] B.M.

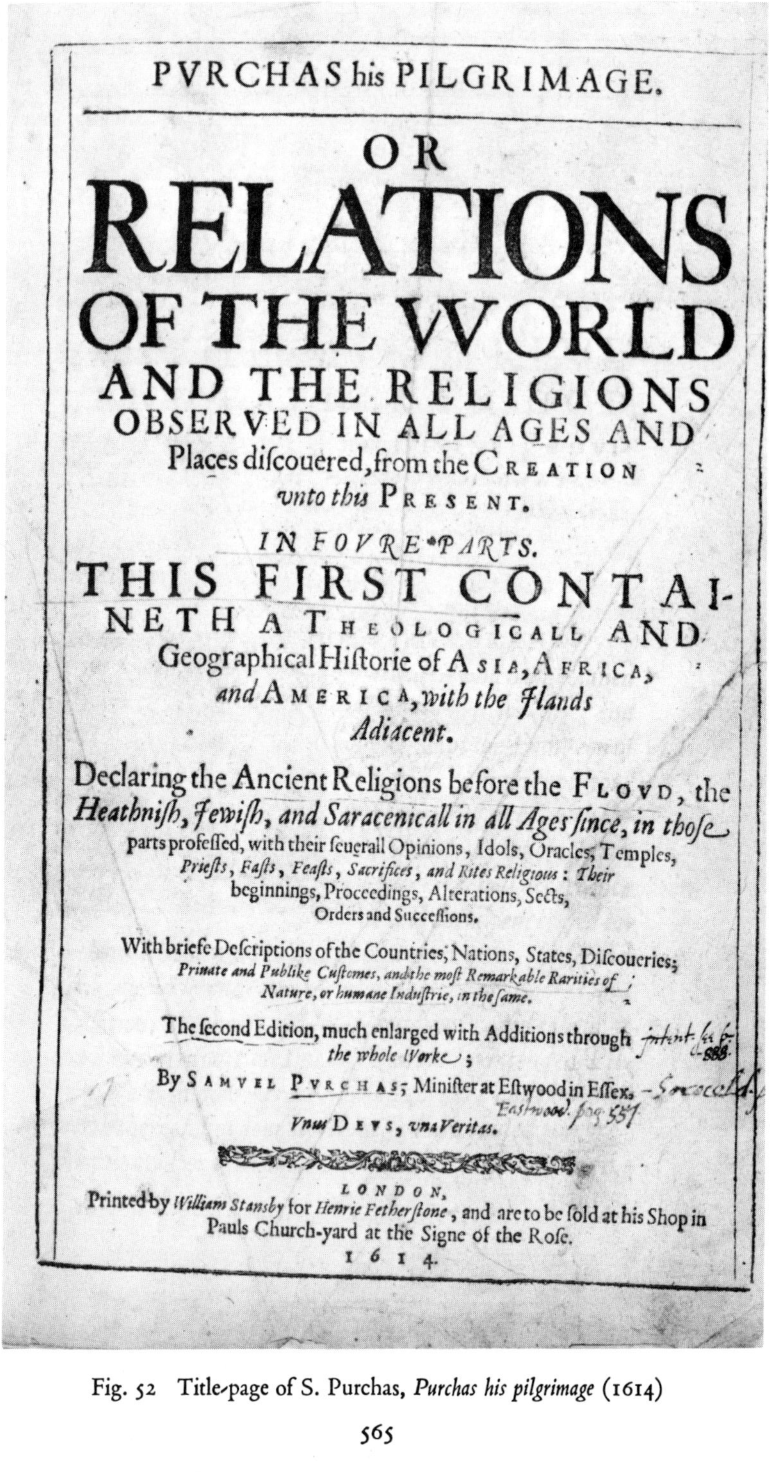

PVRCHAS his PILGRIMAGE.

OR
RELATIONS
OF THE WORLD
AND THE RELIGIONS
OBSERVED IN ALL AGES AND
Places difcouered, from the CREATION
vnto this PRESENT.

IN FOVRE PARTS.

THIS FIRST CONTAI-
NETH A THEOLOGICALL AND
Geographical Hiftorie of ASIA, AFRICA,
and AMERICA, *with the Ilands*
Adiacent.

Declaring the Ancient Religions before the FLOVD, the
Heathnifh, Jewifh, and *Saracenicall in all Ages fince,* in thofe
parts profeffed, with their feuerall Opinions, Idols, Oracles, Temples,
Priefts, Fafts, Feafts, Sacrifices, and *Rites Religious :* Their
beginnings, Proceedings, Alterations, Sects,
Orders and Succeffions.

With briefe Defcriptions of the Countries, Nations, States, Difcoucries;
Priuate and Publike Cuftomes, and the moft Remarkable Rarities of
Nature, or humane Induftrie, in the fame.

The fecond Edition, much enlarged with Additions through
the whole Worke ;

By SAMVEL PVRCHAS; Minifter at Eftwood in Effex.

Vnus DEVS, *vna Veritas.*

LONDON,
Printed by *William Stansby* for *Henrie Fetherftone*, and are to be fold at his Shop in
Pauls Church-yard at the Signe of the Rofe.
1 6 1 4.

Fig. 52 Title-page of S. Purchas, *Purchas his pilgrimage* (1614)

565

Pitiscus, Bartholomew. Trigonometry: or The doctrine of triangles. First written in Latine, by Bartholomew Pitiscus...and now translated into English, by Ra[lph] Handson [or Hanson].

For Iohn Tappe (1614).

Collation: A⁴, *², B⁴, C–M⁸, N⁴, O⁸, P–Q⁴, R², *A–L*⁴, *M*²

[S.T.C. 19967] B.M.

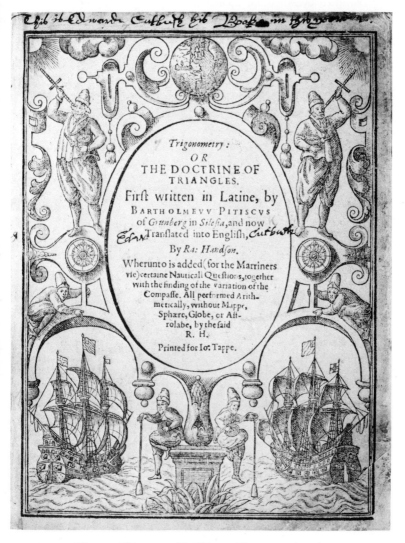

Fig. 53   Title-page of B. Pitiscus, *Trigonometry* (1614)

Arthus, Gothard. Dialogues in the English and Malaiane languages.

Translated by Augustine Spalding.

Felix Kyngston for William Welby, 1614.

Collation: ¶², A², B–K⁴, L²

[S.T.C. 810] B.M.

[The word-list had been taken by Arthus from Frederick de Houtman, *Spraeck ende woord-boeck, in de Maleysche ende Madagaskarsche talen* (Amsterdam, 1603).]

DIALOGVES
IN THE ENGLISH
AND MALAIANE
LANGVAGES:

OR,

CERTAINE COMMON FORMES
OF SPEECH, FIRST WRITTEN IN
Latin, Malaian, and Madagaſcar tongues, by the diligence
and painfull endeuour of Maſter GOTARDVS ARTHVSIVS,
*a Dantisker, and now faithfully tranſlated into the Engliſh
tongue by* AVGVSTINE SPALDING *Merchant,
for their ſakes, who happily ſhall hereafter
vndertake a voyage to the
Eaſt-Indies.*

AT LONDON,
Imprinted by FELIX KYNGSTON for WILLIAM
WELBY, and are to bee ſold at his ſhop in Pauls
Church-yard, at the ſigne of the Swan.
1614.

Fig. 54   Title-page of G. Arthus, *Dialogues* (1614)

569

III

Works, the publication of which Hakluyt may have influenced

Where no specific acknowledgement or reference is contained in a pamphlet or book to the influence of a person other than the author it is obviously risky to assert, without direct evidence, that such a person was involved in the publication. Yet in the case of Hakluyt so much of his activity was concentrated in the circulation of knowledge on particular aspects of extra-European activity and so concerned with publicity for specific aspects of English endeavour in certain of these fields that we are more likely to underestimate than overestimate his influence on the publications which took place inside those fields, at least during the period down to about 1600, after which he appears to have slackened off his propaganda efforts and devoted himself primarily to the collection of materials for the never completed third edition of his *Principal navigations*. It would be true to say that we know next to nothing at present about his relations with the book-sellers of London at this period. How far did he encourage certain of them to publish within fields in which he himself was interested, to what extent did he recommend books to them to be translated, did he indeed find patrons who would bless publications and so make them possible without himself appearing as a sponsor? These are questions which are still open to investigation, but only a few hints can be obtained from the preliminary matter to the books listed in the previous section. We can, however, see certain phases of interest in Hakluyt's own activities which can point perhaps to his responsibility, or possible responsibility, for certain types of publicity at certain times.

The first series of American enterprises with which Hakluyt was associated was that linked with Sir Humphrey Gilbert, Sir George Peckham and Christopher Carleill, 1580–4. His own contributions and the publications he is known to have influenced, as already noticed, make it likely that he had also some degree of responsibility for others. Since, for example, he spon-sored Stephen Parmenius at Oxford and introduced him to Gilbert in 1582 we might strongly suspect that Hakluyt opened the way to him for the publication of his *De nauigatione Humfredi...carmen* in June 1582, though whether he had anything to do with Parmenius' subsequent eulogy of England and of its Queen in his *Paean* on the 112th Psalm later in the same year is less easy to say. Again, since he was closely involved in the discussions in which his narrative was elicited, it is highly likely that he was concerned in the publication of David Ingram's *A true discourse of the aduentures & trauailes of David Ingram* (1583), known to us only as an entry in Humphrey Dyson's notebooks, but which Hakluyt was to reprint in 1589. Similarly, his connection with Christopher Carleill was so close that he may well have had a hand in the appearance of one or both of the editions of Carleill's *A discourse vpon the intended voyage to the hithermoste partes of America* (1583) (its other edition was entitled *A breef and sommarie discourse vpon the entended voyage to the hethermoste parts of America*). In the same, or a very similar, category was Sir George Peckham's *A true reporte, of the late discoueries*, which appeared late in 1583, with its first use of the evidence of Edward Hayes, which Hakluyt was later to exploit to such good effect. In the case of all these publications we can say that Hakluyt's concern was at least highly probable. In regard to his possible connection with the translation, by one M.S., of Bartolomé de las Casas, *The Spanish colonie* (1583), there is no such link, except that Hakluyt was to exploit the text vigorously in his 'A particuler discourse' in 1584, and could, con-ceivably, have been concerned with its first appearance in English the previ-ous year.

In the period from 1584 to 1590 Hakluyt's association with Sir Walter Ralegh and Thomas Harriot in providing both background information and promotion publicity for the Virginia voyages was very close, but as his centre was Paris rather than London, his own publications largely eman-ated from there and it is difficult to estimate whether he was responsible to the same extent for material, other than his own, which appeared in England before his permanent return in 1588. There are some indications that Ralegh took a hand in publicity himself and that he left to Harriot a substantial part of the collection and dissemination of information, at times which seemed appropriate, in England. At the same time Hakluyt was frequently in England for extended periods in the years 1584-8 and the likelihood of a close association between him and Harriot and of both with Ralegh in the planning of publications is substantial. It is also likely that Hakluyt was responsible for some at least of the material which John Hooker inserted into his contributions to Holinshed's *Chronicles* in 1587. Whether he had anything to do with the publication, which Giacomo de Castelvetro polished, of Guilio Casare Stella, *Columbeidas* (1585), with its dedication to Ralegh, is less easy to indicate. Again, though he had brought the narra-tive of the Espejo expedition to light by his publications in Paris, he cannot be specifically associated with, though he may have influenced, the transla-tion by A. F. of *New Mexico. Otherwise the voyage of Anthony of Espeio* (1587). More probably, he was involved in the discussions with Harriot and

Ralegh which preceded the publication of Thomas Harriot's *A brief and true report of the new found land of Virginia* (1588), which had apparently been held over from 1587 on account of changing circumstances in the sequence of Roanoke voyages. His major contribution here was clearly the introduction of Theodor de Bry to the drawings of John White and Jacques le Moyne. The stimulation of Le Moyne to prepare a text on French Florida and the junction of Harriot's pamphlet with a selection of the White drawings on the Roanoke voyages were also in some degree Hakluyt's work and were to result in the striking continental publicity which the English and French ventures to North America were to receive in 1590 and 1591. But these, like Hakluyt's own contributions in his *Principall navigations* (1589), belong to other categories.

More casually, his influence may be discerned in Thomas Nichols' *A pleasant description of the Fortunate Islands called the islands of Canaria* (1583). His connections with the somewhat turbulent clergyman, Hugh Broughton, who contributed verses to the preliminaries of both editions of *The principall navigations*, may have exercised some influence on Broughton's *A concent of scripture* [1589 or 1590] – or at least on its maps, and conceivably on other works, even though these were not in favour with the English ecclesiastical establishment to which Hakluyt was usually and profitably subservient.

Hakluyt's responsibility for systematic publicity for other groups of voyages is rather less capable of being substantiated. Certainly he regarded the translation by Thomas Hickock of Cesare Federici, *The voyage and trauaile of M. Caesar Frederick...into the East India* (1588), as of seminal importance for the diffusion of English knowledge of this area, but his association with its appearance is not confirmed. He was also a pioneer in the 1590s in keeping an English public closely informed of Dutch activities in the East Indies which he wished England would emulate or surpass. Here his influence is directly evident in his efforts to get Linschoten into print, but it is also very likely that he had a hand in the appearance, also in translations by William Phillip, of Cornelius Houtman, *The description of a voyage made by certaine ships of Holland vnto the East Indies* (1598) and its sequel, Cornelius Geraldson, *An addition to the sea iournal or nauigation of the Hollanders vnto Iaua* (1598). Whether subsequent pamphlets were the result of his efforts, or affected by him, or whether they reflected the creation of an independent market for pamphlets on the Dutch efforts is less clear, but it is possible that *A true report of the gainefull, prosperous and speedy voiage to Iaua in the East Indies* (1599), Jacob Corneliszoon van Neck, *The iournall, or dayly register...of the voyage...which sayled from Amsterdam the first day of March,*

1598 (1601) and *A true and perfect relation of the newes sent from Amsterdam the 21. of February, 1603* (1603), in some degree reflected in their publication his influence as well as his example.

Hakluyt's association with the London merchants who planned the competitive East India voyages and obtained the first East India Company charter was, during the years 1598–1603, very close indeed, and there are traces of his propaganda activity on their behalf in the second edition of *The principal navigations* which began to appear in 1598, while his aid in their preparations 1599–1601 is well attested from surviving minutes. It is therefore highly plausible to consider that he was consulted about the appearance of *A letter written to the right worshipfull the gouernors and assistants... in London* (1603) and *A true and large discourse of the voyage of the whole fleete of ships set forth the 20. of Aprill 1601* (1603), though there is no direct evidence in either instance. It is more likely that, by the time *The last East-Indian voyage* (1606) appeared, his influence was less apparent, though he continued to be consulted by the company until 1614.

Hakluyt was, of course, very actively concerned with the revival of North American voyaging after 1600, yet specific connections between him and the publications which preceded and followed the launching of the Virginia Company in 1606 are less easy to pin down than might be imagined. In regard to John Brereton's *A briefe and true relation of the discouerie of the north part of Virginia* (1602), though both editions were padded out with data drawn from his collections and, in a few cases, material from his unpub-lished store of materials, his own hand in the compilation of the book cannot be confirmed and it is more probable that he provided material for Brereton and for his old associate Edward Hayes to use in the book than that he had a direct hand in its shaping himself, though he may very well have advised Ralegh, who was closely concerned, on its publication. It seems rather more likely that he had something directly to do with the appearance of James Rosier, *A true relation of the most prosperous voyage made in this present yeere 1605, by Captaine George Waymouth* (1605), since he eventually handed on to Samuel Purchas a manuscript of the narrative containing a few references, deleted in the published version, which would have recalled to readers the sponsorship of the voyage by a Catholic group and which might have raised suspicions, so soon after the November plot, of the character of further American enterprises which it was intended to foster. The editing of the published version by Hakluyt seems a likely possibility, though it is not directly documented in any way. Hakluyt himself was associated with the Virginia Company by the appearance of his name in the charters of 1606 and 1609, but we have, in the absence of the earlier records of the company, no evidence of the precise part he played in the launching of their early enterprises. What is perhaps a little strange is that his hand cannot so far be traced in any of the publications made under the Company's auspices or for its purposes except in his own *Virginia truly valued* (1609) and the Lok translation of Peter Martyr (1612), though this may well be the result of our ignorance rather than of his inactivity. Certainly he was known to John Smith, who exploited his writings, and to William Strachey. His loan to Purchas of North American materials, first for the briefer references in *Pilgrimage* of 1614, then at great length by later acquisition to enable them to figure largely in the *Pilgrimage* (1625), indicated the continu, ance of his interest in and involvement with the Virginia enterprise.

It might be possible too to speculate on his connections with the appear, ance of certain works in the longish string of books and pamphlets on ocean navigation from the early 1580s onwards in which he had such a deep concern and where he knew many of the authors. But such scientific publications had their own momentum, one tract calling out another and so on, which would render, at this stage at least, an analysis of such publica, tions in an attempt to see his possible influence on certain of them too marginal to be worth the pursuit. So far as voyage literature is concerned the case is rather different. By his collections and his known record of influence on others he is established firmly as a figure to whom reference is likely appreciably and continuously to have been made. Consequently, however much the sequence of travel literature may have been self-generating, we are more likely to underestimate than overestimate his influence on what appeared: it may also be true of course that he had some influence in the non-appearance of works which he judged might be inopportune or preju, dicial to overseas activities in which he had a substantial interest. Over the whole field of travel literature we can however reckon that his knowledge, his collections and his associations with merchants and patrons were widely availed of in the publishing trade. Though there is a decline after about 1606 in his known activities, we know enough about those he engaged in after this date to say clearly that his interests were maintained and that his influence endured until his death.

28

Secondary works on Hakluyt and his circle

L. E. PENNINGTON

Biography

In 1905, Professor Walter Raleigh described Richard Hakluyt as 'the silent man, seated in the dark corner, who is content to listen and remember'.[1] Recent scholars would certainly argue that Raleigh assigned Hakluyt too passive a role, but there is nonetheless a certain truth in his statement. For more than two centuries, Richard Hakluyt has in one respect eluded scholars. Though his works have been examined, particularly in recent years, in increasingly close (though still not definitive) detail, no one has succeeded in capturing Hakluyt the man. We know next to nothing of his personal life or of what must have been his extensive clerical activities; no one has been able to delineate his character;[2] we do not even know what he looked like. The problem is that we lack both direct and indirect evidence. His own papers have disappeared, and what little he tells us of himself in his writing is to further whatever theme he is pursuing at the moment. The possible indirect sources provide few keys. Though we can reconstruct his large circle of acquaintances among scholars, politicians, promoters, and mariners, most of the papers of these individuals and the groups with which they were connected have not survived.[3] It is surprising, even, how

[1] Walter Raleigh, 'The English voyages of the sixteenth century', in *The principal navigations* (12 vols., Hakluyt Society, Glasgow, 1903–5), XII, 75. The essay was later reprinted separately (Glasgow, 1910). All citations are from the 1903–5 edition. Raleigh argued that no biography of Hakluyt in the usual sense was possible (p. 74). George Bruner Parks, his only full-scale biographer, agreed (*Richard Hakluyt and the English voyages* (New York, 1928; 2nd ed., New York, 1961), pp. 231–2).

[2] Almost the only attempt to do so, and a weak one at that, was by E. G. R. Taylor in her introduction to *The original writings and correspondence of the two Richard Hakluyts* (2 vols., Hakluyt Society, 1935), I, 65–6.

[3] D. B. Quinn has pointed out that there are no significant collections of papers of those with whom Hakluyt was connected in the Virginia ventures of the 1580s (D. B. Quinn, ed., *The Roanoke voyages, 1584–1590* (2 vols., Hakluyt

seldom contemporaries mentioned him. Sir Philip Sidney's remark that he had proved a good trumpet for the Virginia venture, and Samuel Purchas's claim that his works had saved the East India Company £20,000, are so frequently quoted not because they are typical, but because they are so rare. When Michael Drayton referred to him as 'industrious Hakluyt', he summed up the opinion of an age, an age which knew him, as we know him, almost exclusively through his works.

Within half a century of his death, even the facts of Hakluyt's life were in disarray. Thomas Fuller claimed that he had died 'in the beginning of King James's reign',[1] and Anthony à Wood confused him with his elder cousin.[2] His works fared little better, as interest in them declined from the seventeenth to the early years of the nineteenth century.[3] William Oldys was almost alone in providing an effective outline of his life and achievements as well as an assessment of his works, and his article on Hakluyt in *Biographia Britannica* in 1757 remained the basic biographical study for nearly a century.[4] No real renewal of Hakluyt's reputation occurred until after 1800, when the

Society, 1955), I, 10–11). The same situation appears to exist in regard to a number of Hakluyt's later connections. We do not have, for example, any papers of Sir Thomas Smith, or of the Virginia Company of London in its early years.

[1] Thomas Fuller, *The worthies of England* (1662; reprinted, 1952, ed. John Freeman), p. 224.

[2] Anthony à Wood, *Athenae Oxonienses*, II (1691; reprinted, 1815, ed. Philip Bliss), 186–7. (A more recent summary of Hakluyt's career in Oxford is in Joseph Foster, *Alumni Oxoniensis* (4 vols., Oxford, 1891–2), II, 627.)

[3] J. A. Williamson has argued that a principal reason for the decline was that most travel literature of this period was concerned with Pacific discovery, on which Hakluyt had had little to say. He has also suggested that the Hakluyt method of orderly presentation of facts was not sufficiently flamboyant or romantic to suit the tastes of the day ('Richard Hakluyt' in *Richard Hakluyt and his successors*, ed. Edward Lynam (Hakluyt Society, 1946), pp. 43–5). The best summary of voyage collections during this period, particularly in their relation to Hakluyt, is G. R. Crone and R. A. Skelton, 'English collections of voyages and travels', in *Richard Hakluyt*, ed. Lynam, pp. 63–140. A crosssection view of seventeenth- and eighteenth-century comments on Hakluyt may be obtained from C. W. Moulton, ed., *Library of literary criticism of English and American authors*, I (New York, 1910), 445–6.

[4] *Biographia Britannica*, IV (1757), 2561–74. Oldys had earlier published his *Life of Sir Walter Raleigh* (1733), which had drawn extensively on Hakluyt. See also his comments on the *Principal navigations* in *The British Librarian*, no. 3 (1737), 137n. The remainder of the last article, pp. 136–58, is a description of the contents of that work.

appearance of R. H. Evans' edition of the *Principal navigations* (1809–12) opened a new period of study and assessment. At last, as J. A. Williamson remarked,[1] the popular taste for romantic travel literature had apparently run its course, and scholars were ready to turn to the study of discovery and exploration for its own sake. Even so, no biographical work developed which threw significant fresh light on Hakluyt's career before the introduction by John Winter Jones to his *Divers voyages* in 1850 at last superseded Oldys.

Throughout the nineteenth century, the secondary bibliography of Hakluyt took on both bulk and significance partly as the result of a series of controversies on specific problems affecting four groups of voyages which figured prominently in his works. The origin of the most important of these disputes went back to 1753. In the course of diplomatic negotiations with France, England had argued a claim to North America based on the Cabot voyages as they were set out in Hakluyt. The French replied in 1755–7 with a series of volumes denying the British claim and impugning the consistency and accuracy of Hakluyt's accounts.[2] Some seventy-five years later Richard Biddle, a Pittsburgh, Pennsylvania, lawyer, set out to vindicate the Cabot claim and, presumably, Hakluyt. But very soon Hakluyt became his chief villain. Briefly, his charge was that Hakluyt had systematically altered dates and accounts in his works, and had suppressed evidence so as to give to John Cabot the credit for a discovery that rightfully belonged to Sebastian.[3]

The defence of Hakluyt (and John Cabot) surfaced almost immediately,[4] and moved to a climax as the 400th anniversary of the Cabot discoveries

---

[1] In *Richard Hakluyt,* ed. Lynam, p. 45.

[2] *Mémoires des commissaires…sur les possessions & les droits respectifs des deux couronnes en Amerique* (4 vols., Paris, 1755–7). See especially vol. IV.

[3] *A memoir of Sebastian Cabot* (Philadelphia, 1831). The Biddle thesis did achieve a certain currency, and reached the peak of polemic in James F. Nicholls, *The remarkable life, adventures, and discoveries of Sebastian Cabot, of Bristol, the founder of Great Britain's maritime power, discoverer of America, and its first colonizer* (1869). Nicholls was a Bristol librarian.

[4] Patrick Fraser Tytler, *Historical view of the progress of discovery on the more northern coasts of America…to which is added an appendix, containing notes on a late memoir of Sebastian Cabot, with a vindication of Richard Hakluyt* (Edinburgh and London, 1832, reprinted, New York, 1836), pp. 333–60. The attitude of much of the profession was summed up by John Winter Jones who in 1850 called Biddle's attack the 'solitary exception to the feeling of admiration for the labours of an honest, upright man' (Jones, ed., *Divers voyages touching the discovery of America and the islands adjacent* (Hakluyt Society, 1850), introduction, p. ii).

approached.[1] When the smoke had finally cleared Hakluyt stood accused at most of some carelessness, and silent but correct alteration of his sources.[2]

[1] For the John Cabot–Hakluyt side of the controversy, see especially the following: Charles Deane, 'Remarks of Mr. Charles Deane', *American Antiquarian Society Proceedings,* no. 48 (1867), 47–50, note; J. G. Kohl, *A history of the discovery of the east coast of North America (Documentary History of the State of Maine,* I (1869)), 130–1, 206–7, 224; George Dexter, 'The testimony of Fabyan's Chronicle to Hakluyt's account of the Cabots', *American Antiquarian Society Proceedings,* new series, I (1881), 436–41; Samuel Edward Dawson, 'The voyages of the Cabots in 1497 and 1498', *Transactions of the Royal Society of Canada,* XII, sec. 2 (1894), 51–112, especially 54, 66–7, 89–92, 96–7, 101–2, 104–7; R. H. Major, 'The true date of the English discovery of the American continent under John and Sebastian Cabot', *Archaeologia,* XLIII (1871), 17–42, especially 41–2; Henry Harrisse, *John Cabot, the discoverer of North America, and Sebastian his son* (1896), pp. 23–5, 440–8; Harrisse, *The discovery of North America* (2 vols., London and Paris, 1892), I, 1–45; Harrisse, *Jean et Sébastian Cabot: leur origene et leurs voyages* (Paris, 1882; reprinted Chicago, 1968), pp. 24–35, 106–8, 151–6; Henry Stevens, *Sebastian Cabot – John Cabot = o* (Boston, 1870); C. R. Beazley, *John and Sebastian Cabot* (1898; reprinted, New York, 1964), especially pp. 168–9, 176–7, 206, 252–3; G. E. Weare, *Cabot's discovery of North America* (London and Philadelphia, 1897), pp. 244–77; Fridtjof Nansen, *In Northern Mists,* II (London and New York, 1911), ch. 14, especially pp. 319–33. Almost all of these authors agreed, in spite of their reservations, that Biddle had made a significant contribution to the study of the Cabots. The most prominent recent scholar of the Cabots, J. A. Williamson, has, it would appear, given the last word on the Hakluyt muddle. See his *The voyages of the Cabots and the English discovery of Northern America under Henry VII and Henry VIII* (1929), pp. 37–8, 150–2, 239; and his more recent *The Cabot voyages and the Bristol discovery under Henry VII* (Hakluyt Society, 1962), pp. 95–8, 124–31, and doc. 31, pp. 220–3. Williamson's works reflects the decreasing interest of Cabot researchers in the Hakluyt controversy.

[2] The best sketch of the nineteenth-century Cabot controversy is George Parker Winship, 'Some facts about John and Sebastian Cabot', *American Antiquarian Society Proceedings,* XIII (1900), pp. 409–28, and I follow him here. Except for the sources indicated in the three notes immediately above, the bibliography of the dispute is far too extensive (and in many cases too peripheral) to be reproduced here. It may best be followed in Charles Deane's 'Critical essay on the sources of information' attached to his article 'The voyages of the Cabots' in *Narrative and critical history of America,* ed. Justin Winsor (8 vols., Boston, 1884–9, reprinted, New York, 1967), III, 7–58, and in George Parker Winship, *Cabot bibliography, with an introductory essay on the careers of the Cabots* (New York and London, 1900).

Three other notable disputes took their cues at least partially from Hakluyt materials. These concerned the supposed voyages of Madoc, the Zeni, and Verrazzano. In 1794 Jeremy Belknap charged that Hakluyt had seized upon the Madoc legend in a misguided attempt to overthrow the fame of Columbus and the eminence of Spain.[1] The quarrel continued[2] until Thomas Stephens devastated the legend in 1893 with the publication of a book written many years before.[3]

Belknap had also raised some questions regarding Hakluyt's Zeni accounts.[4] John Winter Jones, in editing *Divers voyages* for the Hakluyt Society in 1850, declined to annotate the Zeni materials on the grounds that 'the object of the Hakluyt Society is to extend the knowledge of the bold and energetic and successful efforts of early discoverers, not to bring prominently forward clumsy compilations and absurd fictions'.[5] In 1898 Fred W. Lucas argued that the whole Zeni affair was one of the most ingenious and

---

[1] *American biography*, I (Boston, 1794), 58–66.

[2] See especially Benjamin F. Bowen, *America discovered by the Welsh in 1170 A.D.* (Philadelphia, 1876) and Rasmus B. Anderson, *America not discovered by Columbus* (Chicago, 1891), which lists some 71 items discussing the subject, pp. 142–9. See also the extended bibliographical discussion in Winsor, *Narrative and critical history*, I, 109–11.

[3] *Madoc: an essay on the discovery of America by Madoc* (London and New York, 1893). He had attacked the Madoc myth as early as 1849 (*Literature of the Kymry* (1849)). The controversy has by no means ended. The fullest recent defence of the Madoc claim, which uses Hakluyt as important evidence, is Richard Deacon's *Madoc and the discovery of America: some new light on an old controversy* (New York, 1966). David Williams has been the principal critic of the legend in recent years, though in a rather indirect way. See his 'John Evans' strange journey', *American Historical Review*, LIV (1949), 277–95, 508–29; and *John Evans and the legend of Madoc, 1770–1779* (Cardiff, 1963). For the present state of scholarship on the matter, see Robert R. Rea, 'Madogwys forever: the present state of the Madoc controversy', *Alabama Historical Quarterly*, XXX (1968), 6–17; D. B. Quinn, in *Dictionary of Canadian Biography*, I (Toronto, 1965), 677–8.   [4] *American biography*, I, 67–85.

[5] *Divers voyages*, p. 90, note. Another Society editor, R. H. Major, took the opposite view in 1873 when he edited *The voyages of the Venetian brothers Nicolò and Antonio Zeno* (Hakluyt Society, 1873), and upheld the validity of the voyages. Major aimed his evidence primarily at the Danish hydrographer, Capt. C. C. Zahrtmann, whose 'Remarks on the voyages to the northern hemisphere, ascribed to the Zeni of Venice', *Journal of the Royal Geographical Society*, V (1835), 102–28, had found the Zeni accounts fraudulent. Interestingly enough, Zahrtmann used 'The libelle of Englyshe polycye', which Hakluyt published, as evidence against their authenticity (pp. 121–2).

successful literary frauds ever to gull the public.[1] Lucas' book appeared to settle the matter, but since then the question has risen again,[2] and in 1964, one of the foremost Hakluyt scholars, E. G. R. Taylor, defended, if not very convincingly, the authenticity of the voyages.[3]

The question of the Verrazzano voyages involved Hakluyt somewhat less. It was first raised by Buckingham Smith in 1864.[4] The chief defence came from J. C. Brevoort, whose *Verrazano the navigator* was published in 1874.[5] Henry Murphy's *The voyage of Verrazzano*[6] and his later *Inquiry into the authenticity of Verrazzano's claims*[7] were the last serious attempts to deny the validity of the voyages. Murphy's argument fell, for the most part, on deaf ears, and the voyages have seldom been questioned since that time.[8]

While the disputes over the Cabots, Madoc, the Zeni, and Verrazzano had excited considerable indirect interest in Hakluyt, and had led to some re-evaluation of his skills as an editor, all of this was peripheral to the main factor in the expansion of the secondary literature on Hakluyt which was the founding in 1846 of the Hakluyt Society for the purpose of editing and publishing accounts of discoveries and explorations, including those in

---

[1] *The annals of the voyages of the Venetian brothers Nicolo and Antonio Zeno* (1898). Lucas argued that Hakluyt was skeptical of the voyages (pp. 31–3).

[2] See particularly William H. Hobbs, 'Zeno and the cartography of Greenland', *Imago Mundi*, VI (1949), 15–19; Hobbs, 'The fourteenth-century discovery of America by Antonio Zeno', *Scientific Monthly* LXXII (1951), 24–31; Frederick J. Pohl, *The Sinclair expedition to Nova Scotia in 1398* (Pictou, Nova Scotia, 1950); and Pohl, *The Viking explorers* (New York, 1966), appendix, pp. 218–30. For the view that the voyages were fictitious, see W. H. Babcock, *Legendary islands of the Atlantic* (New York, 1922), pp. 124–43; and Tryggvi J. Oleson, *Early voyages and northern approaches* (Toronto, 1963), pp. 108–10.

[3] 'A fourteenth-century riddle – and its solution', *Geographical Review*, LIV (1964), 573–6.

[4] *An inquiry into the authenticity of documents concerning a discovery in North America claimed to have been made by Verrazzano* (New York, 1864). Smith had read the paper before a meeting of the New York Historical Society in October 1864, but he died before he could revise and expand it for publication.

[5] (New York, 1874).

[6] (New York, 1875). Murphy's work was intended as an answer to Brevoort.

[7] (New York, 1903).

[8] See Harrisse, *Discovery of North America*, I, 214–28; II, 541–3, 553–5. For other nineteenth-century literature on the subject, see B. F. De Costa, 'Bibliography of Verrazano', *Magazine of American History*, VI (1881), 68–70, reprinted *Acta Cartographica*, VI (1969), 111–13; and George Dexter; 'Critical essay on the sources of information' attached to his article 'Cortereal, Verrazano, Gomez, Thevet', in *Narrative and critical history*, ed. Winsor, IV, 17–28.

Hakluyt. In spite of this apparent worthy purpose, its efforts met with at least one severe critic. This was James Anthony Froude. He charged that the first volumes of the Society had done more to paralyse than to excite interest in Hakluyt, who had produced, in his now famous phrase, 'the Prose Epic of the English nation'.[1]

The Society's editors, and particularly R. H. Major, took umbrage at what seemed to be a charge of incompetence, and the dispute rattled on for some eighteen years until Major made a public answer for the Society.[2] Actually, Major may have missed one of Froude's main points. That he had charged the editors with incompetence was true enough. But it might be claimed that the main burden of his complaint lay elsewhere. Froude believed that the *Principal navigations* was an epic for the English people, and that the purpose of the Society ought to be to appeal to popular taste rather than mere scholarly interest. In short, Froude appeared to object not only to incompetent editing, but to scholarly editing.

If this was Froude's view, it fortunately did not prevail. The Society's efforts over the next 125 years produced more than fifty volumes bearing directly or indirectly on Hakluyt or his accounts and writings.[3] Quality was sometimes uneven, and many of the introductions, particularly in earlier years, were more summaries than critical analyses or evaluations. As G. R. Crone has pointed out, the early editors tended to be amateurs, the amateurs gave way to antiquarians, and the antiquarians have in turn given way to those who edit in terms of the broader geographical and economic situation in which the works first appeared.[4]

Whether through the activities of the Society or the trend of the times, interest in and analysis of Hakluyt and his works continued to increase, and

[1] 'England's forgotten worthies', first published in *Westminster Review* (1852) and reprinted in *Short studies on great subjects* (1867). The citation is from the London, 1891 edition, I, 443–501.

[2] Following the republication of the essay in *Short studies* in 1867. For Major's answer, see his edition of *Select letters of Christopher Columbus* (Hakluyt Society, 1870), preface, pp. i–iv. A good account of the dispute, and of the history of the Society is William Foster, 'The Hakluyt Society: A retrospect, 1846–1946', *Richard Hakluyt,* ed. Lynam, pp. 141–70. See also C. R. Markham, 'The jubilee of the Hakluyt Society', *Geographical Journal*, IX (1897), 169–78.

[3] As these volumes will be taken up in other sections of this essay, it seems unnecessary to list them here.

[4] The best summary of the editorial work of the Society is Crone's '"Jewells of Antiquitie": the work of the Hakluyt Society', *Geographical Journal,* CXXVIII (1962), 321–4. See also Edward Lynam, 'The present and the future', *Richard Hakluyt,* ed. Lynam, pp. 183–4.

over the next one hundred years there appeared a number of articles attempt-
ing biographical and historical assessments. Among the best were those by
E. Hallam Moorhouse, Albert Gray, J. A. Williamson, Louis B. Wright,
Edward Lynam, E. G. R. Taylor, and Keith Feiling.[1]

Also influential were the publications of numerous editions of lesser and
greater parts of Hakluyt's writings. They ranged from Edmund Goldsmid's
sixteen volume edition[2] to selections from Hakluyt for juveniles.[3] A number

[1] E. Hallam Moorhouse, 'The tercentenary of Richard Hakluyt', *Cornhill
Magazine*, XLI (1916), 560–8; Albert Gray, *An address on the occasion of the
tercentenary of the death of Richard Hakluyt...with a note on the Hakluyt family*
(Hakluyt Society, 1917); Williamson, 'Richard Hakluyt', in *Richard Hakluyt*,
ed. Lynam, pp. 9–46; Louis B. Wright, *Religion and Empire* (Chapel Hill,
N.C., 1943), ch. 2; Edward Lynam, 'Hakluyt and the Elizabethan seaman',
Geographical Magazine, XIX (1947), 361–8; E. G. R. Taylor, 'Richard Hakluyt',
Geographical Journal, CIX (1947), 165–71; Taylor, 'Richard Hakluyt and
England's sea story', *Geographical Magazine*, XXXV (1963), 694–703; Keith
Feiling, 'Richard Hakluyt', *In Christ Church Hall* (1960), pp. 1–9. The last
two are especially graceful popularizations. See also C. R. Markham 'Address
by Sir Clements Markham on the fiftieth anniversary of the foundations of the
Society' (1896) (also *Revised on the occasion of the sixty-fifth anniversary* (Hakluyt
Society, 1911), *Geographical Journal*, IX, 169–73; J. H. Reynolds, 'The ter-
centenary of Richard Hakluyt', *Geographical Journal*, XLVIII (1916), 449–56;
C. H. Coote and C. R. Beazley, 'Hakluyt, Richard', *Encyclopaedia Britannica*,
XII (eleventh edition, Cambridge and New York, 1910), 828–9; W. P. M.
Kennedy, 'Richard Hakluyt: The spirit of our race', *Canadian Magazine*, XLVI
(1916), 491–5; J. K. Laughton, 'Hakluyt', *Dictionary of national biography*,
VIII (1921), 895–6; Samuel Eliot Morison, 'Promoters and precursors: Richard
Hakluyt, Captain John Smith, and Morton of Merrymount', *Builders of the
Bay Colony* (New York, 1930), pp. 3–6; Charles F. Mullett, 'The Hakluyt
Society: its first hundred years', *Scientific Monthly*, LXIII (1946), 423–7; H. R.
Trevor-Roper, 'The Homer of Herefordshire', *New Statesman*, LVI (1958),
419–20; G. R. Crone, 'Hakluyt, Richard', *Encyclopaedia Britannica*, X (Chicago
and London, 1970), 1126–7. See also J. A. Williamson, *The ocean in English
history* (Oxford, 1941), pp. 76–81; Walter Oakeshott, *Founded upon the seas*
(Cambridge, 1942), pp. 27–31; Boies Penrose, *Travel and discovery in the Renaissance, 1420–1620* (Cambridge, Mass., 1955), pp. 316–19; R. N. Routh, ed.,
Who's who in history (Oxford, 1969), II, 444.

[2] Edmund Goldsmid, ed., *The principal navigations...collected by Richard Hakluyt*
(16 vols., Edinburgh, 1885–90). See also Goldsmid's *The voyages of the English
nation to America before the year 1600. From Hakluyt's collection of voyages* (1598–1600)
(4 vols., Edinburgh, 1889–90). Both were poorly edited.

[3] Frank Elias, ed., *First voyages of famous memory; passages from the 'Principal
navigations' of Richard Hakluyt* (1911); Lawrence Irving, ed., *A selection of the*

of these contained introductions and an occasional note,[1] but only a few made even a passing contribution to the study of Hakluyt.[2] The same was true of the twelve volume reprint of the second edition of the *Principal navigations* published under the imprint of the Society by arrangement with James MacLehose. Its reputation for accuracy is undisputed, but it lacks any critical apparatus. Professor Walter Raleigh's concluding essay was largely a graceful attempt to escape the antiquarian approach, and placed Hakluyt in the setting of the age of voyaging, poetry, and imagination by operating on a plane of high generalization. Indeed, his section which dealt directly with Hakluyt seemed to indicate that there was little that could be said about him.[3]

In the period before the mid 1920s, only Foster Watson gave extended attention to the circumstances of Hakluyt's life and works. He published several articles during the first world war,[4] and in 1924, the first biography of Hakluyt.[5] It was intended as a popularization, and the *Annual Bulletin of*

principal voyages... *set out with many embellishments* (London and New York, 1926); Frank Knight, ed., *They told Mr. Hakluyt* (London and New York, 1964).

[1] See, for example, *Voyagers' tales from the collections of Richard Hakluyt* (Cassels' National Library, 1892); E. E. Speight ed., *Hakluyt's English voyages* (1905); *The principal navigations,* with an introduction by John Masefield (8 vols., 1907; completed by two additional volumes, London and New York, 1927–8); Richard Wilson, ed., *Stories from Hakluyt* (London and Toronto, n.d.); Albert M. Hyamson, ed., *Elizabethan adventurers upon the Spanish Main* (1912); A. S. Mott, ed., *Hakluyt's voyages* (Boston and New York, 1929); Janet Hampden, ed., *Richard Hakluyt: Voyages & documents* (1958); John Hampden, ed., *The Tudor venturers* (1970); John Beeching, ed., *Voyages and discoveries* (1972).

[2] The editions of Hakluyt materials which do contain worthwhile introductions, and in some instances critical notes are the following: Edward J. Payne, ed., *Voyages of the Elizabethan seamen to America: Thirteen original narratives from the collection of Hakluyt* (1880; re-edited, 2 vols., Oxford, 1893–1900; with notes by C. R. Beazley, Oxford, 1907); C. R. Beazley, ed., introduction to *Voyages and travels* (vols. X–XI of *An English Garner,* ed. Thomas Seccombe, London, 1903, reprinted, 2 vols., New York, 1964); Irwin R. Blacker, *Hakluyt's voyages* (New York, 1965); D. B. and A. M. Quinn, edd. *Virginia Voyages from Hakluyt* (1973), and, outstandingly, Federico Marenco, *I viaggi inglesi...di Richard Hakluyt,* vol. I (Milan, 1966), in progress.

[3] *Principal navigations,* XII, 74–92.

[4] 'Richard Hakluyt and his debt to Spain', *Fortnightly Review,* new series, C (1916), 827–40; 'Hakluyt and Mulcaster', *Geographical Journal,* XLIX (1917), 48–53; 'Richard Hakluyt: A pioneer of colonization', *United Empire,* VIII (1917), 225–38.

[5] *Richard Hakluyt* (1924).

Historical Literature found it 'slight and disappointing'. But it was not without merit, particularly in its re-evaluation of the idea that Hakluyt was violently anti-Spanish.[1]

The period before the mid 1920s was, however, more a period of preparation than of definitive scholarly accomplishments. But the period of accomplishment was at hand. Many scholars would contribute to it, but the writings of George Bruner Parks, E. G. R. Taylor and David Beers Quinn were to be the most prominent. It is perhaps appropriate that one of them was a professor of literature, one of geography (first trained as a chemist), and one of history.

Parks was first in the field. From 1922 to 1926 he published three articles on Hakluyt,[2] and in 1928 he published *Richard Hakluyt and the English voyages*.[3] Its chief contribution was an examination of Hakluyt's career in the movement of overseas enterprise and particularly in regard to his activities as scholar, consultant, and propagandist. Parks also attempted to present the record of Hakluyt's literary activities, most of which he found to be in the promotional vein. Recent scholarship has modified his work in a few particulars, and supplemented it in several, and his interpretations have been occasionally challenged. But within the context in which he wrote, he is not likely to be superseded.

Richard Hakluyt and the English voyages by no means answered all questions. In her review of the book, E. G. R. Taylor suggested that Parks failed to give proper attention to two major questions: what were Hakluyt's personal connections with the promoters of overseas activity and with the intellectual groups supporting it, and secondly, what were the standards and methods by which he carried on his editorial work?[4]

---

[1] *Ibid.*, pp. 48–57.

[2] 'Hakluyt's Mission in France, 1583–1588', *Washington University Studies* Humanistic Series, IX (1922), 165–84; 'The ancestry of Richard Hakluyt', *Notes and Queries*, CXLVI (1924), 335–7; 'The forerunners of Hakluyt', *Washington University Studies*, Humanistic Series, XIII (1926), 335–70. Parks has also published a number of later articles bearing on Hakluyt. They include: 'The two versions of Settle's Frobisher narrative', *Huntington Library Quarterly*, II (1938), 59–65; 'George Peele and his friends as "ghost"-poets', *Journal of English and Germanic Philology*, XLI (1942), 527–36; 'The occasion of Milton's "Muscovia"', *Studies in Philology*, XL (1943), 399–404; 'The contents and sources of Ramusio's "Navigationi"', *Bulletin of the New York Public Library*, LIX (1955), 279–313. Parks' *The English traveler to Italy*, I (Rome, 1954) gives some attention (pp. 148–9) to a few of Hakluyt's medieval accounts.

[3] A second edition, slightly revised, appeared in 1961.

[4] The review appeared in *Geographical Journal*, LXXIII (1929), 572–4.

Taylor herself was preparing the answer to the first question. Her *Tudor geography, 1485–1583* stressed the role of the intellectual group (including Hakluyt) which surrounded John Dee.[1] Her *Late Tudor and early Stuart geography, 1583–1650* traced the Hakluyt circle,[2] as did her excellent introduction to *The original writings and correspondence of the two Richard Hakluyts*,[3] the body of which provided a convenient collection of almost all the material on the writings of the Hakluyt cousins.

Taylor also tackled the question of Hakluyt as editor, though for the most part in rather general terms,[4] but this question fell chiefly to D. B. Quinn. Raleigh had pointed out in his 1905 essay the need to compare Hakluyt's accounts with the texts he had used as sources,[5] and some of the early efforts of the Society had been along this line. But the problem was not this simple. It was also a matter of comparing the different Hakluyt versions of the same account. And even this was not the end. Scholars had tended to regard Hakluyt as the compendium, and to look no further than his works for their source material. Later research of a number of scholars, particularly in the Spanish archives and in the records of the High Court of Admiralty, proved the completely erroneous nature of this view.[6] Finally, there was, as G. R. Crone put it, the problem of putting Hakluyt's writing not in some framework of antiquarian isolation, but in the matrix of men and ideas in which they had come forth.[7] All of these problems Quinn attempted to handle.

He started modestly enough in 1940 with his edition of *The voyages and colonising enterprises of Sir Humphrey Gilbert*,[8] which among other things,

---

[1] (1930), especially chs. 5–7.

[2] (1934), chs. 1–3. Mention should also be made of her *The mathematical practitioners of Tudor & Stuart England* (Cambridge, 1954), which, while it does not deal with Hakluyt, does deal with many of the mathematicians at work during his time, with some of whom he had connections. See also her *The haven-finding art* (London, 1956; New York, 1957), pp. 196, 225–6.

[3] See also her 'Richard Hakluyt' in *Geographical Journal*, CIX, 165–71.

[4] *Late Tudor and early Stuart geography*, chs. 2–3. Her more specific considerations of Hakluyt's editorial work include the following: *The troublesome voyage of Captain Edward Fenton* (Hakluyt Society, 1959), which in effect compares the accounts in the two editions of the *Principal navigations* with other source materials on the voyage; and 'Master Hore's voyage of 1536', *Geographical Journal*, LXXVII (1931), 469–70, which does the same for that affair.

[5] *Principal navigations*, XII, 91.

[6] For an enumeration of their contributions to the study of Hakluyt's editing, see the section 'Works published', below.

[7] *Geographical Journal*, CXXVIII, 323–4.   [8] (2 vols., Hakluyt Society, 1940).

concerned itself with the Gilbert–Hakluyt connection (as set out by Taylor and Parks), and the comparison, and in some cases the collating, of accounts and propaganda of Gilbert and his associates as they appeared in Hakluyt's publications. His *The Roanoke voyages, 1584–1590*[1] was a far more ambitious attempt. Using Hakluyt's accounts as a base, he collated them with each other, and compared them with Spanish and High Court of Admiralty and other records. The result was by far the most complete picture of Hakluyt's editing and his involvement in a colonial attempt that we have had.

While Quinn has published a number of articles bearing on Hakluyt,[2] his principal contribution since *The Roanoke voyages* has been the republication of the first edition of the *Principall navigations* (with R. A. Skelton)[3] and a new edition of *Divers voyages*.[4] Both are facsimile editions, and do not carry the extensive annotations that marked his two earlier works. But the introductory essays, which he admits are more tentative than final, are still the last word we have on Hakluyt as editor at this time.

Through the works of Parks, Taylor, and Quinn, and to a lesser extent those of their predecessors and contemporaries, we now probably know all we are likely to find out about Richard Hakluyt the man. With regard to his works, we are, as has been pointed out above, in the ironic position of

[1] (2 vols., Hakluyt Society, 1955).

[2] For those which involve Hakluyt or his accounts in various ways, see 'Preparations for the 1585 Virginia voyage', *William and Mary Quarterly,* third series, VI (1949), 208–36; 'The failure of Raleigh's American colonies', *Essays in British and Irish history in honour of James Eadie Todd,* edd. H. A. Cronne et al. (1949), pp. 61–85; 'Christopher Newport in 1590', *North Carolina Historical Review,* XXIX (1952), 305–16; (with Jacques Rousseau), 'Hakluyt et le mot "esquimau"', *Revue d'histoire de l'Amérique française,* XII (1959), 597–601; (with Jacques Rousseau), 'Les toponymes amérindiens da Canada 1591–1602', *Cahiers de Géographie de Québec,* X (1966), 263–77. 'Edward Hayes, Liverpool colonial pioneer', *Transactions of the Historic Society of Lancashire and Cheshire,* CXI (1959), 25–45; 'The voyage of Etienne Bellenger to the maritimes in 1583: A new document', *Canadian Historical Review,* XLIII (1962), 328–43; 'Sailors and the sea', *Shakespeare Survey,* XVII (1964), 21–36; 'England and the St. Lawrence, 1577 to 1602', *Merchants and Scholars: Essays in the history of exploration and trade,* ed. John Parker (Minneapolis, 1965), pp. 117–43; 'The first Pilgrims', *William and Mary Quarterly,* third series, XXIII (1966), 359–90.

[3] (2 vols., The Hakluyt Society and the Peabody Museum of Salem, 1965.)

[4] (2 vols., Amsterdam, 1967.) The first volume is an essay entitled *Richard Hakluyt, editor.* The second is the facsimile of *Divers voyages* (1582) and *A shorte and briefe narration of the two nauigations...to...Newe Fraunce* (1580).

lacking a critical edition of Hakluyt's prime effort, the second edition of the *Principal navigations*. The undertaking of a critical edition of the entire work would be a monumental task and may well be beyond the abilities of present scholarship. Even should it be accomplished, scholars may then look forward to an even more difficult encounter, the resurrection of Richard Hakluyt from the pages of Samuel Purchas.[1]

Motivation

A question which has much concerned historians, though they have usually more asserted than debated it, is that of Hakluyt's motivating ideas. That patriotism was his principal theme none will deny, but beyond that there are considerable differences of opinion. Some of the differences stem from the nature of Hakluyt's materials. They provide such a wealth of support for every point of view that it is easy to forget the difference between Hakluyt and his accounts. On the other hand, many historians have been prone to assess his motives solely in the context of the 'Discourse of western planting', forgetting that it was written at a particular time and for a particular purpose. Further, his views have too often been considered only within the framework of some monolithic context in which Hakluyt is relegated to the realm of supporting evidence. Historians who have considered Hakluyt within such contexts have seldom seen him in other than simplistic terms. It is perhaps significant that those who have dealt with Hakluyt and his works in detail usually avoid such one-sided characterizations.

Insofar as historians of all shades have generalized on Hakluyt's motives, they have tended to divide into two camps: those who have seen his thinking as essentially concerned with the high strategy of international politics, usually with religious overtones, and those who have viewed him as essentially a pragmatist interested in promoting the economic advancement of England. The latter group had a particular vogue in the first forty years of the twentieth century, reflecting, no doubt, the concern of that day for things economic,[2] and the idea is prominent in the writings of Parks,

---

[1] Parks has estimated that the Hakluyt material in Purchas amounts to 1,625,000 words of the 3,900,000 contained in the work (*Hakluyt*, p. 227, note); and see the list on pp. 84–96 above.

[2] George Louis Beer, *The origins of the British colonial system, 1578–1660* (New York, 1908), chs. 2–3; Beer, 'The early English colonial movement', *Political Science Quarterly*, XXIII (1908), 75–94, 242–58; Raleigh, in *Principal navigations*, XII, 2 (which sees the main thread in all the travel literature as the struggle for com-

Williamson, and Taylor.[1] Since World War II, however, the economic emphasis has been balanced by the political, religious, and strategic argument, and has been reflected in the works of such writers as Rowse,[2] Wright,[3] and Quinn.[4] While these authors have stressed the religious, antiCatholic, and antiSpanish nature of Hakluyt's thought, and have seen him as sympathetic to the forward party, they, and others who have followed this line, have generally been willing to admit that Hakluyt was no pro

mercial supremacy and the search for Cathay); A. P. Newton, 'The beginnings of English colonisation, 1569–1618', *The Cambridge history of the British Empire,* edd. J. Holland Rose *et al.,* I (New York and Cambridge, 1929), 67–70; E. A. J. Johnson, *American economic thought in the seventeenth century* (1932, reprinted New York, 1961), pp. 35–57. Another group of writers has also opposed the view that Hakluyt's ideas were essentially antiSpanish, though they do not particularly advance the economic argument. This was the opinion of Foster Watson (see above, p. 585) and it has been shared, though somewhat obliquely, by Sidney Lee, 'The example of Spain', *Elizabethan and other essays,* ed. F. S. Boas (Oxford, 1929), 199–231; and E. M. Tenison, *Elizabethan England* (14 vols. Royal Leamington Spa, 1933–61), VII, 408–12; VIII, 200, n. 6. Tenison's argument is primarily an attack on Williamson and Taylor for what she considers their too narrow view of the Elizabethan age. William S. Maltby, *The Black Legend in England* (Durham, N.C., 1971), pp. 61–87, and Philip W. Powell, *The tree of hate* (New York and London, 1971), p. 75, revive the view that Hakluyt was bitterly antiSpanish.

[1] Parks, *Hakluyt,* especially chs. 7–9; Williamson, in *Richard Hakluyt,* ed. Lynam, pp. 14–17 (though Williamson at other times stresses the antiSpanish element in Hakluyt – see his *The Age of Drake* (3rd ed., London, 1952), pp. 238–9); Taylor, *Late Tudor and early Stuart geography,* pp. 2–3; Taylor, *Hakluyts,* I, preface, p. vii; introduction, *passim;* Taylor, in *Geographical Journal,* CIX, 165–71. It is doubtless unfair to catagorize Taylor's views so simply, for no one has been more of a proponent of Hakluyt's multiple motives.

[2] *The expansion of Elizabethan England* (London and New York, 1955), ch. 6 and *passim; The Elizabethans and America* (London and New York, 1959), ch. 3.

[3] *Religion and empire,* ch. 2; *The dream of prosperity in colonial America* (New York, 1965), pp. 25–33, 39. The last points up the commonly suggested contrast between the high politics views of the younger Hakluyt and the exclusively economic ideas of the elder.

[4] This would appear to be the burden of his *Roanoke voyages* and of his several articles cited above dealing with the decade of the 1580s which see strategic considerations as the most immediate objective, with economic considerations more of a longterm goal. See also his *Raleigh and the British empire* (London and New York, 1949), pp. 59–62. Quinn's articles on Hakluyt's activities in the late 1590s appear, however, to reflect a somewhat different view.

moter of direct frontal assault on Spain. Of late, Christopher Hill has attempted a comprehensive synthesis of both views in a framework reminiscent of the protestant ethic and the spirit of capitalism.[1]

Geographer, scientist, litterateur, historian

The Hakluyt contribution to the study of geography was a principal topic for Taylor, who gave the fullest attention to the intellectual circles within which he carried on his activities.[2] Indeed, it might well be argued that she saw this as his primary motivation. Wright and Hill have commented at some length concerning the connection between Hakluyt's religious orientation and his scientific viewpoint,[3] while Parks has given an excellent description of his advancement of learning, particularly in the 1590s.[4]

Along more specific lines, Hakluyt's concern with cartography, in spite of the general lack of cartographic aids within his own works, was of great interest to nineteenth century writers, and continues undiminished to the present.[5] Another topic which has received extensive coverage is his

[1] Hill, *Intellectual origins of the English revolution* (Oxford, 1965), ch. 4.

[2] See especially *Hakluyts,* introduction; *Tudor Geography,* chs. 5–7; *Late Tudor and early Stuart geography,* ch. 1; also J. N. L. Baker, *The history of geography* (Oxford, 1963), *passim.*

[3] Wright, *Religion and empire,* pp. 33–8; Hill, *Intellectual origins of the English revolution,* ch. 2.

[4] *Hakluyt,* ch. 13.

[5] For works which discuss several of the maps with which Hakluyt had some connection see J. G. Kohl, *A descriptive catalogue of those maps, charts, and surveys relating to America which are mentioned in vol. III of Hakluyt's great work* (Washington, 1857); A. E. Nordenskiöld, *Facsimile-atlas to the early history of cartography,* trans. Johan A. Ekelöf and C. R. Markham (Stockholm, 1889), pp. 95–6, 103; Emerson D. Fite and Archibald Freeman, *A book of old maps delineating American history* (Cambridge, Mass, 1926), pp. 50–3, 60–5, 90–96, 100–02; R. A. Skelton, *Explorers' maps* (1958), *passim;* Henry Harrisse, *Découverte et évolution cartographique de Terre-Neuve* (London and Paris, 1900), *passim;* Harrisse, *Discovery of North America,* II, *passim;* W. F. Ganong, *Crucial maps in the early cartography and place-nomenclature of the Atlantic coast of Canada* (first printed in *Transactions of the Royal Society of Canada,* 1929–37; reprinted with an introduction, commentary, and map notes by T. E. Layng, Royal Society of Canada, 1964), pp. 438–9, 452–61 (Ganong's work has a number of useful comments on various Hakluyt materials); Henry R. Wagner, *The cartography of the northwest coast of America to the year 1800,* I (Berkeley, Cal., 1937), 82–4, 86–8; Wagner, *Sir Francis*

promotion of the science of navigation,[1] though there has been some tendency to dismiss the subject on the grounds that the English were far better at navigation than Hakluyt believed.[2] D. W. Waters has given

Drake's voyage around the world (San Francisco, 1926), pp. 404–22. For the Thorne and Lok maps contained in *Divers voyages,* see Quinn, *Richard Hakluyt, editor,* pp. 17–26; R. P. Bishop, 'Lessons of the Gilbert map', *Geographical Journal,* LXXII (1928), 237–43; B. F. De Costa, 'The Verrazano map', *Magazine of American History* II (1878), 461–4; and, indirectly, M. Destombes, 'Nautical charts attributed to Verrazzano (1525–1528)', *Imago Mundi,* XI (1954), 57–66; L. C. Wroth, *The voyages of Giovauni da Verrazzano, 1524–1528* (New Haven, 1970). For the map in the 1587 Latin edition of Peter Martyr, see Carl I. Wheat, *Mapping the transmississippi west,* I (San Francisco, 1957), 26, 190. For discussions of the world map in the second edition of the *Principal navigations,* see C. H. Coote, ed., *The map of the world A.D. 1600 called by Shakspere 'the new map, with the augmentation of the Indies'* (Hakluyt Society, 1880); E. J. S. Parsons and W. F. Morris, 'Edward Wright and his work', *Imago Mundi,* III (1939), 68–9 (discusses the respective contributions of Molyneux, Hakluyt, John Davis, and Wright to the map); Lawrence C. Wroth, 'The early cartography of the Pacific', *Papers of the Bibliographical Society of America,* XXXVIII (1944), 171–2 (argues the effect of Drake's circumnavigation on the map, and also on the map in the edition of Martyr); E. G. R. Taylor, 'Early empire building projects in the Pacific Ocean, 1565–1585', *Hispanic-American Historical Review,* XIV (1934), 302–3 (denies the above contention); Taylor, *Haven-finding art,* pp. 223–4; Milton Waldman, *Americana: the literature of American history* (New York, 1925), pp. 103–8 (calls the map the most significant thing in the *Principal navigations*). On the Molyneux globes, see C. R. Markham, ed., *Tractatus de globis et eorum usu* (Hakluyt Society, 1889), especially introduction, p. xxxvi; Helen M. Wallis, 'The first English globe: A recent discovery', *Geographical Journal,* CXVII (1951), pp. 275–90, especially 275–8; Wallis, 'The Molyneux globes', *British Museum Quarterly,* XVI (1951), 89–90 (points out the terrestrial globe was a counterpart of that in *Principal navigations*); Wallis, 'Further light on the Molyneux globes', *Geographical Journal,* CXXI (1955), 304–11; Ruth A. McIntyre, 'William Sanderson: Elizabethan financier of discovery', *William and Mary Quarterly,* third series, XIII (1956), 192–4.

[1] References to the lectureship in navigation are numerous, but see especially Parks, *Hakluyt,* pp. 168–71; Watson, *Geographical Journal,* XLIX, 48–53 (argues he may have taken the idea from Richard Mulcaster). For another Hakluyt contribution to the science of navigation see Taylor, *Haven-finding art,* p. 226.

[2] Moorhouse in *Cornhill Magazine,* XLI, 563, points out that Hakluyt did not realize the major problem of Elizabethan shipping was hygiene rather than navigation. See also Williamson in *Richard Hakluyt,* ed. Lynam, p. 16; Alwyn A. Ruddock, 'The Trinity House at Deptford in the sixteenth century', *English Historical Review* LXV (1950), 458–76, especially 463.

thorough examination to the rutters which appear in his works,[1] while Quinn and Hulton have dealt extensively with his interest in natural sciences, especially as seen in his connection with the publication of the White–Harriot materials by Theodor de Bry.[2]

Hakluyt's role as a man of letters has been the subject of some commentary, though it is again a realm in which his edited materials tend to be mixed indiscriminately with his personal writings. Parks has discussed in detail the reputation of the *Principal navigations* as an epic.[3] W. T. Jewkes and especially Howard Mumford Jones have seen Hakluyt as expressing the rather stereotyped romantic tradition of the renaissance, with all its contradictions,[4] while Sidney Lee has stressed the influence of the French renaissance in Hakluyt's works.[5] A number of writers have commented on the literary qualities of his sea accounts.[6] Wright has set forth the middle-class attractions of his style on his own and later ages,[7] and Hill has argued

[1] Waters, *The art of navigation in Elizabethan and early Stuart times* (London and New Haven, Conn., 1958), pp. 234–5, 261–5. Waters has also pointed out a number of other Hakluyt contributions to the science of navigation. See particularly pp. 92–3, 185, 203, 236, 277, 282–3.

[2] Quinn, *Roanoke voyages*, I, 35–60, and chs. 5–7; Paul H. Hulton and D. B. Quinn, *The American drawings of John White, 1577–1590* (2 vols., London and Chapel Hill, N.C., 1964).   [3] Parks, *Hakluyt*, ch. 15.

[4] Both authors have dealt with Hakluyt within the framework of a general consideration of travel literature. See Jewkes, 'The literature of travel and the mode of romance in the renaissance', *Bulletin of the New York Public Library*, LXVII (1963), 219–36; Jones, *O strange new world* (New York, 1964), especially chs. 1–2, 4–5.

[5] *The French renaissance in England* (New York, 1910), pp. 194, 306, 327–8.

[6] See especially Payne, ed., *Voyages of the Elizabethan seaman* (1893–1900 ed.), introduction; Harold F. Watson, *The sailor in English fiction and drama, 1550–1800* (New York, 1931), ch. 1; Clennell Wilkinson, *The English adventurers* (1931, reprinted, Freeport, N.Y., 1968), ch. 4; William B. White, 'The narrative technique of Elizabethan voyage and travel literature from 1550 to 1603' (unpublished PhD. dissertation, Lehigh University, 1955), which sees the sea narratives as the perfect embodiment of the plain style; Anne Treneer, *The sea in English literature from Beowulf to Donne* (Liverpool and London, 1926), chs. 3–4; William Paxton Ker, 'The Elizabethan voyagers', *Collected Essays of William Paxton Ker*, ed. Charles Whibley, I (1925), pp. 2–9. See also J. E. Dyer, 'The Elizabethan sailorman', *Mariner's Mirror* X (1924), 133–46, which offers an interesting commentary on the type of person who wrote the sea accounts which appear in Hakluyt.

[7] *Middle-class culture in Elizabethan England* (Chapel Hill, N.C., 1935; reprinted, Ithaca, N.Y., 1958), pp. 527–34.

that the plain style of Hakluyt and his accounts was another precursor of Puritanism.[1] In dealing with his personal style, Taylor offered something of a prior demurrer to such claims by pointing out that while Hakluyt's style was plain in his earlier works, the last edition of the *Principal navigations* indicates that he had consciously begun to take on all the embellishments made fashionable by Lyly.[2]

Hakluyt's direct contributions to English literature have been of somewhat less scholarly concern than his influence on the writers of his own and the succeeding ages. Walter Raleigh's essay accompanying the MacLehose edition of the *Principal navigations* was a landmark in this field,[3] and interest in the subject has increased since the 1920s. The most significant contribution has been made by R. R. Cawley, who has given Hakluyt extensive attention in his general works, and has pointed out his influence on specific authors in a number of articles.[4] Rowse, James E. Gillespie, Franklin T. McCann, and indirectly, William Holzhausen[5] have also commented generally, and various writers have indicated Hakluyt's influence on Shakespeare, Drayton, Nash, Strachey, Spencer, Milton, and Defoe.[6]

[1] *Intellectual origins of the English revolution,* especially p. 129.

[2] Taylor, *Hakluyts,* I, 55–7. See also Eleanor Rosenberg's review of *Principall navigations (1589),* ed. Quinn and Skelton, in *Renaissance News,* XIX (1966), 382–7.

[3] *Principal navigations,* XII, 92–120.

[4] Cawley's general works are *The voyagers and Elizabethan drama* (Boston, 1938) and *Unpathed waters: studies in the influence of the voyagers on Elizabethan literature* (Princeton, N.J., 1940). The former is a chaotic work, but extremely suggestive in regard to Hakluyt's influence. The latter is less concerned with Hakluyt. Cawley's articles which touch on Hakluyt include the following: 'Warner and the voyagers', *Modern Philology,* XX (1922), 113–47; 'Drayton and the voyagers', *Publications of the Modern Language Association of America,* XXXVIII (1923), 530–56; 'Shakspere's use of the voyagers in *The Tempest*', *ibid.,* XLI (1926), 688–726. In regard to Milton, see also his *Milton and the literature of travel* (Princeton, N.J., 1951), ch. 3 and *passim.*

[5] Rowse, *Elizabethans and America,* ch. 8; Gillespie, *The influence of overseas expansion on England to 1700* (*Columbia University Studies in History, Economics, and Public Law,* XCI, 1920), chs. 8–10; Franklin T. McCann, *English discovery of America to 1585* (New York, 1952), especially ch. 10, which sees the high point of travel literature influence in Marlowe's *Tamburlaine;* Wilhelm Holzhausen, 'Übersee in den Darstellungsformen des Elizabethanischen Dramas', *Beiträge zur Erforschung der Sprache und Kultur Englands und Nordamerikas,* IV (1928), 155–277.

[6] For Shakespeare, see Lois Whitney, 'Did Shakespeare know *Leo Africanus*?', *Publications of the Modern Language Association of America,* XXXVII (1922), 47–83 (the influence of Hakluyt and his protégé, John Pory); Henry Pemberton,

Hakluyt was very conscious of the importance of language as a bridge between Europeans and the non-European world and helped to further the knowledge of explorers and merchants by including vocabularies of foreign languages and retaining significant foreign words in narratives he printed. Indeed as late as 1614 he fostered the publication of an important Malay vocabulary in England. His vocabularies have, not surprisingly, been exploited by modern linguistic students.[1]

Shakspere and Sir Walter Ralegh (Philadelphia and London, 1914), chs. 10–15, which argues that Ralegh wrote Shakespeare's plays, and uses, among other evidence, the great familiarity of the author with Hakluyt's works; Charles M. Gayley, *Shakespeare and the founders of liberty in America* (New York, 1917), pp. 71–6, which suggests a possible personal connection between Hakluyt and Shakespeare; Fred Sorensen, '"The masque of the Muscovites" in *Love's Labour's Lost*', *Modern Language Notes*, L (1935), 499–501. On Drayton, see Joseph Quincy Adams, 'Michael Drayton's "To the Virginia voyage"', *Modern Language Notes*, XXXIII (1918), 405–8; Gerhard Friedrich, 'The genesis of Michael Drayton's ode "To the Virginia voyage"', *ibid.*, LXXII (1957), 401–6; Michael D. West 'Drayton's "To the Virginian Voyage": from heroic pastoral to mock-heroic', *Renaissance Quarterly*, XXIV (1971), 501–6. On Nash see R. B. McKerrow, ed., *The works of Thomas Nash*, v (Oxford, 1910, reprinted, Oxford, 1958), introduction, pp. 125, 127, 135. On Strachey, see S. G. Culliford, *William Strachey, 1572–1621* (Charlottesville, Va., 1965), pp. 148–50, 162, 172–7, 186, which sees Strachey as borrowing heavily from Hakluyt, but without acknowledgement. On Spencer, see Lois Whitney, 'The literature of travel in the *Faerie Queene*', *Modern Philology*, XIX (1921), 145, 157–9. On Milton, see Elbert N. S. Thompson, 'Milton's knowledge of geography', *Studies in Philology*, XVI (1919), 151–5; H. Mutschmann, *Studies concerning the origin of 'Paradise Lost'* (Dorpat, 1924), pp. 5–47, 67–8; Parks 'The Occasion of Milton's "Muscovia"' in *Studies in Philology*, XL, 399–404. For Defoe see Arthur W. Secord, *Studies in the narrative method of Defoe* (*University of Illinois Studies in Language and Literature*, IX, no. 1, 1924), 29–30, 69–71, 86–90, 114, 127, 138, 230–1.

[1] Vocabularies of West African languages appearing in Hakluyt are examined, with early vocabularies from other sources, by David Dalby and P. E. H. Hair, '"Le langaige de Guynee": a sixteenth century vocabulary from the Pepper Coast', *African Language Studies*, v (1964), 174–91 (Towerson's Kra and Akan vocabularies), and P. E. H. Hair, 'An ethnolinguistic inventory of the Lower Guinea coast before 1700: Part II', *African Language Review*, VIII (1969), 225–56 (Towerson's Akan vocabulary). A pioneer in the use of Hakluyt vocabularies was John Abercrombie, 'The earliest list of Russian Lapp words', *Journal de la Société Finno-Ougrienne*, XIII (Helsinki, 1895), 1–10; and much later T. I. Itkonen, 'Wörterbuch des Kolta- und Kolalappischen', *Lexica Societatis Fenno-ugricae*, XV (Helsinki, 1958), utilized the same material. Hakluyt's

While Hakluyt's role in the promotion of science and as a geographer and man of letters have been extensively assessed, almost no attention has been given to his possible contributions to the discipline of history. Most historians have considered him a kind of archivist, and have regarded his works in that light. Louis B. Wright, a confirmed Hakluyt proponent, ignored him completely in his discussion of 'The Elizabethan taste for history',[1] and recent discussions of Tudor historiography have given him only the slightest attention.[2] The only worthwhile, though quite inadequate, study of Hakluyt as an historian was published by J. Hamard in 1948.[3] He saw Hakluyt's works as combining a renaissance search for truth with a utilitarian view that closely approached the idea of progress.

Russian words are discussed by H. Leeming, 'Russian words in 16th-century English sources', *Slavonic and East European Review,* XLVI (1968), 1–30; XLVII (1969), 11–36. The Frobisher Eskimo word-list has attracted attention from W. Thalbitzer, 'Fra grønlandsforskningens første dage', *Festskrift udgivet af Københavns Universitet* (September 1932), p. 11; and V. Stefansson, *The three voyages of Martin Frobisher* (2 vols., 1938), II, 233–6. Notes on the Eskimo words in the John Davis narratives were first made by H. Rink, in *The voyages and works of John Davis the navigator,* ed. A. H. Markham (Hakluyt Society, 1880), and later by C. W. Schultz-Lorentzen, in John Davis, *Trerejser til Grønland i Aarene 1585–7,* translated by G. N. Bugge (Det Grønslandske Selskabs Skrifter, VII, København, 1930). James A. Geary, 'The language of the Carolina Algonkian tribes', *The Roanoke voyages, 1584–90,* edited by D. B. Quinn, II (1955), 873–900, analyses the linguistic material on eastern North America in the Hakluyt narratives.

[1] *Journal of Modern History,* III (1931), 175–97.
[2] See, for example, L. F. Dean, *Tudor theories of history writing (University of Michigan Contributions in Philosophy,* no. 1, 1947), which ignores Hakluyt completely, and F. J. Levy, *Tudor historical thought* (San Marino, Cal., 1967), which gives him only the slightest attention (pp. 144, 208).
[3] 'Richard Hakluyt, historien', *Les Langues Modernes,* XLII (1948), 249–59. It might be argued that the Hakluyt's role as a philosopher of history is inherent in Hill's *Intellectual origins of the English revolution.* Hill makes the same point in 'God's Englishmen and his empire', a review of Janet Hampden's edition of Hakluyt, in which he claims that Hakluyt was one of those chiefly responsible for the Protestant legend of English history. (*The Spectator,* CC (1958), 809.)

Activities and connections

The indispensable works on most aspects of Hakluyt's career are the main writings of E. G. R. Taylor,[1] and Parks' *Hakluyt*.[2] The Hakluyt family background is best followed in Parks,[3] who is also the chief guide for Hakluyt's activities at Oxford from 1570 to 1583.[4] John Lambert has described the financial aid he received from the Skinners' Company, while Tom Girtin has done the same for the Clothworkers'.[5] Hakluyt has generally been credited with giving the first lectures in geography at Oxford, but this has been challenged by J. N. L. Baker.[6] J. G. Underhill and Santiago Magariños have argued that Hakluyt received his interest in Spanish writings primarily from his group of associates at Oxford.[7]

The influence of the elder Hakluyt and his role in bringing the younger into geographical circles are covered in Parks and Taylor,[8] the latter of

[1] *Tudor geography, passim; Late Tudor and early Stuart geography*, especially ch. 1; *Hakluyts*, I, introduction, 1–66.

[2] Aside from the text of the work, appendices I–II, pp. 233–59, which contain year by year summaries of the known activities of both Hakluyts, are particularly helpful. They are not, in many respects, superseded by the 'Chronology' given above, pp. 265–331.

[3] *Hakluyt*, pp. 56–9. See also Parks in *Notes and Queries*, CXLVI, 335–7; Reynolds in *Geographical Review*, XLVIII, 453–6; Eric St John Brooks, 'Origin of the name Hakluyt', *Notes and Queries*, CLXVI (1934), 240; Gray, *Address on the occasion of the tercentenary of the death of Richard Hakluyt...with a note on the family*, pp. 13–19.

[4] *Hakluyt*, pp. 59–62, 66–7. See also Taylor, *Hakluyts*, I, 11–12.

[5] John Lambert, ed., *Records of the Skinners of London* (1933), pp. 373–5; Tom Girtin, 'Mr. Hakluyt, scholar at Oxford', *Geographical Journal*, CXIX (1953), 208–12; Girtin, *The golden ram: a narrative history of the Clothworkers' Company*, (1958), pp. 53–6. Girtin suggests that the Clothworkers' support may indicate that Hakluyt came not from the prosperous background suggested by Parks but from a relatively poor one.

[6] 'The history of geography in Oxford', *The history of geography* (Oxford, 1963), pp. 119–22. For an argument that Hakluyt entered into what was already an ardent community of students of astronomy and cosmography, see Mark H. Curtis, *Oxford and Cambridge in transition* (Oxford, 1959), pp. 234–41.

[7] Underhill, *Spanish literature in the England of the Tudors* (New York, 1899), ch. 5 and pp. 262–6, 309–11, 317–24, 331–2; Magariños 'Inglaterra y los historiadores de Indias', *Ensayos hispano-ingleses. Homenaje a Walter Starkie* (Barcelona, 1948), 168–70.

[8] Parks, *Hakluyt*, especially chs. 3–5; Taylor, *Hakluyts*, I, introduction, *passim*.

whom is also best for the Dee connection with all its ramifications.[1] Taylor also considered Hakluyt's possible early connections with the Muscovy and Levant groups,[2] and argued that he offered a plan for seizing the Strait of Magellan in 1578.[3] This last has been accepted and amplified by Helen M. Wallis, but Williamson has expressed some doubt as to whether the plan was actually Hakluyt's.[4] Hakluyt's role in the plans of Gilbert and his associates was noted by W. G. Gosling in his biography of Gilbert published in 1911,[5] but it remained for Parks, Taylor, and especially Quinn to delineate his very active efforts in that affair.[6]

No single aspect of Hakluyt's career has received more attention than his activities on behalf of Ralegh's Virginia colony. Prior to 1877, his link with Ralegh before 1587 was unsuspected, but the accidental discovery of Hakluyt's so-called 'Discourse of western planting' by Leonard Woods and its publication in the former year proved to be an historical landmark. The Woods–Charles Deane introduction and notes are still of some use, but the tract itself is very imperfectly printed.[7] Taylor's is a far better edition.[8]

The 'Discourse' has been one of the most commented upon documents of the time, though most such commentaries are quite superficial. Among the better or more interesting ones, a number of which go beyond the tract in examining the Ralegh–Hakluyt connection on British colonial theory, are those by Hill, Beer, Wright, Rowse, A. P. Newton, K. E. Knorr,

---

[1] *Tudor geography*, chs. 5–7. See also Peter J. French, *John Dee* (London, 1972), ch. 7.

[2] *Hakluyts*, I, 19–20, 28–9; *Tudor geography*, pp. 129–37.

[3] *Hakluyts*, I, 16–18 and doc. 24, pp. 139–46.

[4] Wallis, 'English enterprise in the region of the Strait of Magellan', *Merchants and scholars*, ed. Parker, pp. 193–220; Williamson in *Richard Hakluyt*, ed. Lynam, pp. 27–8.

[5] *The life of Sir Humphrey Gilbert, England's first empire builder* (1911), especially chs. 10–15.

[6] Parks, *Hakluyt*, pp. 78–84; Taylor, *Hakluyts*, I, 21–8; Quinn, *Gilbert*, I, introduction, 62–7, 76–80; D. B. Quinn and Neil M. Cheshire, edd., *The new found land of Stephen Parmenius* (Toronto, 1972). See also the related documents in the last three works.

[7] Charles Deane, ed., *A discourse concerning western planting* (with an introduction by Leonard Woods), (Cambridge, Mass., 1877). The tract was also issued under a slightly different title ('A discourse on western planting') as vol. II of *A documentary history of the State of Maine* (*Maine Historical Society Collections*, second series, 1877.)

[8] *Hakluyts* II, doc. 46, pp. 211–326.

and Max Savelle,[1] in addition to Taylor and Parks.[2] While Parks, especially, has argued an economic interpretation of the document, the weight of recent opinion has seen it as the perfect blueprint of a colonial theory. But Quinn's 1949 article on 'The failure of Ralegh's American colonies' pointed out that the ideas expressed by Hakluyt were generally unsuited to the situation, and contributed significantly to the failure of the colony.[3] This, together with Quinn's full study of the numerous Hakluyt links with Ralegh in his *Roanoke voyages*, has helped to reduce the 'Discourse' to its proper perspective.[4]

The involvement with Ralegh was sandwiched in and around Hakluyt's mission to France with Sir Edward Stafford. The fullest discussion of the mission is by Parks, who claims that Hakluyt went to France (as the best place other than Spain) to compile a colonial dossier.[5] As Parks indicates, the mission involved a close relationship with Sir Francis Walsingham,[6] and to a lesser extent with William Cecil, Lord Burghley.[7] It is a pity that no one has been able to trace more exactly, and especially in the realm of ideas, the relationship between Hakluyt and those two giants of

[1] Hill, *Intellectual origins of the English revolution*, chs. 2, 4; Beer, *Origins of the British colonial system*, ch. 2; Wright, 'Elizabethan politics and colonial enterprise', *North Carolina Historical Review*, XXXII (1955), 259–65; Wright, *Religion and empire*, pp. 43–50; Rowse, *Elizabethans and America*, pp. 45–8; Newton, *Cambridge history of the British Empire*, edd. Rose *et al.*, I, 67–70; Knorr, *British colonial theories, 1570–1859* (Toronto, 1944, reprinted, Toronto, 1963), ch. 2; Savelle, *The origins of American diplomacy* (New York and London, 1967), pp. 27–9.

[2] Taylor, *Hakluyts*, I, 33–6; Parks, *Hakluyt*, ch. 7.

[3] In *Essays in British and Irish history*, edd. Cronne *et al.*, pp. 64–9.

[4] In addition to Quinn's *Roanoke voyages*, see his 'Some Spanish reactions to Elizabethan colonial enterprises', *Transactions of the Royal Historical Society*, fifth series, I (1951), 1–23; and 'The first pilgrims' in *William and Mary Quarterly*, third series, XXIII (1966), 359–90.

[5] *Hakluyt*, chs. 8–9. See also his 'Hakluyt's mission in France, 1583–1588' in *Washington University Studies*, IX, 165–84; and Quinn in *Canadian Historical Review*, XLIII, 335–8.

[6] Other than in Parks, the connection with Walsingham may best be traced in the introductory materials and documents in Taylor, *Hakluyts*, and Quinn, *Roanoke voyages*.

[7] Quinn in his introduction to the *Principall navigations* sketches the Burghley role in the Paris mission (p. xv) but is in error in claiming no letter from Hakluyt to Burghley survives (see Taylor, *Hakluyts*, II, doc. 60, pp. 379–80). Tom Girtin suggests that Hakluyt may have served as a commercial spy for Burghley while in Paris (*Geographical Journal*, CXIX, 211–12). See also Williamson in *Richard Hakluyt*, ed. Lynam, p. 32, and Taylor, *Hakluyts*, I, 31–48.

Elizabethan politics.[1] Nor do we know much about Hakluyt's other personal connections in the 1580s. One interesting relationship of that decade which has been quite fully described is that with the colonial promoter Edward Hayes. It was one which endured for twenty years.[2]

Hakluyt's activities in the last decade of the sixteenth century have become increasingly clear, and we can now see him as much more active than we formerly suspected. Parks sees the period as a time when he func, tioned as a consultant geographer and promoter of research and learning.[3] In both of these roles he operated on an international scale, and a number of scholars have contributed to further clarification of such connections at this and other times.[4] Little has been done in recent years with regard to Hakluyt's

[1] The works of the great student of Burghley and Walsingham, Conyers Read, shed little light on the subject. His ch. 18 in vol. III of *Mr. Secretary Walsingham and the policy of Queen Elizabeth* (Oxford, 1925) on English maritime enter, prise has only a brief mention of Hakluyt (p. 404), though the work does later discuss Walsingham's patronage of discovery publications (pp. 433–5).

[2] Quinn in *Transactions of the Historic Society of Lancashire and Cheshire*, CXI, 25–45. For his dealings with the privateers see K. R. Andrews, 'New light on Hakluyt', *Mariner's Mirror*, XXXVII (1951), 299–308, and *English privateering voyages, 1588–95* (Hakluyt Society, 1959), *passim*.

[3] *Hakluyt*, chs. 11, 13. Also Williamson in *Richard Hakluyt*, ed. Lynam, pp. 37–8; Taylor, *Hakluyts*, I, 48–54; II, docs. 69–72, pp. 415–25.

[4] For his consultations with the Dutch over the possible North,east Passage, see J. H. de Stoppelaar, *Balthaser de Moucheron* (The Hague, 1901), pp. 103–11; Charles de Lannoy and Herman van der Linden, *Historie de l'expansion coloniale des peuples européens*, II (Brussels, 1911), 31–4; Van Nouhuys, 'The ship's council on the expedition of Pet and Jackman on July 27th, 1580', *Mariner's Mirror*, XVI (1930), 411–14, which challenges some of Parks' contentions on the information supplied to the Dutch by Hakluyt in the 1590's; John Parker, *Van Meteren's Virginia, 1607–1612* (Minneapolis, 1961), pp. 12–13, 18, 26; Ernest C. Abbe and Frank J. Gillis, 'Henry Hudson and the early exploration and mapping of Hudson Bay, 1610–1631', *Merchants and scholars*, ed. Parker, pp. 91–3, which suggest the Dutch got information on the 1610–11 Hudson expedition through Hakluyt. For the John White – Thomas Harriot materials, and Hakluyt's connection with them and De Bry, see Laurence Binyon, 'The drawings of John White, governor of Raleigh's Virginia colony', *Walpole Society Publications* XIII (1924–25), 19–24; Stefan Lorant, *The new world: the first pictures of America made by John White* (New York, 1946), pp. 30–1, 182; and especially Quinn, *Roanoke voyages*, I, 35–60 and chs. 5–6, and Hulton and Quinn, *The American drawings of John White*. See also H. Averdunk and J. Müller,Reinhard, *Gerhard Mercator und die Geographen unter seinen nachkommen*

activities with the East India Company, and Parks and Taylor remain the standard.[1] One new connection that has emerged is Hakluyt's involvement with a plan of settlement in the Canadian maritime area.[2]

Hakluyt has long been considered a primary link between the Ralegh Virginia attempts and the Virginia Company of London. His particular interest in the voyages preliminary to the Jamestown settlement and in the settlement itself have been studied and commented upon by a number of scholars, of whom Warner F. Gookin and Philip L. Barbour have recently been most prominent.[3] With the founding of Jamestown, knowledge

(*Petermanns Geographische Mitteilungen Ergänzungsheft*, no. 182, 1914), pp. 49, 114–15; R. A. Skelton, 'Mercator and English geography in the 16th century', *Duisberger Forschungen*, VI (1962), 158–68.

[1] Parks, *Hakluyt*, ch. 12, is excellent. See also Taylor, *Hakluyts*, II, docs. 78, 81, pp. 465–8, 476–82; C. R. Markham, ed., *The voyages of Sir James Lancaster, Kt. to the East Indies* (Hakluyt Society, 1877), introduction, pp. iii–iv; Markham, *A memoir on the Indian surveys* (1878, reprinted, Amsterdam, 1968), pp. 1–2, 400; William Foster, *John Company* (1926), p. 4; William Foster, 'Samuel Purchas', in *Richard Hakluyt*, ed. Lynam, pp. 52–3. Markham and Foster debate Hakluyt's supposed role as historiographer of the Company. On his contributions to Far Eastern documentation see Donald F. Lach, *Asia in the making of Europe*, I, bk 1 (Chicago, 1965), 212–15.

[2] Quinn, 'England and the St. Lawrence', in *Merchants and Scholars*, ed. Parker, pp. 123–9, 138–40; 'The first pilgrims' in *William and Mary Quarterly*, third series, XXIII, 368–72, 384.

[3] For Hakluyt's connection with the voyages preliminary to settlement, and possible responsibility for the accounts of them, as well as with the Virginia Company, see Fulmer Mood, 'Richard Hakluyt and John Brierton', *New England Historical and Genealogical Register*, LXXXIII (1929), 505–7; Warner F. Gookin, 'Who was Bartholomew Gosnold?', *William and Mary Quarterly*, third series, VI (1949), 410–15; Gookin, 'Notes on the Gosnold family', *Virginia Magazine of History and Biography*, LVII (1949), 312–14; Gookin, 'The first leaders at Jamestown', *ibid.*, LVIII (1950), 186–7; Gookin (with footnotes and concluding part by Philip L. Barbour), *Bartholomew Gosnold: discoverer and planter* (Hampden, Conn., and London, 1963), pp. 22–3, 26–35, 57–61, 105, 177–87, 205–6, *passim*; K. O. Emery 'Bartholomew Gosnold and Richard Hakluyt', *The Cape*, I (1967), 9–11; Parks, *Hakluyt*, pp. 203–7, 217–19; B. F. De Costa, 'Gosnold and Pring', *New England Historical and Geneological Register*, XXXII (1878), 78–9; Alexander Brown, ed., *The genesis of the United States* (2 vols., Boston and New York, 1897), *passim*, but especially the cross-referenced biographical sketches at the end of vol. II; Conway Whittle Sams, *The conquest of Virginia: the second attempt* (Norfolk, Va., 1929), *passim*; Walter H. Stowe, 'The Reverend Richard Hakluyt...and the first charter of Virginia',

of Hakluyt's activities becomes very shadowy, and thereafter we catch only an occasional glimpse of him.[1] An air of mystery hangs over his final personal relationship about which we should like to know a great deal more: that with Samuel Purchas.[2]

Publications

George Bruner Parks has in the past done more than any other researcher to ferret out the totality of Hakluyt's publishing activities.[3] Parks has argued the essentially propagandistic nature of Hakluyt's works, and most writers have agreed to a lesser or greater extent.[4] The theme still awaits a definitive study, though Howard Mumford Jones, John Parker, and the present writer have given it attention within the framework of broader studies.[5]

Historical Magazine of the Protestant Episcopal Church, XXVI (1957), 10–14; D. B. Quinn, ed., 'A list of books purchased for the Virginia Company', *Virginia Magazine of History and Biography,* LXXVII (1969), 349–50; Taylor, *Hakluyts,* II, doc. 87, pp. 492–6; Philip L. Barbour, ed., *The Jamestown voyages under the first charter, 1606–1609,* I (Hakluyt Society, 1969), 1–7, 15, 22–3, 62–4.

[1] Especially in regard to renewed interest in the North-west Passage and in one or two instances with the Virginia and East India Companies. See Parks, *Hakluyt,* pp. 206–13; Taylor, *Hakluyts,* I, 62–4; II, docs. 88, 92, pp. 497–9, 510.

[2] *Ibid.,* I, 64–5; Taylor, *Late Tudor and early Stuart geography,* pp. 56–9; Parks, *Hakluyt,* pp. 223–9. See also Barbour, *Jamestown voyages,* I, 5–7.

[3] The works are considered in various places throughout his *Hakluyt,* but see especially his list of Hakluyt's publications in appendix III, pp. 262–7. Brief listings of Hakluyt's publications, including their various editions, are also contained in Edward Godfrey Cox. *A reference guide to the literature of travel* (3 vols., Seattle, Wash., 1935–49), I–II, *passim.* Boies Penrose's *Travel and discovery in the renaissance, 1420–1620* (Cambridge, Mass., 1952) discusses many of the works in their original editions. The final chapter is an excellent summary of the whole of renaissance geographical literature.

[4] In addition to Parks, Hakluyt's propaganda motive has been most stressed in Williamson, *The ocean in English history* (Oxford, 1941), ch. 3, and Wright, *Religion and empire,* ch. 2. Taylor has tended to regard the propagandistic intent of Hakluyt's publications as somewhat overplayed. See particularly her review of Parks' *Hakluyt* in *Geographical Review,* LXXIII, 572–4.

[5] Jones, 'The colonial impulse: an analysis of the "promotion" literature of colonization', *American Philosophical Society Proceedings,* XC (1946), 131–61, much of which was incorporated and expanded in his later *O strange new world;* Parker, *Books to build an empire* (Amsterdam, 1965), *passim;* Pennington, 'The origins of English promotional literature for America, 1553–1625' (unpublished

Hakluyt's published writings readily divide themselves into two categories: his collections, including *Divers voyages* and the two editions of the *Principal navigations,* and the books from foreign sources, usually in the form of trans-lations, which he either did himself or caused to be done. The latter group has been insufficiently studied, and it is here that Parks' biography has been particularly useful, as he has shown Hakluyt's connection with a multitude of publications on overseas discovery and exploration in the period from 1580 to 1614. A few other writers have viewed all or several of his translations,[1] but for the most part they have been dealt with individually or in small groups.

John Florio's *A shorte and briefe narration* (1580), a translation from the French of the first two voyages of Jacques Cartier, was Hakluyt's first publishing effort. James Phinney Baxter and H. P. Biggar have compared this and later Cartier-Roberval accounts appearing in Florio and in Hak-luyt's collections with manuscript copies,[2] while Taylor and Frances A. Yates have discussed his relationship with Florio.[3] A somewhat later connection, that between Hakluyt and Marco-Antonio Pigafetta, whose *Itinerario* Hakluyt caused to be published in 1585, has been suggested by Franz Babinger.[4]

The Spanish, French, and Latin editions of Antonio de Espejo, René de

PhD. dissertation, University of Michigan 1962), chs. 4–8. The last two view Hakluyt's propaganda efforts as generally unsuccessful, though for different reasons.

[1] Parker, *Books to build an empire, passim;* Pennington, 'Origins of English pro-motional literature', chs. 4–5; Mood, 'The English geographers and the Anglo-American frontier in the seventeenth century', *University of California Publications in Geography,* VI (1932–44), 386–8. Reference should also be made to the various considerations of Hakluyt within the framework of the general translating activities of the day. See Mary Augusta Scott, *English translations from the Italian* (Boston, 1916), pp. 373–86, 396; Henry Thomas, 'English translations of Portuguese books before 1640', *Library,* fourth series, VII (1926), 5–8; Gustav Ungerer, 'The printing of Spanish books in Elizabethan England', *ibid.,* fifth series, XX (1965), 180–2, 211–15; Underhill, *Spanish literature in the England of the Tudors,* pp. 34–6, and especially ch. 5.

[2] Baxter, *A memoir of Jacques Cartier* (New York, 1906); Biggar, *The voyages of Jacques Cartier* (*Publications of the Public Archives of Canada,* XL, 1924).

[3] Taylor, *Hakluyts,* I, 21–2; Yates, *John Florio* (Cambridge, 1934), pp. 55–60. See also R. C. Simonini, Jr., *Italian scholarship in renaissance England* (Chapel Hill, N.C., 1952), p. 58. For a full discussion of the accounts of the two voyages, see Ganong, *Crucial maps,* pp. 248–354.

[4] 'Marcantonio Pigafetta', *Miscellanea in onore di Roberto Cessi,* II (Rome, 1958), 89–96.

Laudonnière, and Peter Martyr, respectively, for which Hakluyt was responsible during his Paris mission, as well as his English edition of Laudonnière, have received treatment from Parks, Quinn, and Taylor, all of whom see them as part of the campaign for Ralegh's Virginia.[1] *The historie of the great and mightie kingdom of China,* which Robert Parke translated from the work of Juan González de Mendoza at Hakluyt's suggestion, has been the subject of a Society edition.[2] An excellent discussion of the sources and influence of the original work (Parke's was one of forty-six editions) is contained in Donald F. Lach's *Asia in the making of Europe.*[3] There is no extended treatment of Abraham Hartwell's *A reporte of the kingdom of the Congo* (1597), translated from Filippo Pigafetta at Hakluyt's instigation.[4]

Two of the four translations from the Dutch sponsored by Hakluyt in the period from 1597 to 1609, as well as Pory's translation of Leo Afri-canus, Hakluyt's own translation of Antonio Galvano (Galvão), and Edward Grimston's translation of José de Acosta have been issued in critical editions by the Society.[5]

[1] Parks, *Hakluyt,* ch. 9; Taylor, *Hakluyts,* I, 40–41; Quinn, *Roanoke voyages,* I, 7 and *passim.* See also Francis A. MacNutt, trans. and ed., *De orbe novo,* I (New York, 1912), introduction, for an excellent discussion of Martyr and his work; and Eleanor Rosenberg, 'Giacopo Castelvetro: Italian publisher in Elizabethan England and his patrons', *Huntington Library Quarterly,* VI (1943), 119–48, especially pp. 127–32, which indicates a possible Hakluyt link with another publication intended to promote the Virginia venture.

[2] George T. Staunton, ed., *The history of the great and mighty kingdom of China* (introduction by R. H. Major; 2 vols., Hakluyt Society, 1853–54). The work does no more than suggest Hakluyt's role.

[3] Vol. I, bk 2 (Chicago, 1965), pp. 742–94; vol. II, bk I (1970), pp. 34–5.

[4] The French translation, ed, Willy Bal, *Description du royaume de Congo,* 2nd edition, Louvain and Paris, 1965, has valuable notes.

[5] C. T. Beke (ed.), *A true description of three voyages by the northeast...by Gerrit de Veer* (Hakluyt Society, London, 1853; 2nd edition, ed. Koolemans Beynan, Hakluyt Society, 1876); A. C. Burnell and P. A. Tiele, edd., *The voyage of John Huyghen van Linschoten to the East Indies* (2 vols., Hakluyt Society, 1885); Robert Brown, ed., *The history and description of Africa...[by] Leo Africanus... done into English in the year 1600, by John Pory* (3 vols., Hakluyt Society, 1896); C. R. D. Bethune, ed., *The discoveries of the world from their first original... published in England by Richard Hakluyt* (Hakluyt Society, 1862), which gives some indication of Hakluyt's editing by collating his work with an original Portuguese text, though not one used by Hakluyt; C. R. Markham, ed., *The natural & moral history of the Indies, by Father Joseph de Acosta. Reprinted from the English translated edition of Edward Grimston, 1604* (2 vols., Hakluyt Society, 1880). For the suggestion that Hakluyt may have had some connection with the last,

Hakluyt's publications on behalf of the Virginia Company have also received extensive attention. His translation of the Gentleman of Elvas' account of the Soto expedition (*Virginia richly valued*) was republished by the Society.[1] Buckingham Smith's re-translation of the original permits a comparison with the Hakluyt version.[2] There has also been some contro-versy over the reliability of the Elvas account as compared with others of the Soto expeditions.[3] The best modern edition of the Hakluyt-sponsored Erondelle translation of Marc Lescarbot's *Nova francia* is by H. P. Biggar.[4] Neither of Hakluyt's final efforts, the 1612 Michael Lok translation of Peter Martyr and the *Dialogues in the English and Malaiane languages*, have received more than cursory treatment.[5]

The weight of historical interest in Hakluyt has fallen mainly on his collections, though seldom on any one of the collections as a whole. For more than a century, the only critical edition of one of these in its entirety was John Winter Jones' edition of *Divers voyages*, published by the Hakluyt Society in 1850. The work has been superseded in its introductory material by the facsimile edition published by Theatrum Orbis Terrarum in 1967, with an introductory volume by D. B. Quinn, which analyses Hakluyt's role as editor. Several other writers have examined *Divers voyages* in detail, with particular emphasis on its promotional aspects.[6]

see Parks, *Hakluyt*, p. 217. On Hakluyt's Dutch translations, see also T. de Vries, *Holland's influence on English language and literature* (Chicago, 1916), pp. 253–60, and Parks, *Hakluyt*, pp. 164–5, 222, 264–6.

[1] William B. Rye, ed., *The discovery and conquest of Terra Florida* (Hakluyt Society, 1851), is from the second Hakluyt edition of 1611.

[2] Smith's retranslation is available in *Narratives of the career of Hernando de Soto in the conquest of Florida* (New York, 1866). There have been a number of other editions of Smith's translation. The most convenient is in F. W. Hodge and T. H. Lewis, *Spanish explorers in the southern United States, 1528–1543* (New York, 1907, reprinted, New York, 1959), pp. 127–272.

[3] It was attacked by Jared Sparks in his 'Life of Father Marquette', *Library of American Biography*, x (New York, 1873), 267–71, and R. B. Cunninghame Graham, *Hernando de Soto* (London, 1903), especially pp. 56–7. Defences of it are by Rye, *Discovery and conquest*, introduction, and E. G. Bourne, ed., *Narratives of the career of Hernando de Soto* 1 (New York, 1904), introduction, pp. vii–xvii.

[4] *Nova Francia* (New York and London, 1928). Unfortunately, the introduction and notes are of limited value.

[5] Parks, *Hakluyt*, pp. 159, 222–3, 267; Taylor, *Hakluyts*, 1, 63–4.

[6] One of the earliest examinations of *Divers voyages* was John Payne Collier, 'On Richard Hakluyt and the American discoveries', *Archaeologia*, xxxiii (1849),

The 1589 *Principall navigations* has generally been the most ignored of Hakluyt's collections. But since the Quinn–Skelton edition of 1965, it is probably the work of Hakluyt we understand the best, at least in its totality. Their work is especially valuable for its analysis of Hakluyt's source materials, many of which have a carry-over to his second edition. Even so, earlier evaluations of the first edition by Parks and Taylor should not be ignored.[1] As previously indicated, there have been no reasonably definitive evaluations of the whole of Hakluyt's second edition. Observations are confined to general comments, and again the best are by Parks and Taylor.[2]

Most Hakluyt scholarship has been confined to analysis, critique, and expansion of particular accounts or groups of accounts in his various collections. With regard to the travel relations and tracts written prior to the Elizabethan age, A. W. Pollard illustrated Mandeville by using other Hakluyt accounts on Rubruquis, Carpini, and Odoric, though without critical analysis.[3] Malcolm Letts, Josephine Waters Bennett, and Quinn have made suggestions on the version of Mandeville Hakluyt used.[4] The Beazley edition of the journeys of Carpini and Rubruquis was the beginning of the projected edition of the *Principal navigations* which was cancelled because of the forthcoming MacLehose edition.[5] The work is a detailed comparison of manuscript versions with those in the *Principal navigations*.

283–92. Modern examinations include Taylor, *Hakluyts*, I, 22–7; Parks, *Hakluyt*, pp. 68–74; Parker, *Books to build an empire*, 108–11; Pennington, 'Origins of English promotional literature', ch. 6.

[1] Parks, *Hakluyt*, ch. 10; Taylor, *Late Tudor and early Stuart geography*, ch. 2.

[2] Parks, *Hakluyt*, chs. 14–15; Taylor, *Hakluyts*, I, 54–8, and more especially *Late Tudor and early Stuart geography*, ch. 3. For other recent general evaluations, see Blacker, *Hakluyt's voyages*, introduction; W. Nelson Francis, 'Hakluyt's *Voyages*: an epic of discovery', *William and Mary Quarterly*, third series, XII (1955), 447–55.

[3] Pollard, *The travels of John Mandeville* (1900).

[4] Bennett, *The rediscovery of Sir John Mandeville* (New York, 1954), pp. 103–4, 245–6; Letts, ed., *Mandeville's travels: texts and translations*, II (Hakluyt Society, 1953), 514; Letts, *Sir John Mandeville: the man and his book* (1949), pp. 123–4; Quinn and Skelton, *Principall navigations* (1589), I (1965), xxvi–xxvii.

[5] *The texts and versions of John de Plano Carpini and William de Rubruquis as printed for the first time by Hakluyt in 1598* (Hakluyt Society, 1903). See also W. W. Rockhill, ed., *The journey of William of Rubruck...with two accounts of the earlier journey of John of Pian de Carpine* (Hakluyt Society, 1900). For the Odoric account, see Henry Yule ed., *Cathay and the way thither*, II (2nd edition, ed. Henri Cordier, Hakluyt Society, 1913).

The materials on the alleged voyages of the Zeni have been cited earlier, as have those on Madoc and Cabot. Probably the most famous of Hakluyt's early English materials are those of Robert Thorne, on which Taylor commented extensively.[1] A number of the lesser early English pieces have been covered by a variety of authors.[2]

Among the late sixteenth-century sections, the relations of English travel to Muscovy have been recognized as the fullest, and in past years their accuracy was generally unquestioned.[3] With one notable exception, even Russian writers offered no more than a few caveats.[4] Lately, however, a good deal of scepticism has arisen. T. S. Willan has pointed out that they

---

[1] *Tudor geography*, pp. 10–13 and ch. 3; 'Roger Barlow: a new chapter in early Tudor geography', *Geographical Journal*, LXXIV (1929), 157–66; *A briefe summe of geographie* (Hakluyt Society, 1932), introduction, pp. xxii–xlvi. See also Williamson, *Voyages of the Cabots*, pp. 255–67.

[2] On the King Alfred account, see Richard Hennig, *Terrae Incognitae*, II (Leiden, 1950), 202–15. Though not directly concerned with Hakluyt, two worthwhile studies of 'The libel of English policy' are George Warner, *The libelle of Englyshe polycye* (Oxford, 1926) and G. A. Holmes, 'The "Libel of English policy"', *English Historical Review*, LXXVI (1961), pp. 193–216. See also Parks, *English travelers in Italy*, pp. 148–9; G. L. Marcus, 'The first English voyages to Iceland', *Mariner's Mirror*, XLII (1956), 313–18; David W. Becker, 'An error in Hakluyt', *Notes and Queries*, CC (1955), 140–1. D. W. Prowse, *A history of Newfoundland* (London and New York, 1895), pp. 41–2; Williamson, *Voyages of the Cabots*, pp. 268–71; and Taylor in *Geographical Journal*, LXXVII, 469–70, discuss the Hakluyt version of the Hore voyage from contradictory points of view.

[3] E. Delmar Morgan and C. H. Coote, edd., *Early travels to Russia and Persia by Anthony Jenkinson and other Englishmen* (2 vols., Hakluyt Society, 1886) and Edward A. Bond, ed., *Russia at the close of the sixteenth century* (Hakluyt Society, 1856) provide some critical analysis of many of Hakluyt's Russian accounts. Armand J. Gerson, *The organization and early history of the Muscovy Company*, and E. V. Vaughan, *English trading expeditions into Asia*, both in *University of Pennsylvania Studies in the History of English Commerce in the Tudor Period* (1912) reflect the total dependence on Hakluyt as a source.

[4] J. Hamel, *England and Russia*, trans. J. S. Leigh (London, 1854) is extremely sceptical of Hakluyt and raises questions about the interpretations inherent in his documents, but Inna Lubimenko, 'England's part in the discovery of Russia', *Slavonic Review*, VI (1927), 104–18, finds the English accounts of Russia, including those in Hakluyt, more sympathetic and impartial than those of the travellers of other nations. V. O. Klyuchevskiy, *Skazaniya inostrantsev o moskovskom gosudarstvye* (Moscow, 1916), pp. 17–18, and Yu. V. Got'ye, *Angliyskiye puteshestvenniki v moskovskom gosudarstve v XVI veke* (Leningrad, 1938), pp. 16–18, tend to agree. The latter is an edition of Hakluyt's Russian accounts.

give no more than a sketchy account of the amount of trade between England and Muscovy,[1] Robert O. Lindsay has charged Hakluyt in one instance with careless, if not dishonest, editing,[2] and Karl Heinz Ruffman has seen his Russian accounts as a totally inaccurate view of the Muscovite State.[3]

With regard to the Asia relations, Lach has placed Hakluyt within the context of Asian travel literature of the day.[4] The exploits of Ralph Fitch, John Newbery, and Thomas Stevens have received the most attention.[5] The Cesare Federici account of Thomas Hickock, which Hakluyt used, has been analysed by Emilio Teza and Lach.[6] There has also been considerable interest in comparing Hakluyt's Turkish materials with other manuscript accounts.[7]

[1] 'Trade between England and Russia in the second half of the sixteenth century', *English Historical Review*, LXIII (1948), 307–21. However, Willan does defend the accuracy of Hakluyt. See his *The early history of the Russia Company* (Manchester, 1956), pp. 11–13. The same work contains valuable analysis of various Russian embassages reported by Hakluyt. See also Walter Kirchner, 'Commercial relations between Russia and Europe, 1400 to 1800', *Indiana University Publications in Russian and East European Studies,* XXXIII (1966), pp. 10–11, 252, n. 13, which claims that the exaggerated Hakluyt accounts overstress the economic importance of the White Sea trade.

[2] 'Richard Hakluyt and *Of the Russe common wealth*', *Papers of the Bibliographical Society of America,* LVII (1963), 312–27, but see pp. 475–6, above.

[3] *Das Russlandbild im England Shakespeares (Göttinger Bausteine zur Geschichtswissenschaft,* Heft VI, 1952), *passim.*

[4] *Asia in the making of Europe,* I, bk 1 (Chicago, 1965), 148–288.

[5] J. Courtenay Locke, ed., *The first Englishmen in India* (1930); William Foster, *Early travels in India, 1583–1619* (Oxford, 1921), pp. 1–47; Foster, *England's quest of eastern trade* (1933), especially pp. 79, 87–8, 106–8; Ram Chandra Prasad, *Early English travellers in India* (Delhi, 1965), pp. 1–65; H. G. Rawlinson, *British beginnings in western India, 1579–1657* (Oxford, 1920), pp. 22–9; J. Horton Ryley, *Ralph Fitch* (1899); Cecil Tragen, *Elizabethan venture* (1953), pp. 146–8; Lach, *Asia in the making of Europe,* I, bk 1, 478–82.

[6] Teza, 'I viagge de Cesare dei Fedrici e la versione inglese dell' Hitchcock', *Atti de reale instituto veneto di scienze, lettere ed arti,* eighth series, XI (1908–9), 327–37; Lach, *Asia in the making of Europe,* I, bk 1, 469–73.

[7] H. G. Rosedale, *Queen Elizabeth and the Levant Company* (1904); H. G. Rawlinson, 'The embassy of William Harborne to Constantinople, 1583–8', *Transactions of the Royal Historical Society,* fourth series, V (1922), 1–27; Albert L. Rowland, *England and Turkey: the rise of diplomatic and commercial relations (University of Pennsylvania Studies in English Commerce and Exploration in the Reign of Elizabeth,* 1924), introduction, pp. xii–xviii; Paul Wittek, 'The Turkish documents in Hakluyt's "Voyages"', *Bulletin of the Institute of Historical Research,*

The African voyages in Hakluyt have received the least attention, perhaps as Williamson has shown, because we have mistakenly believed Hakluyt reported all English efforts in that area.[1] J. W. Blake's *Europeans in West Africa, 1450–1560* is an excellent assessment of a number of Hakluyt's earlier African accounts.[2] Winthrop D. Jordan's *White over Black* argues that the African materials in Hakluyt and in Pory's translation of Leo Africanus bear a principal responsibility for establishing the prejudice against negroes in early America.[3]

The new world as it appears in Hakluyt's collections is, of course, the main area of scholarly interest. The Society's editions of the Frobisher and Davis voyages give considerable attention to Hakluyt,[4] and there have been other writings touching on these accounts.[5] Hakluyt's relations of the Gilbert and Ralegh colonization ventures have been dealt with by almost all of the authors discussed above who have written generally on Hakluyt, and there have been numerous reprints of the Virginia voyages, few or none of them of critical value before Quinn. The standard works are therefore Quinn's editions of *The voyages and colonising enterprises of Sir Humphrey Gilbert* and his *Roanoke voyages*, both of which contain very full bibliographies.

By all odds the most popular of Hakluyt's accounts are those concerning the trading voyages to Spanish America and the raiding expeditions. The

XIX (1942–43), 121–39; William A. Jackson, 'Humphrey Dyson's library, or, some observations on the survival of books', *Bibliographical Society of America Papers*, XLIII (1949), 285–6; Akdes N. Kurat, *Türk-Ingiliz münasabetlerinin baslangici ve gelismesi (1553–1610)* (Ankara, 1953); Susan A. Skilliter, 'Three letters from the Ottoman "Sultana" Safiye to Queen Elizabeth I', in S. M. Stern, ed., *Documents from Islamic chanceries* (Oxford, 1965), pp. 120–33.

[1] 'England and the opening of the Atlantic', in *Cambridge History of the British Empire,* edd. Rose *et al.,* I, 44. Williamson claims Hakluyt reported no more than one-quarter of the Guinea voyages.

[2] (2 vols., Hakluyt Society, 1942).

[3] (Chapel Hill, N.C., 1968); pp. 3–43, 594–5.

[4] Richard Collison, ed., *The three voyages of Martin Frobisher in search of a passage to Cathaia and India by the north-west, A.D. 1576–8* (Hakluyt Society, 1867); Vilhjalmur Stefansson and Eloise McCaskill, *The three voyages of Martin Frobisher,* 2 vols. (1938); A. H. Markham, ed., *The voyages and works of John Davis* (Hakluyt Society, 1880).

[5] See especially Parks in *Huntington Library Quarterly,* II, 59–65. Taylor, 'The northern passages', *The great age of discovery,* ed. A. P. Newton (1932), pp. 201–6, deals with the influence of the polar theories ascribed by Hakluyt to Nicholas of Lynn.

general view of early historians on these ventures is best examined in Payne and Beazley.[1] Julian Corbett assessed some of the Hakluyt accounts of the Drake voyages,[2] while the circumnavigation as reported in the two editions of the *Principal navigations* has been analysed by a number of writers.[3] C. R. Markham edited the various voyages of the Hawkins family as reported in Hakluyt[4] and the adventures of the survivors of the third slaving expedition, and particularly those of David Ingram, have been studied extensively.[5]

[1] Payne, *Voyages of the Elizabethan seamen* (1893–1900 ed.), introduction to vols. I and II and to individual voyages; Beazley, *Voyages and travels* (1964 ed.), introductions to vols. I and II.

[2] Corbett, *Drake and the Tudor navy* (2 vols., 1899) I, 406–7; II, appendices, 411, 426–7; Corbett, ed., *Papers relating to the navy during the Spanish War, 1585–1587,* Navy Records Society XI (1898).

[3] Wagner, *Sir Francis Drake's voyage around the World,* especially pp. 232–45, 290; Zelia Nuttall, ed., *New light on Drake* (Hakluyt Society, 1914), pp. 13–14, 149, 256–71; John W. Robertson, *Francis Drake & other early explorers along the Pacific coast* (San Francisco, 1927), especially pp. 24–5, 97–100, 133–5, 163–7, 171–3; E. G. R. Taylor, 'More light on Drake', *Mariner's Mirror,* XVI (1930), 138–9; Willis Holmes Kerr, 'The treatment of Drake's circumnavigation in Hakluyt's "Voyages"', *Bibliographical Society of America Papers,* XXXIV (1940), 281–302; K. R. Andrews, 'The aims of Drake's expedition of 1577–80', *American Historical Review,* LXXII (1968), 724–41.

[4] *The Hawkins' voyages during the reigns of Henry VIII, Queen Elizabeth and James I* (Hakluyt Society, 1878), pp. 3–81.

[5] Opinions of Ingram's journey and the credence to be given his account have tended to improve. See B. F. De Costa, 'Ingram's journey through North America in 1567–69', *Magazine of American History,* IX, (1883), 168–76; Williamson, *Hawkins* (1927), pp. 837–8, is scornful; John Bartlett Brebner, *The explorers of North America* (New York, 1933), pp. 142–5, sees the journey as an important fraud; Quinn, *Gilbert,* I, 64–5, is hostile; Herbert Wendt, *In search of Adam,* trans. James Cleogh (Boston, 1956), pp. 525–6, E. deGolyer, *The journey of three Englishmen across Texas in 1568* (El Paso, Texas, 1947), Rayner Unwin, *The defeat of John Hawkins* (New York and London, 1960), pp. 293–312, are favourable; D. B. Quinn and T. Dunbabin, *Dictionary of Canadian Biography,* I (1965), 380–1, are sceptical. S. E. Morison's view in *The European discovery of America: the northern voyages* (New York and London, 1971), pp. 497–8, 489, that there is something in it, but not too much, probably reflects current opinion. The relations of the captured seamen whose accounts appear in Hakluyt are dealt with in the light of Spanish documents in Frank Aydelotte, 'Elizabethan seamen in Mexico and ports of the Spanish Main', *American Historical Review,* XLVIII (1942), 1–19; P. E. H. Hair, 'An Irishman before the Mexican inquisition, 1574–5', *Irish Historical Studies,* XVII (1971),

Several authors have examined various other accounts.[1]

Much of the best scholarship of recent years has been done in searching out and analysing Hakluyt's omissions in regard to these voyages. The works of Gordon Connell-Smith,[2] I. A. Wright,[3] and K. R. Andrews[4] have been especially valuable in rounding out the *Principal navigations,* and have therefore made useful suggestions concerning Hakluyt's editing methods. Several others have also contributed on a lesser scale.[5] It is an area which will undoubtedly continue to make a significant contribution to the re-evaluation of Richard Hakluyt.

297–319; Julio Jiménez Rueda, *Corsarios franceses e ingleses en la Inquisición de la Nueva España, siglo XVI* (Mexico City, 1945). Spanish versions of the principal narratives from Hakluyt on Mexico are in Joaquín García Icazbalceta, ed. and trans., *Relaciones de varios viajeros Ingleses en la ciudad de Mexico y otros lugares de la Nueva España* (Madrid, 1963). On Robert Tomson, see G. R. G. Conway, ed., *An Englishman and the Mexican Inquisition, 1556–1560* (Mexico City, 1927), which finds the Hakluyt version accurate in the light of other evidence.

[1] Taylor, *Troublesome voyage of Captain Edward Fenton;* C. R. Markham, *Voyages of Sir James Lancaster,* pp. 1–56; William Foster, ed.; *The voyages of Sir James Lancaster to Brazil and the East Indies, 1591–1603* (Hakluyt Society, 1940), introduction, pp. xxiii, 1–74; C. Lethbridge Kingsford, ed., 'The taking of the *Madre de Dios*', *Miscellany,* II (N.R.S., 1912), introduction, 87–98. On the Cadiz expedition, see Charles E. Armstrong, 'The "Voyage to Cadiz" in the second edition of Hakluyt's "Voyages"', *Bibliographical Society of America Papers,* XLIX (1955), 254–62; Julian Corbett, *The successors of Drake* (London and New York, 1900), appendix, pp. 439–45.

[2] 'English merchants trading to the New World in the early sixteenth century', *Bulletin of the Institute of Historical Research,* XXIII (1950), 53–67; 'Robert Reneger: precursor de Drake', *Anuario de Estudios Americanos,* VII (1955), 73–93; *Forerunners of Drake: a study of English trade with Spain in the early Tudor period* (1954), especially introduction, pp. xii–xiv.

[3] *Spanish documents concerning English voyages to the Caribbean, 1527–1568* (Hakluyt Society, 1929); *Documents concerning English voyages to the Spanish Main, 1569–1580* (Hakluyt Society, 1932); *Further English voyages to Spanish America, 1583–1594* (Hakluyt Society, 1951).

[4] 'New light on Hakluyt', *Mariner's Mirror,* XXXVII (1951), 299–308; *English privateering voyages to the West Indies, 1588–1595* (Hakluyt Society, 1959); *Elizabethan privateering* (Cambridge, 1964); *Drake's voyages* (1967); *The last voyage of Drake and Hawkins* (Hakluyt Society, 1972).

[5] R. G. Marsden, 'Voyage of the "Barbara" of London to Brazil in 1540', *English Historical Review,* XXIV (1909), 96–100; T. S. Willan, *Studies in Elizabethan foreign trade* (Manchester, 1959), pp. 5–9, 98–106; T. N. Marsh, 'An unpublished Hakluyt manuscript?', *New England Quarterly,* XXXV (1962), 247–52; Quinn in *Canadian Historical Review,* XLIII, 328–43.

29
Works published by the Hakluyt Society 1846-1973

arranged by E. L. C. Mullins[1]

Hakluyt Society, First Series

[1]   The observations of Sir Richard Hawkins, knt., in his voyage into the South Sea in the year 1593. Reprinted from the edition of 1622. Edited by C. R. Drinkwater Bethune. 1847.

The text edited 'with only such slight alterations as were necessary where the sense of the author had been obviously marred by a misprint'. For second edition see 57 below.

[2]   Select letters of Christopher Columbus, with other original documents, relating to his four voyages to the New World. Translated and edited by R. H. Major. 1847.

Five letters by Columbus describing his first, third, and fourth voyages; another by Dr. Chanca, physician, descriptive of the second voyage; and an extract from the will of Diego Mendez, one of Columbus's officers on the fourth voyage. With Spanish texts. For second edition see 43 below; for third edition see Second Series 65, 70 below.

[3]   The discovery of the large, rich, and beautiful empire of Guiana, with a relation of the great and golden city of Manoa (which the Spaniards call El Dorado), etc., performed in the year 1595, by Sir W. Raleigh, knt., ...Reprinted from the edition of 1596, with some unpublished documents relative to that country. Edited by Sir Robert H. Schomburgk. 1848.

With Anon. 'Of the voyage for Guiana', probably written in 1596, and Ralegh's journal of the second voyage, 1617-18. Typographical errors of the 1596 text have been corrected.

[4]   Sir Francis Drake his voyage, 1595, by Thomas Maynarde, together with the Spanish account of Drake's attack on Puerto Rico. Edited by W. D. Cooley. 1849.

With translation of the Spanish document.

---

[1] This material © the Royal Historical Society and Mr Mullins.

[5]   Narratives of voyages towards the north-west, in search of a passage
to Cathay and India, 1496 to 1631, with selections from the early records of
the Honourable the East India Company and from MSS in the British
Museum. [Edited by] Thomas Rundall. 1849.
   Accounts of the voyages of Cabot, Davis, Frobisher, and others, drawn
   chiefly from the works of Hakluyt, Purchas, Harris, and Foxe.

[6]   The historie of travaile into Virginia Britannia, expressing the cosmographie and comodities of the country, togither with the manners and
customes of the people, gathered and observed as well by those who went
first thither as collected by William Strachey, gent., the first secretary of the
colony. Now first edited by R. H. Major. 1849.
   From B.M., Sloane MS 1622.

[7]   Divers voyages touching the discovery of America and the islands
adjacent, collected and published by Richard Hakluyt, prebendary of
Bristol, in the year 1582. Edited, with notes and an introduction, by John
Winter Jones. 1850.
   The original printed text.

[8]   Memorials of the empire of Japon in the 16 and 17 centuries. Edited,
with notes, by Thomas Rundall. 1850.
   Documents, including a description of Japan in the sixteenth century
   and the letters of William Adams, 1611–17.

[9]   The discovery and conquest of Terra Florida by Don Fernando de
Soto and six hundred Spaniards his followers, written by a gentleman of
Elvas, employed in all the action, and translated out of Portuguese by
Richard Hakluyt. Reprinted from the edition of 1611. Edited, with notes
and an introduction and a translation of a narrative of the expedition by
Luis Hernández de Biedma, factor to the same, by William B. Rye. 1851.
   The translation of Hernández de Biedma's narrative is made from
   Ternaux-Compans' *Recueil de pièces sur la Floride* (Paris, 1841).

[10]   Notes upon Russia, being a translation of the earliest account of that
country, entitled *Rerum Muscoviticarum commentarii*, by the Baron Sigismund
von Herberstein, ambassador from the court of Germany to the grand prince
Vasiley Ivanovich, in the years 1517 and 1526. Translated and edited, with
notes and an introduction, by R. H. Major, Vol. I. 1851.
   The first edition of the *Commentarii* appeared in Vienna in 1549, but it is
   not clear which edition was used for this translation. Continued in 12
   below.

[11] The geography of Hudson's Bay, being the remarks of Captain W. Coats, in many voyages to that locality, between the years 1727 and 1751; with an appendix containing extracts from the log of Capt. Middleton on his voyage for the discovery of the north-west passage in H.M.S. *Furnace*, in 1741–2. Edited by John Barrow. 1852.

[12] Notes upon Russia...Vol. II. 1852.
With an appendix of documents. translated and in part collected by Richard Eden and printed from the 1577 edition of his *History of travayle in the West and East Indies*, revised by Richard Willes.

[13] A true description of three voyages by the north-east towards Cathay and China, undertaken by the Dutch in the years 1594, 1595, and 1596, by Gerrit de Veer. Published at Amsterdam in the year 1598, and in 1609 translated into English by William Phillip. Edited by Charles T. Beke. 1853.
With an appendix of documents printed by Hakluyt and Purchas. See also 54 below.

[14] The history of the great and mighty kingdom of China and the situation thereof, compiled by the padre Juan González de Mendoza, and now reprinted from the early translation of R. Parke. Edited by Sir George T. Staunton, with an introduction by R. H. Major. [Vol. I.] 1852.
From the 1588 black-letter edition, after the Madrid edition, 1586.

[15] The history of the great and mighty kingdom of China....Vol. II. 1854.

[16] The world encompassed by Sir Francis Drake; being his next voyage to that to Nombre de Dios. Collated with an unpublished manu-script of Francis Fletcher, chaplain to the expedition. [Edited] with appen-dices illustrative of the same voyage, and introduction, by W. S. W. Vaux. 1854.
From the 1628 edition 'collected out of the notes of Master Francis Fletcher', collated with British Museum, Sloane MS 61.

[17] History of the two Tartar conquerors of China, including the two journeys into Tartary of Father Ferdinand Verbiest in the suite of the Emperor Kang-hi, from the French of Père Pierre Joseph d'Orléans, of the company of Jesus; to which is added Father Pereira's journey into Tartary in the suite of the same emperor, from the Dutch of Nicolaas Witsen.

Translated and edited by the Earl of Ellesmere, with an introduction by R. H. Major. 1854.

The first is from the 1688, Paris, edition; the narrative of Father Pereira's journey and the text of two letters by Father Verbiest are from the 1692, Amsterdam, edition.

[18] A collection of documents on Spitzbergen and Greenland, comprising a translation from F. Martens' *Voyage to Spitzbergen,* a translation from Isaac de la Peyrère's *Histoire du Groenland,* and *God's power and providence in the preservation of eight men in Greenland nine months and twelve dayes.* Edited by Adam White. 1855.

The first is from an English collection published in 1694, the second from the *Relation du Groenland* (Paris, 1663), the third is the text of Edward Pelham's tract (London, 1631).

[19] The voyage of Sir Henry Middleton to Bantam and the Maluco islands, being the second voyage set forth by the governor and company of merchants of London trading into the East-Indies, from the edition of 1606. Annotated and edited by Bolton Corney. 1854.

The 1606 title-page begins: *The last East-Indian voyage.* The appendix includes commissions, letters of James I addressed to foreign rulers, and other documents. See also Second Series 88 below.

[20] Russia at the close of the sixteenth century, comprising the treatise *Of the Russe common wealth,* by Dr. Giles Fletcher, and the travels of Sir Jerome Horsey, knt., now for the first time printed entire from his own manuscript. Edited by Edward A. Bond. 1856.

The first is a reprint of the London, 1591, edition, the second relates to the late sixteenth century. With additional documents descriptive of Russia and the missions of the two writers.

[21] History of the New World, by Girolamo Benzoni, of Milan, shewing his travels in America, from A.D. 1541 to 1556, with some particulars of the island of Canary. Now first translated, and edited by W. H. Smyth. 1857.

Text originally published at Venice, 1572.

[22] India in the fifteenth century, being a collection of narratives of voyages to India in the century preceding the Portuguese discovery of the Cape of Good Hope, from Latin, Persian, Russian, and Italian sources, now first translated into English. Edited, with an introduction, by R. H. Major. 1857.

The travels of Abd-er-Razzak, 1442, Nicoló Conti, Athanasius Nikitin, and Hieronimo di Santo Stefano.

[23] Narrative of a voyage to the West Indies and Mexico in the years 1599–1602, with maps and illustrations, by Samuel Champlain. Translated from the original and unpublished manuscript, with a biographical notice and notes, by Alice Wilmere. Edited by Norton Shaw. 1859.
Text written c. 1602.

[24] Expeditions into the valley of the Amazons, 1539, 1540, 1639. Translated and edited, with notes, by Clements R. Markham. 1859.
The expeditions of Gonzalo Pizarro, Francisco de Orellana, and Father Cristóbal de Acuña.

[25] Early voyages to Terra Australis, now called Australia: a collection of documents, and extracts from early manuscript maps, illustrative of the history of discovery of the coasts of that vast island, from the beginning of the sixteenth century to the time of Captain Cook. Edited, with an introduction, by R. H. Major. 1859.
From Spanish and Dutch sources and relating to Spanish and Dutch enterprises. With a separate supplementary pamphlet on the discovery of Australia by the Portuguese in 1601, by the same author, reprinted from Archaeologia, XXXVIII.

[26] Narrative of the embassy of Ruy González de Clavijo to the court of Timour, at Samarcand, A.D. 1403–6. Translated, for the first time, with notes, a preface, and an introductory life of Timour Beg, by Clements R. Markham. 1859.

[27] Henry Hudson the navigator: the original documents in which his career is recorded. Collected, partly translated, and annotated, with an introduction, by G. M. Asher. 1860.

[28] The expedition of Pedro de Ursua and Lope de Aguirre in search of El Dorado and Omagua in 1560–1. Translated from Fray Pedro Simón's Sixth historical notice of the conquest of Tierra Firme by William Bollaert. With an introduction by Clements R. Markham. 1861.
From the Spanish text, published at Cuenca, 1627.

[29] The life and acts of Don Alonzo Enríquez de Guzmán, a knight of Seville, of the order of Santiago, A.D. 1518 to 1543. Translated from an original and inedited manuscript in the National Library at Madrid, with notes and an introduction, by Clements R. Markham. 1862.
Includes accounts of travel in Europe and Peru.

[30] The discoveries of the world, from their first original unto the year of Our Lord, 1555, by Antonio Galvano, governor of Ternate. Corrected,

quoted, and published in England, by Richard Hakluyt, 1601. Now reprinted, with the original Portuguese text, and edited by [C. R. D.] Bethune. 1862.

[31] Mirabilia descripta. The wonders of the east, by Friar Jordanus, of the order of preachers and bishop of Columbum in India the Greater, c. 1330. Translated from the Latin original, as published at Paris in 1839, in the *Recueil de voyages et de mémoires,* of the Society of Geography, with the addition of a commentary, by Henry Yule. 1863.

[32] The travels of Ludovico di Varthema in Egypt, Syria, Arabia Deserta and Arabia Felix, in Persia, India, and Ethiopia, A.D. 1503 to 1508. Translated from the original Italian edition of 1510, with a preface, by John Winter Jones, and edited, with notes and an introduction, by George Percy Badger. 1863.

[33] The travels of Pedro de Cieza de León, A.D. 1532–50, contained in the first part of his chronicle of Peru. Translated and edited, with notes and an introduction, by Clements R. Markham. 1864.
    From the Antwerp, 1554, edition. Continued from another source in 68 below.

[34] Narrative of the proceedings of Pedrarias Dávila in the provinces of Tierra Firme or Castilla del Oro, and of the discovery of the South Sea and the coasts of Peru and Nicaragua, written by the *adelantado* Pascual de Andagoya. Translated and edited, with notes and an introduction, by Clements R. Markham. 1865.
    Text written c. 1514.

[35] A description of the coasts of east Africa and Malabar in the beginning of the sixteenth century, by Duarte Barbosa, a Portuguese. Translated from an early Spanish manuscript in the Barcelona library, with notes and a preface, by the Hon. Henry E. J. Stanley. 1866.
    Text written c. 1514. See Second Series 44, 49 below.

[36] Cathay and the way thither. Being a collection of medieval notices of China, translated and edited by Henry Yule, with a preliminary essay on the intercourse between China and the western nations previous to the discovery of the Cape route. Vol. I. 1866.
    Containing the travels of Friar Odoric of Pordenone, 1316–30, and letters and reports from missionary friars from Cathay and India, 1292–1338, in English translation.

[37]   Cathay and the way thither. Vol. II. 1866.
Contemporary notices of Cathay under the Mongols, from Rashíduddín; Pegolotti's notices of the land route to Cathay and of Asiatic trade in the 14th century; Marignolli's recollections of eastern travel; Ibn Batuta's travels in Bengal and China; Benedict Goës' journey from Agra to Cathay; all in English translation, with Latin and Italian texts of Odoric's narrative. But see Second Series 33, 37, 38, 41 below.

[38]   The three voyages of Martin Frobisher, in search of a passage to Cathaia and India by the north-west, A.D. 1576–8, reprinted from the first edition of Hakluyt's *Voyages,* with selections from manuscript documents in the British Museum and State Paper Office. By Richard Collinson. 1867.
With Edward Sellman's account of the third voyage, and a list of Frobisher relics deposited with the Royal Geographical Society, by C. F. Hall. The additional documents relate to numerous aspects of the financing and fitting out of the expeditions.

[39]   The Philippine Islands, Moluccas, Siam, Cambodia, Japan, and China, at the close of the sixteenth century, by Antonio De Morga. Translated from the Spanish, with notes and a preface, and a letter from Luis Vaez de Torres describing his voyage through the Torres straits, by the Hon. Henry E. J. Stanley. 1868.
From a transcription of the Mexico, 1609, edition. The appendix includes a brief continuation of the history of the Philippines, particularly with regard to government and commerce, to 1868. See Second Series 140 below.

[40]   The fifth letter of Hernán Cortés to the Emperor Charles V, containing an account of his expedition to Honduras. Translated from the original Spanish by Pascual de Gayangos. 1868.
A.D. 1526.

[41]   First part of the royal commentaries of the Yncas, by the Ynca Garcillasso de la Vega. Translated and edited, with notes and an introduction, by Clements R. Markham. Vol. I: Containing Books I, II, III, and IV. 1869.
From the Lisbon, 1609, edition. Continued in 45 below.

[42]   The three voyages of Vasco da Gama, and his viceroyalty. From the *Lendas da India* of Gaspar Correa; accompanied by original documents. Translated from the Portuguese, with notes and an introduction, by Henry E. J. Stanley. 1869.
The additional documents, mainly letters and reports to the king of Portugal, are in Portuguese.

[43]   Select letters of Christopher Columbus...Second edition. 1870.
A revised translation of the documents in 2 above, with the editor's reply to Froude's strictures in the *Westminster Review* (1852), and in his *Short studies on great subjects*, vol. II.

[44]   History of the Imâms and Seyyids of 'Omân, by Salîl-ibn-Razîk, from A.D. 661–1856. Translated from the original Arabic and edited, with notes, appendices, and an introduction, continuing the history down to 1870, by George Percy Badger. 1871.

[45]   First part of the royal commentaries of the Yncas....Vol. II: Containing Books V, VI, VII, VIII, and IX. 1871.

[46]   The Canarian, or, book of the conquest and conversion of the Canarians in the year 1402, by Messire Jean de Bethencourt, kt., lord of the manors of Bethencourt, Reville, etc., councillor and chamberlain in ordinary to Charles V and Charles VI, composed by Pierre Bontier, monk, and Jean le Verrier, priest. Translated and edited, with notes and an introduction, by Richard Henry Major. 1872.
With fifteenth century French text.

[47]   Reports on the discovery of Peru I: Report of Francisco de Xeres, secretary to Francisco Pizarro. II: Report of Miguel de Astete on the expedition to Pachacamac. III: Letter of Hernando Pizarro to the Royal Audience of Santo Domingo. IV: Report of Pedro Sancho on the partition of the ransom of Atahuallpa. Translated and edited, with notes and an introduction, by Clements R. Markham. 1872.
Documents, *c.* 1533.

[48]   Narratives of the rites and laws of the Yncas. Translated from the original Spanish manuscripts, and edited, with notes and an introduction, by Clements R. Markham. 1873.
By Cristobál de Molina, *c.* 1570–84, Juan de Santa Cruz (an Indian), *c.* 1620, Francisco de Avila, 1608, and Polo de Ondegardo, *c.* 1560.

[49a]   Travels to Tana and Persia, by Josafa Barbaro and Ambrogio Contarini. Translated from the Italian by William Thomas, clerk of the council to Edward VI, and by S. A. Roy, and edited, with an introduction, by Lord Stanley of Alderley. 1873.
[49b]   A narrative of Italian travels in Persia in the fifteenth and sixteenth centuries. Translated and edited by Charles Grey. 1873.
Bound together, separately paginated. The second contains accounts by Caterino Zeno, Giovan Maria Angiolello, Vincentio d'Alessandri, and an unknown merchant.

[50]   The voyages of the Venetian brothers Nicolò and Antonio Zeno, to the northern seas in the 14th century, comprising the latest known accounts of the lost colony of Greenland, and of the north-men in America before Columbus. Translated and edited, with notes and an introduction, by Richard Henry Major. 1873.

   With the Italian text of the Zenos' narrative, and the Danish and Latin texts of Ivar Bardsen's description of Greenland in the fourteenth century, and English translation.

51. The captivity of Hans Stade of Hesse, in A.D. 1547–1555, among the wild tribes of eastern Brazil. Translated by Albert Tootal and annotated by Richard F. Burton. 1874.

   From the 1557, Marburg, edition.

52. The first voyage round the world, by Magellan. Translated from the accounts of Pigafetta and other contemporary writers. Accompanied by original documents, with notes and an introduction, by Lord Stanley of Alderley. 1874.

   Includes the log-book of Francisco Alvo or Alvaro, Pigafetta's treatise on navigation and his account of the voyage, Gaspar Correa's account, other anonymous narratives, and documents relating to the cost and other aspects of the expedition.

53. The commentaries of the great Afonso Dalboquerque, second viceroy of India. Translated from the Portuguese edition of 1774, with notes and an introduction, by Walter de Gray Birch. [Vol. I.] 1875.

   Continued in 55, 62, 69 below.

54. The three voyages of William Barents to the Arctic regions, 1594, 1595, and 1596, by Gerrit de Veer. First edition by Charles T. Beke, 1853. Second edition, with an introduction, by Koolemans Beynen. 1876.

55. The commentaries of the great Afonso Dalboquerque... Vol. II. 1877.

   Part ii of the 1774 edition.

56. The voyages of Sir James Lancaster, kt., to the East Indies, with abstracts of journals of voyages to the East Indies, during the seventeenth century, preserved in the India Office, and the voyage of Captain John Knight, 1606, to seek the north-west passage. Edited by Clements R. Markham. 1877.

   The abstracts relate to the voyages of Keeling and Hawkins, Sharpie, Sir Henry Middleton, Thomas Love, Nicholas Downton, and Ralph Cross. There is a calendar of ships' journals of the seventeenth century and a list of ships employed by the East India Company in the same period. See Second Series 85 below.

57. The Hawkins' voyages during the reigns of Henry VIII, Queen Elizabeth, and James I. Edited, with an introduction, by Clements R. Markham. 1878.

A new edition of 1 above, with narratives of the voyages of Sir Richard Hawkins' grandfather William, of his father Sir John, and of his cousin William Hawkins, from MSS and printed editions.

58. The bondage and travels of Johan Schiltberger, a native of Bavaria, in Europe, Asia, and Africa, 1396–1427. Translated from the Heidelberg MS edited in 1859 by Karl Friedrich Neumann, by J. Buchan Telfer, with notes by P. Bruun, and a preface, introduction and notes by the translator and editor. 1879.

59[a]. The voyages and works of John Davis, the navigator. Edited, with an introduction and notes, by Albert Hastings Markham. 1880.

Includes *The worldes hydrographical description* (1595), *The seamans secrets* (1607), a list of works on navigation available before and during the reign of Elizabeth, and her letters patent to Adrian Gilbert and others for the exploration of the north-west passage.

59[b] The map of the world, A.D. 1600, called by Shakspere 'the new map, with the augmentation of the Indies', to illustrate the voyages of John Davis. 1880.

Bound separately, with notes by C. H. Coote.

60. The natural and moral history of the Indies, by Father Joseph de Acosta. Reprinted from the English translated edition of Edward Grimston, 1604, and edited, with notes and an introduction, by Clements R. Markham. Vol. 1: The natural history (Books I, II, III, and IV). 1880.

Concerned chiefly with Mexico and Peru. Pagination of this and the following is continuous.

61. The natural and moral history of the Indies....Vol. II: The moral history (Books V, VI, and VII). 1880.

62. The commentaries of the great Afonso Dalboquerque....Vol. III. 1880.

Part iii of the 1774 edition. With descriptions of Malacca and Goa transcribed from Pedro Barretto de Resende's *Livro do estado da India oriental*.

63. The voyages of William Baffin, 1612–1622. Edited, with notes and an introduction, by Clements R. Markham. 1881.

From narratives and journals by John Gatonbe, Robert Fotherby, and others, with Baffin's letters, journals, and other observations, and various treatises on the probability of a north-west passage.

64. Narrative of the Portuguese embassy to Abyssinia during the years 1520–1527, by Father Francisco Alvarez. Translated from the Portuguese, and edited, with notes and an introduction, by Lord Stanley of Alderley. 1881.

65. The historye of the Bermudaes or Summer islands. Edited, from a MS in the Sloane collection, British Museum, by Sir J. Henry Lefroy. 1882.

A.D. 1609–22. By Nathaniel Butler. Additional documents include a note on constitutional procedure at the first general assembly held at St George's, 1 August 1620.

66. Diary of Richard Cocks, Cape-merchant in the English factory in Japan, 1615–1622, with correspondence. Edited by Edward Maunde Thompson. Vol. I. 1883.

Ends December 1617. Continued to 1622 in the following, with Cocks' correspondence with the East India Company and others.

67. Diary of Richard Cocks...Vol. II. 1883.

68. The second part of the chronicle of Peru by Pedro de Cieza de León. Translated and edited, with notes and an introduction, by Clements R. Markham. 1883.

Continues the narrative in 33 above.

69. The commentaries of the great Afonso Dalboquerque...Vol. IV. 1884.

Part iv of the 1774 edition. With Portuguese descriptions of places and fortresses in Portuguese India, and a pedigree of Albuquerque from British Museum MSS.

70. The voyage of John Huyghen van Linschoten to the East Indies, from the old English translation of 1598. The first book, containing his description of the East. Vol. I. Edited by Arthur Coke Burnell. 1885.

71. The voyage of John Huyghen van Linschoten...Vol. II. Edited by P. A. Tiele. 1885.

72. Early voyages and travels to Russia and Persia by Anthony Jenkinson and other Englishmen, with some account of the first intercourse of the English with Russia and Central Asia by way of the Caspian Sea. Edited by E. Delmar Morgan and C. H. Coote. Vol. I. 1886.

> From the MSS of Jenkinson and other agents of the Muscovy Company in the second half of the sixteenth century, and including correspondence between Elizabeth I and Ivan IV, and reports to Cecil and the council.

73. Early voyages and travels to Russia and Persia...Vol. II. 1886.

74. The diary of William Hedges, esq., afterwards Sir William Hedges, during his agency in Bengal, as well as on his voyage out and return overland, 1681–1687. Transcribed, with introductory notes, etc., by R. Barlow, and illustrated by copious extracts from unpublished records, etc., by Henry Yule. Vol. I: The diary, with index. 1887.

> Continued in 75, 78 below.

75. The diary of William Hedges, esq....Vol. II, containing notices regarding Sir William Hedges, documentary memoirs of Job Charnock, and other biographical and miscellaneous illustrations of the time in India. 1888.

76. The voyage of François Pyrard, of Laval, to the East Indies, the Maldives, the Moluccas, and Brazil. Translated into English from the third French edition of 1619, and edited, with notes, by Albert Gray, assisted by H. C. P. Bell. Vol. I. 1887.

> A.D. 1601 – arrival at Goa, 1608. Continued in 77, 80 below.

77. The voyage of François Pyrard....Vol. II, pt. I. 1888.

> A.D. 1608 – departure from Goa, 1610.

78. The diary of William Hedges, esq....Vol. III, containing documentary contributions to a biography of Thomas Pitt, governor of Fort St George; with collections on the early history of the Company's settlement in Bengal; and on early charts and topography of the Húglí river. 1889.

> With pedigree of Pitt of Blandford St Mary and Pitt of Stratfieldsay, and index to vols. II and III.

79[a]. Tractatus de globis et eorum usu. A treatise descriptive of the globes constructed by Emery Molyneux, and published in 1592, by Robert Hues. Edited, with annotated indices and an introduction, by Clements R. Markham. 1889.

79[b] Sailing directions for the circumnavigation of England, and for a voyage to the straits of Gibraltar, from a 15th century MS. Edited, with an account of the MS, by James Gairdner, and a glossary by E. Delmar Morgan. 1889.

> Bound together, separately paginated. The first contains the text of the English translation, *A learned treatise of globes* by John Chilmead (1638), (the translation 'is usually attributed to Edmund Chilmead with apparent corrections'); the title-page of the Latin original is dated 1594.

80. The voyage of François Pyard...Vol. II, pt. 2. 1890.

> A.D. 1610-11, the return to France. With treatise on animals, trees, and fruits, and advice upon the voyage to the East Indies.

81. The conquest of the river Plate, 1535-1555. I: Voyage of Ulrich Schmidt to the rivers La Plata and Paraguai, from the original German edition, 1567. II: The commentaries of Alvar Núñez Cabeza de Vaca, from the original Spanish edition, 1555. Translated, with notes and an introduction, by Luís L. Domínguez. 1891.

82. The voyage of François Leguat, of Bresse, to Rodriquez, Mauritius, Java, and the Cape of Good Hope. Transcribed from the first English edition [1708]. Edited and annotated by Pasfield Oliver. Vol. I. 1891.

> A.D. 1689-93. Continued for 1693-8 in the following.

83. The voyage of François Leguat...Vol. II. 1891.

84. The travels of Pietro della Valle in India. From the old English translation of 1664, by G. Havers. Edited, with a life of the author, an introduction and notes, by Edward Grey. [Vol. II.] 1892.

> Letters 1-3, 1623. Letters 4-8, 1623-4, are in the following.

85. The travels of Pietro della Valle in India. Vol. II. 1892.

86. The journal of Christopher Columbus during his first voyage, 1492-93, and documents relating to the voyages of John Cabot and Gaspar Corte Real. Translated, with notes and an introduction, by Clements R. Markham. 1893.

> With Paolo Toscanelli's sailing directions in letters to Columbus, and documents. relating to Sebastian Cabot.

87. Early voyages and travels in the Levant. I: The diary of Master Thomas Dallam, 1599-1600. II: Extracts from the diaries of Dr. John Covel, 1670-1679. With some account of the Levant Company of Turkey merchants. Edited, with an introduction and notes, by J. Theodore Bent. 1893.

88. The voyages of Captain Luke Foxe, of Hull, and Captain Thomas James, of Bristol, in search of a north-west passage, in 1631-32; with narratives of the earlier north-west voyages of Frobisher, Davis, Weymouth, Hall, Knight, Hudson, Button, Gibbons, Bylot, Baffin, Hawkridge, and others. Edited, with notes and an introduction, by Miller Christy. Vol. 1. 1894.

Containing part of the text of *North-west Fox* (London, 1635).

89. The voyages of Captain Luke Foxe, of Hull, and Captain Thomas James, of Bristol....Vol. II. 1894.

North-west Fox concluded, and the text of *The strange and dangerous voyage of Captaine Thomas James* (London, 1633), with documents relating to early voyages to Hudson's Bay and the north-west.

90. The letters of Amerigo Vespucci and other documents illustrative of his career. Translated, with notes and an introduction, by Clements R. Markham. 1894.

91. Narratives of the voyages of Pedro Sarmiento de Gamboa to the straits of Magellan. Translated and edited, with notes and an introduction, by Clements R. Markham. 1895.

A.D. 1579-89.

92. The history and description of Africa and of the notable things therein contained, written by Al-Hassan Ibn-Mohammed Al-Wezaz Al-Fasi, a Moor, baptised as Giovanni Leone, but better known as Leo Africanus. Done into English in the year 1600 by John Pory, and now edited, with an introduction and notes, by Robert Brown. Vol. I. 1896.

Containing Book I of the original. Vol. II below contains Books II-IV, vol. III contains Books V-IX and Pory's additions.

93. The history and description of Africa...Vol. II. 1896.

94. The history and description of Africa...Vol. III. 1896.

95. The chronicle of the discovery and conquest of Guinea, written by Gómes Eannes de Azurara. Now first done into English by Charles Raymond Beazley and Edgar Prestage. Vol. 1: Chapters 1-40, with an introduction on the life and writings of the chronicler. 1896.

Written *c.* 1450. Concluded in 100 below.

96. Danish Arctic expeditions, 1605 to 1620. In two books Book I: The Danish expeditions to Greenland in 1605, 1606, and 1607; to which is added Captain James Hall's voyage to Greenland in 1612. Book II: The

expedition of Captain Jens Munk to Hudson's Bay in search of a north-west passage in 1619–20. Edited, with notes and introductions, by C. C. A. Gosch. Book I. 1897.

97. Danish Arctic expeditions, 1605 to 1620. Book II. 1897.

98. The Christian topography of Cosmas, an Egyptian monk. Translated from the Greek, and edited, with notes and introduction, by J. W. McCrindle. 1897.

99. A journal of the first voyage of Vasco da Gama, 1497–1499. Translated and edited, with notes, and introduction and appendices, by E. G. Ravenstein. 1898.

    With letters of King Manuel and Girolamo Sernigi, 1499, and early seventeenth-century Portuguese accounts of da Gama's first voyage.

100. The chronicle of the discovery and conquest of Guinea. Vol. II: Chapters 41–97, with an introduction on the early history of African exploration, cartography, etc. 1899.

Hakluyt Society, Second Series

1. The embassy of Sir Thomas Roe to the court of the Great Mogul, 1615–1619, as narrated in his journal and correspondence. Edited by William Foster. Vol. I. 1899.

    Pagination of this and the following is continuous. Superseded by the new and revised edition, Oxford University Press, 1926.

2. The embassy of Sir Thomas Roe...Vol. II. 1899.

3. The voyage of Sir Robert Dudley, afterwards styled Earl of Warwick and Leicester and Duke of Northumberland, to the West Indies, 1594–1595, narrated by Capt. Wyatt, by himself, and by Abram Kendall, master. Edited by George F. Warner. 1899.

4. The journey of William of Rubruck to the eastern parts of the world, 1253–55, as narrated by himself, with two accounts of the earlier journey of John of Pian de Carpine. Translated from the Latin and edited by William Woodville Rockhill. 1900.

5. The voyage of Captain John Saris to Japan, 1613. Edited by Sir Ernest M. Satow. 1900.

    Saris's journal, with two of his reports to the East India Company, a letter, and extracts from Purchas.

6. The strange adventures of Andrew Battell of Leigh, in Angola and the adjoining regions. Reprinted from *Purchas his pilgrimes*. Edited, with a concise history of Kongo and Angola, by E. G. Ravenstein. 1901.

Late sixteenth – early seventeenth century. With part of Anthony Knivet's account of his adventures in the same countries.

7. The discovery of the Solomon Islands by Alvaro de Mendaña in 1568. Translated from the original Spanish manuscripts. Edited by Lord Amherst of Hackney, and Basil Thomson. Vol. I. 1901.

Four narratives, two of them by or attributed to Mendaña's companions, Hernando Gallego and Pedro Sarmiento. Three further narratives, including one by Gómez Catoira, are in the following. Pagination is continuous.

8. The discovery of the Solomon Islands...Vol. II. 1901.

9. The travels of Pedro Teixeira; with his 'Kings of Harmuz', and extracts from his 'Kings of Persia'. Translated and annotated by William F. Sinclair, with further notes and introduction by Donald Ferguson. 1902.

Late sixteenth – early seventeenth century.

10. The Portuguese expedition to Abyssinia in 1541–1543, as narrated by Castanhoso, with some contemporary letters, the 'short account' of Ber-múdez, and certain extracts from Correa. Translated and edited by R. S. Whiteway. 1902.

11. Early Dutch and English voyages to Spitsbergen in the seventeenth century, including Hessel Gerritsz. *Histoire du pays nommé Spitsberghe,* 1613, translated into English, for the first time, by Basil H. Soulsby; and Jacob Segersz. van der Brugge, *Journael of dagh register,* Amsterdam, 1634, trans-lated into English, for the first time, by J. A. J. de Villiers. Edited by Sir W. Martin Conway. 1904.

With affidavits by English merchants and seamen relating to happenings at Spitsbergen in 1618, and two documents telling of events there in 1634–5, taken from P.R.O., State Papers Domestic.

12. A geographical account of countries round the bay of Bengal, 1669 to 1679, by Thomas Bowrey. Edited by Sir Richard Carnac Temple, bart. 1905.

13. The voyage of Captain Don Felipe González in the ship of the line *San Lorenzo,* with the frigate *Santa Rosalia* in company, to Easter Island in 1770–1; preceded by an extract from Mynheer Jacob Roggeveen's official

log of his discovery of and visit to Easter Island in 1722. Transcribed, translated, and edited by Bolton Glanvill Corney. 1908.

Journals, instructions, minutes, and despatches, with an extract from the journal of Lieut. George Peard, of H.M.S. *Blossom, 1825.*

14. The voyages of Pedro Fernandez de Quiros, 1595 to 1606. Translated and edited by Sir Clements Markham. Vol. I. 1904.

Three narratives of voyages to the Pacific. Two further narratives, including one by Torquemada, and an appendix of letters and memoranda addressed to Philip III, are in the following. Pagination is continuous.

15. The voyages of Pedro Fernandez de Quiros, 1595 to 1606. Vol. II. 1904.

16. The journal of John Jourdain, 1608–1617, describing his experiences in Arabia, India, and the Malay archipelago. Edited by William Foster. 1905.

An account of the East India Company's fourth voyage; with an appendix containing William Revett's account of the Seychelles, 1609, and reports on other places by merchants and seamen of the same period.

17. The travels of Peter Mundy in Europe and Asia, 1608–1667. Edited by Sir Richard Carnac Temple, bart. Vol. I: Travels in Europe, 1608–1628. 1907.

With an appendix of extracts from the writings of seventeenth-century travellers to the Levant. Continued in 35, 45, 46, 55, 78 below.

18. The East and West Indian mirror; being an account of Joris van Speilbergen's voyage round the world, 1614–1617, and the Australian navigations of Jacob le Maire. Translated and edited by J. A. J. de Villiers. 1906.

From the Dutch edition of 1619.

19. A new account of East India and Persia; being nine years' travels, 1672–1681, by John Fryer. Edited by William Crooke. Vol. I. 1909.

Composed in the form of letters and first published in 1698. This volume contains letters I–III. Continued in 20, 39 below.

20. A new account of East India and Persia. Vol. II. 1912.

Letters IV–V, with a chapter on Indian history and customs, and another on coins, weights, and precious stones.

21. The Guanches of Tenerife, the holy image of our Lady of Candelaria, and the Spanish conquest and settlement, by the friar Alonso de Espinosa, of the order of preachers. Translated and edited by Sir Clements Markham. 1907.

> Written 1580–90, first published at Seville in 1594. With a bibliography of the Canary Islands, 1341–1907.

22[a]. History of the Incas, by Pedro Sarmiento de Gamboa, and the execution of the Inca Tupac Amaru, by Captain Baltasar de Ocampo. Translated and edited by Sir Clements Markham. 1907.

> The first was dedicated to Philip II in 1572; the second was written in 1610. Pagination continues in the following.

22[b]. Supplement. A narrative of the vice-regal embassy to Vilcabamba, 1571, and of the execution of the Inca Tupac Amaru, December 1571, by Friar Gabriel de Oviedo, of Cuzco, 1573.

> Another eye-witness account. Issued separately, 1908.

23. The true history of the conquest of New Spain, by Bernal Díaz del Castillo, one of its conquerors. Edited and published in Mexico by Genaro García. Translated into English and edited by Alfred Percival Maudslay. [Vol. I.] 1908.

> Books I–IV, A.D. 1517–19, concerning the discovery and expeditions of Francisco Hernández de Córdova and Hernán Cortés, the march inland, and the war in Tlaxcala. Continued in 24, 25, 30, 40 below.

24. The true history of the conquest of New Spain. Vol. III. 1910.

> Books V–IX, A.D. 1519–20, concerning the march to Mexico, the stay there, the expedition against Narváez, the flight from Mexico, and the halt at Tepeaca.

25. The true history of the conquest of New Spain. Vol. III. 1910.

> A box of maps and plans, several dating from the sixteenth century, of the valley and city of Mexico.

26. Storm van 'sGravesande. The rise of British Guiana. Compiled from his despatches by C. A. Harris and J. A. J. de Villiers. Vol. I. 1911.

> Extracts from despatches by Laurens Storm van 'sGravesande to the directors of the Zeeland Chamber of the West India Company, 1738–72, selected to illustrate the rise and expansion of the colony, with a detailed introduction. This volume ends with the despatch dated 15 March 1760. For May 1760 to September 1772, see the following. Pagination is continuous.

27. Storm van 'sGravesande. Vol. II. 1911.

28. Early Spanish voyages to the strait of Magellan. Translated and edited by Sir Clements Markham. 1911.

Narratives of the second voyage through the strait, commanded by the Comendador Loaysa and Sebastián del Cano, 1524–6, the third voyage, under the command of Simón de Alcazaba, 1534–5, and the reconnaissance by Bartolomé and Gonzalo de Nodal, 1618–19; with a fragment relating to the expedition sent by the bishop of Plasencia under Alonso de Camargo, 1539–41.

29. Book of the knowledge of all the kingdoms, lands, and lordships that are in the world, and the arms and devices of each land and lordship, or of the kings and lords who possess them, written by a Spanish Franciscan in the middle of the XIV century. Published for the first time, with notes by Marcos Jiménez de la Espada, in 1877. Translated and edited by Sir Clements Markham. 1912.

30. The true history of the conquest of New Spain. Vol. IV. 1912.

Books X–XIII, relating the siege and capture of Mexico, 1521, and the ensuing settlement.

31. The war of Quito, by Pedro de Cieza de León, and Inca documents. Translated and edited by Sir Clements Markham. 1913.

Book III, A.D. 1543–44, of Cieza's 'Civil wars of Peru'. The additional documents continue the narrative to c. 1568.

32. The quest and occupation of Tahiti by emissaries of Spain during the years 1772–1776, told in despatches and other contemporary documents. Translated and compiled, with notes and an introduction, by Bolton Glanvill Corney. Vol. I. 1913.

Instructions, minutes, despatches, and other documents from Spanish and English archives, relating to exploration of the East Indies. Continued in 36, 43 below.

33. Cathay and the way thither...New edition, revised throughout in the light of recent discoveries, by Henri Cordier. Vol. II: Odoric of Pordenone. 1913.

The first issued volume of a revised edition of First Series 36, 37 above. The appendix contains a Latin and an Italian text of Friar Odoric's travels in the early fourteenth century. Continued in 37, 38, 41 below.

34. New light on Drake: a collection of documents relating to his voyages of circumnavigation, 1577–1580. Translated and edited by Zelia Nuttall. 1914.

Spanish official documents, depositions by prisoners, documents relating to Nuño da Silva, etc.

35. The travels of Peter Mundy...Vol. II: Travels in Asia, 1628–1634. 1914.

36. The quest and occupation of Tahiti...Vol. II. 1915.

37. Cathay and the way thither...New edition, revised. Vol. III: Missionary friars; Rashíduddín; Pegolotti; Marignolli. 1914.
Letters and reports of missionary friars from Cathay and India, 1292–1338; Cathay under the Mongols, from Rashíduddín's history, c. 1300–7; Pegolotti's notices of the land route to Cathay, c. 1330–40; and John d'Marignolli's recollections of eastern travel, 1338–53, taken from his 'Chronicle of Bohemia'.

38. Cathay and the way thither...New edition, revised. Vol. I: Preliminary essay on the intercourse between China and the western nations previous to the discovery of the Cape route. 1915.
With numerous supplementary extracts from writers of the first to the sixteenth century.

39. A new account of East India and Persia. Vol. III. 1915.
Letters v (continued)–VIII.

40. The true history of the conquest of New Spain. Vol. v. 1916.
Books XIV–XVII, relating the expedition to Honduras, the return to Mexico, the rule of the Audiencia there, and the record of the conquistadores, with an appendix including the fifth letter of Cortés to the Emperor Charles V, 1526.

41. Cathay and the way thither...New edition, revised. Vol. IV: Ibn Batuta; Benedict Goës; index. 1916.
Ibn Baṭṭūṭa's travels in Bengal and China, c. 1347, and the journey of Goës from Agra to Cathay, 1602–7, with an index to all volumes.

42. Civil wars of Peru, by Pedro de Cieza de León. Part IV, bk. II: The war of Chupas. Translated and edited by Sir Clements R. Markham. 1918.
This forms part of the original Book II. See 54 below.

43. The quest and occupation of Tahiti. Vol. III: The diary of Máximo Rodríguez. 1919.
With the memorial submitted by Rodríguez to the viceroy of Peru, 1788.

44. The book of Duarte Barbosa. An account of the countries bordering on the Indian ocean and their inhabitants, written by Duarte Barbosa, and completed about the year 1518 A.D. Translated from the Portuguese and edited by Mansel Longworth Dames. Vol. I, including the coasts of east Africa, Arabia, Persia, and western India as far as the kingdom of Vijaya٫ nagar. 1918.

With a translation of chapter 2, History of Rander, from Narmashankar's 'Principal events of Surat'. Continued in 49 below.

45. The travels of Peter Mundy...Vol. III, pt. 1: Travels in England, western India, Achin, Macao, and the Canton river, 1634–1637. 1919.

46. The travels of Peter Mundy...Vol. III, pt. 2: Travels in Achin, Mauritius, Madagascar, and St. Helena, 1638. 1919.

With his first appendix, consisting of notes on his China voyage, and additional documents. including papers connected with Courteen's Association, and Dutch and Portuguese accounts of the naval action off Goa, 1637.

47. The chronicle of Muntaner. Translated from the Catalan by Lady Goodenough. Vol. I. 1920.

A.D. 1208–85. Continued to 1328 in 50 below. Pagination is continuous.

48. *Memorias antiguas historiales del Perú,* by Fernando Montesinos. Trans٫ lated and edited by Philip Ainsworth Means, with an introduction by Sir Clements R. Markham. 1920.

Text written in the seventeenth century. Chronological tables added.

49. The book of Duarte Barbosa. Vol. II, including the coasts of Malabar, eastern India, further India, China, and the Indian archipelago. 1921.

With translated extracts from João de Barros, *Decadas de Asia.*

50. The chronicle of Muntaner. Vol. II. 1921.

51. Journal of the travels and labours of Father Samuel Fritz in the river of the Amazons between 1686 and 1723. Translated from the Evora MS and edited by George Edmundson. 1922.

With a translation of the Act of Possession of Pedro Teixeira, 1639, and of contemporary references in Portuguese sources to the work of Father Fritz in the Upper Amazon.

52. The journal of William Lockerby, sandalwood trader in the Fijian islands during the years 1808–1809; with an introduction and other papers

connected with the earliest European visitors to the islands. Edited by Sir Everard Im Thurn and Leonard C. Wharton. 1925.

The additional documents include Samuel Patterson's account of the wreck of the *Eliza*, 1808, the journal of the missionaries from the *Hibernia*, 1809, Captain Richard Siddon's experiences in Fiji in 1809–15, and extracts from periodical publications, 1804–15.

53. The life of the Icelander Jón Ólafsson, traveller to India, written by himself and completed about 1661 A.D., with a continuation by another hand up to his death in 1679. Translated from the Icelandic edition of Sigfús Blöndal, by Bertha S. Phillpotts. Vol. I: Life and travels: Iceland, England, Denmark, White Sea, Faroes, Spitzbergen, Norway, 1593–1622. Edited by the translator. 1923.

Continued in 68 below.

54. Civil wars in Peru, by Pedro de Cieza de León. The war of Las Salinas. Translated, with an introduction, by Sir Clements Markham. 1923.

Book I of Cieza de León's chronicle.

55. The travels of Peter Mundy...Vol. IV: Travels in Europe, 1639–1647. 1925.

With Mundy's second appendix, including a note on English change-ringing.

56. Colonising expedition to the West Indies and Guiana, 1623–1667. Edited by V. T. Harlow. 1925.

Journals, narratives, and descriptions relating to British colonization in St Christophers, Nevis, Barbados, Tobago, Trinidad, and Guiana, and to Admiral de Ruyter's raid in the West Indies, 1664–5.

57. Francis Mortoft, his book. Being his travels through France and Italy, 1658–1659. Edited by Malcolm Letts. 1925.

58. The papers of Thomas Bowrey, 1669–1713,...Pt. 1: Diary of a six weeks' tour in 1698 in Holland and Flanders. Pt. 2: The story of the *Mary Galley*, 1704–1710. Edited by Sir Richard Carnac Temple, bt. 1927.

59. Travels of Fray Sebastien Manrique, 1629–1643. A translation of the *Itinerario de las missiones orientales* with introduction and notes by C. Eckford Luard, assisted by H. Hosten. Vol. 1: Arakan. 1927.

Continued in 61 below.

60. A relation of a voyage to Guiana, by Robert Harcourt, 1613, with

Purchas' transcript of a report made at Harcourt's instance on the Marrawini district. Edited, with introduction and notes, by Sir C. Alexander Harris. 1928.

61. Travels of Fray Sebastien Manrique, 1629–1643. Vol. ii: China, India, etc. 1927.

62. Spanish documents concerning English voyages to the Caribbean, 1527–1568. Selected from the archives of the Indies at Seville by Irene A. Wright. 1929.
In English translation.

63. The desert route to India; being the journals of four travellers by the great desert caravan route between Aleppo and Basra, 1745–1751. Edited by Douglas Carruthers. 1929.
The journals of William Beawes, Gaylard Roberts, Bartholomew Plaisted, and John Carmichael.

64. New light on the discovery of Australia, as revealed by the journal of Captain Don Diego de Prado y Tovar. Edited by Henry N. Stevens, with annotated translations from the Spanish by George F. Barwick. 1930.
Spanish text, with English translation, of Prado's *Relación* of the voyage begun in company with Quiros and Torres in 1607, with a report of the Spanish council of state concerning Quiros, 1618, and letters of Torres and Prado, 1607–13.

65. Select documents illustrating the four voyages of Columbus, including those contained in R. H. Major's *Select letters of Christopher Columbus.* Translated and edited with additional material, an introduction, and notes, by Cecil Jane. Vol. i: The first and second voyages. 1930.
Continued in 70 below.

66. Relations of Golconda in the early seventeenth century. Edited by W. H. Moreland. 1931.
William Methwold's 'relation', reprinted from *Purchas his pilgrimes* and two other 'relations', one by Antony Schorer, translated from the Dutch.

67. The travels of John Sanderson in the Levant, 1584–1602, with his autobiography and selections from his correspondence. Edited by Sir William Foster. 1931.

68. The life of the Icelander Jón Ólafsson,... Vol. ii: Life and travels: Denmark, England, the Cape, Madagascar, Comoro Is., Coromandel

coast, Tranquebar, St. Helena, Ascension Is., Ireland, Iceland, 1618–1679. Edited by Sir Richard Temple, bart, and Lavinia Mary Anstey. 1932.

69. A brief summe of geographie, by Roger Barlow. Edited, with an introduction and notes, by E. G. R. Taylor. 1932.
Transcript of the MS dedicated to Henry VIII, with a pedigree of Barlow.

70. Select documents illustrating the four voyages of Columbus, . . . Vol. II: The third and fourth voyages. With a supplementary introduction by E. G. R. Taylor. 1933.

71. Documents concerning English voyages to the Spanish main, 1569–1580. I: Spanish documents selected from the archives of the Indies at Seville. II: English accounts: *Sir Francis Drake revived,* and others. Reprinted by Irene A. Wright. 1932.

72. Bombay in the days of Queen Anne; being an account of the settlement written by John Burnell, with an introduction and notes by Samuel T. Sheppard; to which is added Burnell's narrative of his adventures in Bengal; with an introduction by Sir William Foster and notes by Sir Evan Cotton and L[avinia] M. Anstey. 1933.

73. A new voyage and description of the isthmus of America, by Lionel Wafer, surgeon on buccaneering expeditions in Darien, the West Indies, and the Pacific, from 1680 to 1688; with Wafer's secret report, 1698, and Davis's expedition to the gold mines, 1704. Edited, with introduction, notes, and appendices, by L. E. Elliott Joyce. 1934.
The text of the 1699 edition, with slight changes, and additional material.

74. Peter Floris, his voyage to the East Indies in the *Globe,* 1611–1615. The contemporary translation of his journal. Edited by W. H. Moreland. 1934.

75. The voyage of Thomas Best to the East Indies, 1612–14. Edited by Sir William Foster. 1934.
Journals, extracts from journals, and narratives, kept on board the *Dragon* and *Hosiander* by Best and various other persons, with Best's correspondence and extracts from the court minutes of the East India Company.

76. The original writings and correspondence of the two Richard Hakluyts. With an introduction and notes by E. G. R. Taylor. Vol. I. 1935.
Pagination of this and the following is continuous.

77. The original writings...of the two Richard Hakluyts. Vol. II. 1935.

78. The travels of Peter Mundy...Vol. V: Travels in south-west England and western India, with a diary of events in London, 1658–1663, and in Penryn, 1664–1667. Edited by Sir Richard Carnac Temple, bt., and Lavinia Mary Anstey. 1936.

79. *Esmeraldo de situ orbis,* by Duarte Pacheco Pereira. Translated and edited by George H. T. Kimble. 1937.
A Portuguese rutter (or set of rules for navigation), written *c.* 1505–8.

80. The voyages of Cadamosto, and other documents on western Africa in the second half of the fifteenth century. Translated and edited by G. R. Crone. 1937.
The additional documents, in translation, comprise a letter by Antoine Malfante, 1447, an account of the voyages of Diogo Gomes, *c.* 1456, and extracts from João de Barros, *ob.* 1570.

81. The voyage of Pedro Álvares Cabral to Brazil and India. From contemporary documents and narratives. Translated, with introduction and notes, by William Brooks Greenlee. 1938.
Letters, narratives, and extracts from diaries, etc., of 1500–1, chiefly of Portuguese and Venetian origin, in translation.

82. The voyage of Nicholas Downton to the East Indies, 1614–15, as recorded in contemporary narratives and letters. Edited by Sir William Foster. 1939.

83. The voyages and colonising enterprises of Sir Humphrey Gilbert. With an introduction and notes by David Beers Quinn. Vol. I. 1940.
A collection of documents, chiefly from English sources, including a few relating to Ireland. Documents relating to the Munster plantation scheme, 1569, and the Knollys piracy, 1579, are in the following. Pagination is continuous.

84. The voyages...of Sir Humphrey Gilbert. Vol. II. 1940.

85. The voyages of Sir James Lancaster to Brazil and the East Indies, 1591–1603. A new edition, with introduction and notes by Sir William Foster. 1940.
Cf. First Series 56 above. Contains three additional narratives and other documents and omits certain supplementary matter in the earlier edition.

86. Europeans in West Africa, 1540–1560. Documents to illustrate the nature and scope of Portuguese enterprise in West Africa, the abortive

attempt of Castilians to create an empire there, and the early English voyages to Barbary and Guinea. Translated and edited by John William Blake. Vol. I. 1942.

Dealing with Portuguese and Castilian enterprise. Documents relating to early English voyages are in the following. Pagination is continuous.

87. Europeans in West Africa, 1450–1560. Vol. II. 1942.

88. The voyage of Sir Henry Middleton to the Moluccas, 1604–1606. A new and enlarged edition, with an introduction and notes by Sir William Foster. 1943.

Cf. First Series 19 above. The additional material includes an account by Edmund Scott of events at Bantam, 1603–5, and his description of Java.

89. The *Suma oriental* of Tomé Pires: an account of the east from the Red Sea to Japan, written in Malacca and India in 1512–1515; and the Book of Francisco Rodrígues: rutter of a voyage in the Red Sea, nautical rules, almanack and maps, written and drawn in the east before 1515. Translated from the Portuguese MS in the Bibliothèque de la Chambre des Députés, Paris, and edited by Armando Cortesão. Vol. I. 1944.

Containing the translated Books I–V of the *Suma oriental*. Book VI is contained in the following, together with a translation of Rodrígues' Book, the entire Portuguese texts, and a letter from Pires to King Manuel, 1516. Pagination is continuous.

90. The *Suma oriental*...Vol. II. 1944.

91. The voyage of Captain Bellingshausen to the Antarctic seas, 1819–1821. Translated from the Russian. Edited by Frank Debenham. Vol. I. 1945.

The additional section entitled 'Short notes on the colonies of New South Wales', is included in the following. Pagination is continuous.

92. The voyage of Captain Bellingshausen...Vol. II. 1945.

93. Richard Hakluyt and his successors. A volume issued to commemorate the centenary of the Hakluyt Society. Edited by Edward Lynam. 1947.

Containing: (i) Richard Hakluyt, by J. A. Williamson, (ii) Samuel Purchas, by Sir William Foster, (iii) English collections of voyages and travels, 1625–1846, by G. R. Crone and R. A. Skelton, (iv) The Hakluyt Society, 1846–1946: a retrospect, by Sir William Foster, (v) The present and the future [of the Society], by Edward Lynam. Also a list of publications and maps.

94. The pilgrimage of Arnold von Harff, knight, from Cologne, through Italy, Syria, Egypt, Arabia, Ethiopia, Nubia, Palestine, Turkey, France and Spain, which he accomplished in the years 1496 to 1499. Translated from the German and edited, with notes and an introduction, by Malcolm Letts. 1946.

95. The travels of the Abbé Carré in India and the Near East, 1672 to 1674. Translated from the manuscript journal of his travels in the India Office by Lady Fawcett, and edited by Sir Charles Fawcett with the assistance of Sir Richard Burn. Vol. 1: From France through Syria, Iraq and the Persian Gulf to Surat, Goa, and Bijapur, with an account of his grave illness. 1947.
Pagination of this and the two following is continuous, but each has its own introduction.

96. The travels of the Abbé Carré...Vol. 11: From Bijapur to Madras and St Thomé. Account of the capture of Trincomalee Bay and St Thomé by De la Haye, and of the siege of St Thomé by the Golconda army and hostilities with the Dutch. 1947.

97. The travels of the Abbé Carré...Vol. 111: Return journey to France, with an account of the Sicilian revolt against Spanish rule at Messina. 1948.

98. The discovery of Tahiti. A journal of the second voyage of H.M.S. *Dolphin* round the world, under the command of Captain Wallis, R.N., in the years 1766, 1767 and 1768, written by her master, George Robertson. Edited by Hugh Carrington. 1948.

99. Further English voyages to Spanish America, 1583–1594. Documents from the archives of the Indies at Seville illustrating English voyages to the Caribbean, the Spanish Main, Florida, and Virginia. Translated and edited by Irene A. Wright. 1951.

100. The Red Sea and adjacent countries at the close of the seventeenth century, as described by Joseph Pitts, William Daniel, and Charles Jacques Poncet. Edited by Sir William Foster. 1949.
With additional documents. The first narrative is from Pitts' *Religion and manners of the Mahometans* (3rd edition, 1731); Daniel's journal was printed in 1702, Poncet's in 1709.

101. Mandeville's travels: texts and translations. By Malcolm Letts. Vol. 1. 1953.
The Egerton text (B. M. Egerton MS 1982), with an essay on the cosmo⁄

graphical ideas of Mandeville's day by E. G. R. Taylor. The following contains the Paris text (French, with translation), Bodleian text, and extracts from other versions. Pagination is continuous.

102. Mandeville's travels....Vol. II. 1953.

103. The historie of travell into Virginia Britania (1612), by William Strachey, gent. Edited by Louis B. Wright and Virginia Freund. 1953.
Transcript of the Princeton MS, with Strachey's vocabulary of an Algon-quian dialect and an essay on the same by James A. Geary.

104. The Roanoke voyages, 1584–1590. Documents to illustrate the English voyages to North America under the patent granted to Walter Raleigh in 1584. Edited by David Beers Quinn. Vol. I. 1955.
Texts from Hakluyt's *Principall Navigations* (1589), together with the items added by him in 1600 and much additional material, a few docu-ments in summary form. This part takes the narrative to January 1586/7 and includes a descriptive list of John White's drawings of the first colony; the narrative is continued to 1590 and later in the following. Pagination is continuous. Appended to vol. II is an article on the language of the Carolina Algonkian tribes by James A. Geary, with a word-list; a chapter on the archaeology of the Roanoke settlements; a detailed account of the MS. and printed sources; and (in pocket) a map of Ralegh's Virginia.

105. The Roanoke voyages...Vol. II. 1955.
Incorrectly numbered 104 on half-title.

106. South China in the sixteenth century; being the narratives of Galeote Pereira, Fr. Gaspar da Cruz, O.P., Fr. Martín de Rada, O.E.S.A., 1550–1575. Edited by C. R. Boxer. 1953.
Translations, the first based largely on Richard Willes, in his *History of trauayle in the West and East Indies* (1577), the second derived from *Purchas his pilgrimes* (1625), the third by the editor from three sixteenth-century Spanish versions. There are appendices on the identification of 'Chincheo' and 'Aucheo', on the Fukien granite bridges, and on the Amoy ver-nacular and its cognate languages, and also a Chinese glossary and a table of Chinese dynasties and emperors.

107. Some records of Ethiopia, 1593–1646; being extracts from *The history of high Ethiopia or Abassia* by Manoel de Almeida, together with Bahrey's *History of the Galla*. Translated and edited by C. F. Beckingham and G. W. B. Huntingford. 1954.

The selections from Almeida describe the country and its people and the journeys of Jesuit missionaries attempting to enter or leave it.

108. The travels of Leo of Rozmital through Germany, Flanders, England, France, Spain, Portugal and Italy, 1465–1467. Translated from the German and Latin and edited by Malcolm Letts. 1957.

From the German account by Gabriel Tetzel, with supplementary passages from the Latin versions (printed in 1577, 1843 and 1951) of the lost account in Czech by Václav Šašek, both Rozmital's companions.

109. Ethiopian itineraries *circa* 1400–1524, including those collected by Alessandro Zorzi at Venice in the years 1519–24. Edited by O. G. S. Crawford. 1958.

Zorzi's Italian text with translation by C. A. Ralegh Radford, sketch-maps by Frank Addison, editor's introduction, bibliography of books, articles and maps, and a gazetteer for Fra Mauro's map.

110. The travels of Ibn Baṭṭūṭa, A.D. 1325–1354. Translated with revisions and notes, from the Arabic text edited by C. Defrémery and B. R. Sanguinetti, by H. A. R. Gibb. Vol. I. 1958.

North-west Africa, Egypt, Syria, Mecca. Continued in 117, 141 below. Pagination is continuous.

111. English privateering voyages to the West Indies, 1588–1595. Edited by Kenneth R. Andrews. 1959.

Documents (some summarized entirely or in part) relating to twenty-five voyages, drawn mainly from the records of the High Court of Admiralty, with selections from narratives printed by Hakluyt and from a quantity of translations by Miss I. A. Wright of originals (1593–5) in the Archivo General de Indias in Seville intended for her fourth volume on English West Indies voyages (see 66, 71, 99 above) and given by her to the Society. The introduction gives an account of the court itself and of privateering during the Spanish war and in the West Indies. See also 142 below.

112. The tragic history of the sea, 1589–1622. Narratives of the shipwrecks of the Portuguese East Indiamen *São Thomé* (1589), *Santo Alberto* (1593), *São João Baptista* (1622), and the journeys of the survivors in south east Africa. Edited from the original Portuguese by C. R. Boxer. 1959.

The narratives by Diogo do Couto, João Baptista Lavanha and Francisco Vaz d'Almada, translated from the original editions of accounts which were subsequently included in the *História Trágico-Marítima* edited by Bernando Gomes de Brito at Lisbon in 1735–6. Matters treated in the introduction and appendices include the round voyage made by the Indiamen between Lisbon and Goa, the ships and their crews, pay and allowances, provisions, allotment of deck and cargo space, and allowance of liberty chests. See also 132 below.

113. The troublesome voyage of Captain Edward Fenton, 1582–1583. Narratives and documents edited by E. G. R. Taylor. 1959.
Transcripts of all the surviving records of the voyage for China and Cathay sponsored by the Privy Council and intended to establish the first English trading base in the Far East. Includes Fenton's own sea journal (Pepys MS 2133) and the official narrative of Richard Madox.

114. The Prester John of the Indies. A true relation of the lands of the Prester John, being the narrative of the Portuguese embassy to Ethiopia in 1520 written by Father Francisco Alvares. The translation of Lord Stanley of Alderley (1881) revised and edited with additional material by C. F. Beckingham and G. W. B. Huntingford. Vol. I. 1961.
The mission of Dom Rodrigo de Lima, from his landing at Massawa on the west coast of the Red Sea in April 1520 to his re-embarking there six years later, the first European embassy known to have reached the Ethiopian court and returned in safety. Chapters 1–88. Continued in 115 below. Pagination is continuous.

115. The Prester John of the Indies. Vol. II. 1961.
Chapters 89–142, with the narrative of the return to Portugal, a translation of a seventeenth-century Ethiopian description of Aksum, and accounts of the rock-cut churches at Lālibalā, the Ethiopian *tābot* (the altar or ark), and the Ethiopian calendar.

116. The history of the Tahitian mission, 1799–1830, written by John Davies, missionary to the South Sea islands, with supplementary papers of the missionaries. Edited by C. W. Newbury. 1961.
Chapters 6–12 and 14–20 of Davies's unpublished 'History', chapters 1–5 summarized in the editor's introduction, chapter 13 omitted as already in print (see pp. 119–60 of 52 above). The editor's 'Epilogue', continuing the history of the mission to 1860, includes part of Davies's 'Conclusion' and the supplementary correspondence. Appendix I: Origins and genealogy of the Pomare dynasty. Appendix II: A note on missionary codes of law, with a list of codes and regulations of eastern Polynesia.

117. The travels of Ibn Baṭṭūṭa, A.D. 1325–1354. Vol. II. 1962.
Southern Persia, Iraq, southern Arabia, east Africa, the Persian Gulf, Asia Minor, south Russia.

118. The travels and controversies of Friar Domingo Navarrete, 1616–1686. Edited from manuscript and printed sources by J. S. Cummins. Vol. I. 1962.

A translation of the autobiographical portions of the *Tratados historicos*, i.e. the sixth treatise with interpolations from others of the treatises and from his unpublished 'Controversias' and other works. Describes travels in China and the outward and homeward journeys. The origin and nature of the Jesuit–Dominican controversy over the Chinese rites, and its development down to the papal Instruction of 1939, are sum﹣ marized in the editor's introduction. Vol. II, below, includes Navarrete's account of the island of Santo Domingo (1679) and appendices on, *inter alia*, the detention of the missionaries in Canton, 1666–70, and his relations with François Pallu, bishop of Heliopolis, and Richard Cony, governor of St Helena. Pagination is continuous.

119. The travels and controversies of Friar Domingo Navarrete. Vol. II. 1962.

120. The Cabot voyages and Bristol discovery under Henry VII. By James A. Williamson, with the cartography of the voyages by R. A. Skelton. 1962.

Documents from English, Portuguese, and Spanish archives, transcribed or in translation, relating to the Atlantic voyages out of Bristol in 1480 and 1481; the undated discovery of the so﹣called isle of Brasil by Bristol men some time before 1496; the expeditions led by John Cabot in 1496–8; those sent forth by the syndicates of Bristol merchants and Azorean promoters in 1501–6; and the expedition under Sebastian Cabot in 1509 or 1508–9 intended for the discovery of the north﹣west passage. In his introduction the editor modifies or disclaims some of his earlier conclusions on the Cabot voyages.

121. The regiment for the sea and other writings on navigation by William Bourne of Gravesend, a gunner (*c*. 1535–1582). Edited by E. G. R. Taylor. 1963.

Reprints Bourne's two almanacks (for three years, 1571, and for ten years, 1581) and the *Regiment* (1574), with the variants and additions in the 1580 edition. Appended are the surviving portion of John Dee's navigational tables entitled *Canon Gubernauticus* (1558), the wills of Bourne and his wife Dorothy, and a bibliographical description of Bourne's manuscript and printed works by D. W. Waters and R. A. Skelton.

122. Byron's journal of his circumnavigation, 1764–1766. Edited by Robert E. Gallagher. 1964.

The voyage of the *Dolphin,* captain the Hon. John Byron (1723–86). Includes the secret instructions by the Admiralty, a list of the crew, and transcripts of documents relating to the voyage. The appendix, on the Patagonians, includes 'The Patagonian giants' by Helen Wallis and Horace Walpole's *Account of the giants lately discovered* (1776).

123. Missions to the Niger. Edited by E. W. Bovill. Vol. 1: The journal of Friedrich Horneman's travels from Cairo to Murzuk in the years 1797–98. The letters of Major Alexander Gordon Laing, 1824–26. 1964.

With Laing's letters are included his 'Cursory remarks on the course and termination of the great river Niger', his 'Notes on Gadamis', his only surviving letter to his wife, and the report of his death in *L'Etoile,* 2 May 1827. Continued in 128, 129, 130 below.

124. Carteret's voyage round the world, 1766–1769. Edited by Helen Wallis. Vol. 1. 1965.

Derived from the abstract retained by Carteret after his voyage and the journal he compiled from it and other papers in about 1773. Vol. 11 below (pagination is continuous) is a collection of documents, 1756–1811, relating to the preparations, the voyage itself, and to its aftermath.

125. Carteret's voyage round the world. Vol. 11. 1965.

126. La Austrialia del Espíritu Santo. The journal of Fray Martín de Munilla O.F.M. and other documents relating to the voyage of Pedro Fernández de Quiros to the South Sea (1605–1606) and the Franciscan missionary plan (1617–1627). Translated and edited by Celsus Kelly O.F.M., with ethnological introduction, appendix, and other contributions by G. S. Parsonson. Vol. 1. 1966.

The *relación* of Munilla, chaplain and vicar of the Royal Fleet and com- missary of the Franciscans in the Quirós expedition, with extensive introduction. Continued in 127 below. Pagination is continuous.

127. La Austrialia del Espíritu Santo. Vol. 11. 1966.

The *sumario breve* of Juan de Iturbe, followed by documents bearing on the preparations for the expedition, the voyage of Quirós, Quirós in New Spain, negotiations for another expedition, and the missionary plan. Appendix 1: The ships' companies. Appendix 11: The problem of Pouro and Manicolo, by G. S. Parsonson.

128. Missions to the Niger. Vol. II: The Bornu mission, 1822–25, pt. I. 1966.

The pagination of this and 129 and 130 below is continuous: though described as vol. II, pt. I, vol. III, pt. 2, vol. IV, pt. 3, they constitute three parts of the same volume, in which is reprinted the *Narrative of travels and discoveries in northern and central Africa in the years 1822, 1823, and 1824 by Major Denham, Captain Clapperton and the late Doctor Oudney* (2nd edition, 1826), omitting appendices XII–XVI but with extra plates from the first edition. This part begins Major Denham's narrative. Previously unpublished documents relating to the mission are included in the editor's introduction and in the appendix.

129. Missions to the Niger. Vol. III: The Bornu mission, 1822–25, pt. 2. 1966.

Major Denham's narrative, chapters 3–7 and supplementary chapter, with additional documents.

130. Missions to the Niger. Vol. IV: The Bornu mission, 1822–25, pt. 3. 1966.

Captain Clapperton's narrative, with the appendix of letters etc. brought back by Denham and Clapperton as translated from the Arabic by the then interpreter to the Colonial Office, Abraham Salamé, and additional documents.

131. The journal and letters of Captain Charles Bishop on the north-west coast of America, in the Pacific, and in New South Wales, 1794–1799 Edited by Michael Roe. 1967.

Recording the voyage of the *Ruby* from Bristol to Amboyna and of the *Nautilus* from Amboyna to Macao.

132. Further selections from the tragic history of the sea, 1559–1565. Narratives of the shipwrecks of the Portuguese East Indiamen *Aguia* and *Garça* (1559), *São Paulo* (1561), and the misadventures of the Brazil-ship *Santo António* (1565). Translated and edited from the original Portuguese by C. R. Boxer. 1968.

The narratives of Diogo do Couto, Henrique Dias and Afonso Luís. See 112 above.

133. The letters of F. W. Ludwig Leichhardt. Collected and newly translated by M. Aurousseau. Vol. I. 1968.

Full texts of all letters, together with translations of those in German, French and Italian. This part contains the letters written while in Germany, 1832–7, and between 1837 and his departure for Sydney in 1841. Continued in 134, 135 below. Pagination is continuous.

134. The letters of F. W. Ludwig Leichhardt. Vol. II. 1968.
The years of scientific reconnaissance, 1842–4, around Sydney and Newcastle, in the Hunter-Goulburn valley, and to the Moreton Bay district.

135. The letters of F. W. Ludwig Leichhardt. Vol. III. 1968.
Major exploration, from 1844 until his disappearance in 1848, with a table of subsequent events.

136. The Jamestown voyages under the first charter, 1606–1609. Documents relating to the foundation of Jamestown and the history of the Jamestown colony up to the departure of Captain John Smith, last president of the council in Virginia under the first charter, early in October, 1609. Edited by Philip L. Barbour. Vol. I. 1969.
Includes a combined list of original planters to about 1 October 1608. Continued in 137 below. Pagination is continuous.

137. The Jamestown voyages... Vol. II. 1969.

138. Russian embassies to the Georgian kings, 1589–1605. Edited with introduction, additional notes, commentaries and bibliography by W. E. D. Allen. Texts translated by Anthony Mango. Vol. I. 1970.
Documents and commentaries relating to the embassy of Zvenigorodski and Antonov, 1589–90. Vol. II below (pagination is continuous) relates to the embassy of Tatishchev and Ivanov, 1604–5, and includes supplementary documents from the embassy of Sovin and Polukhanov, 1596–9, and genealogical notes and tables.

139. Russian embassies... Vol. II. 1970.

140. Sucesos de las Islas Filipinas by Antonio de Morga. Translated and edited by J. S. Cummins. 1971.
From the first edition, Mexico 1609. See First Series 39 above. The first history of the Spanish Philippines to be written by a layman.

141. The travels of Ibn Baṭṭūta, A.D. 1325–1354. Vol. III. 1971.
Turkestan, Khurasan, Sind, north-western India and Delhi, including his account of the reign of Sultan Muhammad ibn Tughluq.

142. The last voyage of Drake and Hawkins. Edited by Kenneth R. Andrews. 1972.
A sequel, 1595–6, to 111 above. Transcripts or translations of documents,

mainly from manuscripts and including many from the archives at Seville, arranged in eight groups, each with an introduction, viz. (i) preliminaries, (ii) the expeditionary force, (iii) English narratives, (iv) the Canaries, (v) Puerto Rico, (vi) Tierra Firme, (vii) Avellaneda, (viii) aftermath. Appendix: The art of navigation in the age of Drake, by D. W. Waters.

143. George Peard's journal of the voyage of H.M.S. *Blossom* to the Pacific, 1823-8. Edited by B. M. Gough. 1973

Hakluyt Society, Extra Series

[1-12] The principal navigations, voyages, traffiques and discoveries of the English nation made by sea or over-land to the remote and farthest distant quarters of the earth at any time within the compasse of these 1600 yeeres. By Richard Hakluyt. 12 vols., 1903-5.

Slightly modified reprint of the 1598-1600 edition, with contemporary maps, plans and charts in facsimile and, in vol. xii, Walter Raleigh's essay on the life and work of Hakluyt and a full index.

[13] The texts and versions of John de Plano Carpini and William de Rubruquis as printed for the first time by Hakluyt in 1598, together with some shorter pieces. Edited by C. Raymond Beazley. 1903.

An exact reprint of the texts and versions, Latin and English, as printed by Hakluyt, and of shorter pieces, especially the voyages of Ohthere and Wulfstan, which open the final edition of the *Principal navigations,* with critical and explanatory commentary.

[14-33] Hakluytus posthumus, or Purchas his pilgrimes, contayning a history of the world in sea voyages and lande travells by Englishmen and others. By Samuel Purchas. 20 vols., 1905-7.

Slightly modified reprint of the 1625 edition, with the addition of an index in vol. xx.

34. The journals of Capt James Cook on his voyages of discovery. Vol. I: The voyage of the *Endeavour,* 1768-1771. Edited by J. C. Beaglehole. 1955. Second edition, with addenda and corrigenda, 1970.

Admiralty instructions and the journal of the first voyage, with appendices containing (i) Cook's letters and reports describing the voyage, (ii) documents illustrating the Royal Society's interest in the voyage, (iii) drafts and variants of the journal, (iv) extracts from an anonymous journal and from the journals of Robert Molyneux and W. B. Monkhouse, surgeon, (v) a roll of the ship's company, (vi) a calendar of all documents bearing on the voyage other than logs and journals, and (vii) extracts from contemporary newspapers. A pamphlet of addenda and corrigenda was issued in 1968. The separate and unnumbered portfolio [34a] con′ taining 88 reproductions of charts and views drawn on the three voyages, edited by R. A. Skelton and issued with the volume in 1955, also went into a second edition in 1970.

35. The journals of Captain James Cook...Vol. ii: The voyage of the *Resolution* and *Adventure, 1772–1775.* Edited by J. C. Beaglehole. 1961. Second edition, with addenda and corrigenda, 1971.

Admiralty instructions and the journal of the second voyage, with appendices containing (i) Cook's letters and reports, (ii) documents on the controversy over the *Resolution*; (iii) documents on the Board of Longitude and the voyage, (vi) extracts from the journals of Tobias Furneaux, commander of the *Adventure,* James Burney, Charles Clerke, Richard Pickersgill, (v) the journal of William Wales, (vi) verses, 'The Antarctic muse', by Thomas Perry, (vii) rolls of the ships' companies, and (viii) a calendar of documents, 29 August 1771–3 May 1776. A pamphlet of addenda and corrigenda was issued in 1969.

36. The journals of Captain James Cook...Vol. iii: The voyage of the *Resolution* and the *Discovery, 1776–1780.* Edited by J. C. Beaglehole. 2 pts., 1967.

Pt. 1: Admiralty instructions and the journal of the third voyage, with supplementary extracts from journals or logs by James King, Clerke, Burney, Richard Gilbert, Thomas Edgar. Pt. 2: Appendices containing (i) William Anderson's journal, (ii) David Samwell's journal, (iii) extracts from the journals of Clerke, Burney, John Williamson, Edgar, King, and Alexander Home, the latter on Cook as a dietician, (iv) rolls of the ships' companies, and (v) a calendar of documents, 17 February 1774– 29 July 1791. Pagination of the two parts is continuous.

37. The journals of Captain James Cook...Vol. iv: The life of Captain James Cook. By J. C. Beaglehole. 1974.

38. The journal of Christopher Columbus. Translated by Cecil Jane, revised and annotated by L. A. Vigneras with an appendix by R. A. Skelton. Ninety illustrations from prints and maps of the period. 1960.

From the transcription by Cesare de Lollis and Julian Paz for the *Raccolta Colombiana* (1892). Includes Columbus's letter, February–March

1493, describing the results of his first voyage. The appendix is concerned with the cartography of the first voyage.

39. The principall navigations, voiages and discoveries of the English nation, by Richard Hakluyt. Imprinted at London, 1589. A photo-lithographic facsimile with an introduction by David Beers Quinn and Raleigh Ashlin Skelton, and with a new index by Alison Quinn. 1965.
In 2 parts with continuous pagination, the first containing Hakluyt's preliminaries, map, first and second parts, and the editor's introduction; the second the 'third and last part', the 'table alphabeticall', and the new index.

40. The diary of A. J. Mounteney Jephson, Emin Pasha relief expedition, 1887–1889. Edited by Dorothy Middleton, with preface, prologue and epilogue compiled by the editor in collaboration with Maurice Denham Jephson. 1969.
Two-thirds of the complete diary, the omissions supplied by editorial narrative.

41. The journals and letters of Sir Alexander Mackenzie. Edited by W. W. Kaye Lamb. 1970.
Mackenzie's 'general history' of the fur trade 'from Canada to the North-West' and his journal of his expedition from Fort Chipewyan to the Pacific in 1793, reprinted from the 1801 edition, together with his unpublished journal of his expedition from Fort Chipewyan to the Arctic in 1789 and all his known letters or fragments of letters.

42. Ying-yai sheng-lan, [by] Ma Huan, 1433. The overall survey of the ocean's shores. Translated from the Chinese text edited by Feng Ch'eng-Chün with introduction, notes and appendices by J. V. G. Mills. 1970.
'The fullest and most interesting account' of China's overseas expansion in the early fifteenth century, by the interpreter who accompanied the envoy Cheng Ho on his fourth, sixth and seventh expeditions. The appendices treat of (i) southern Asian place-names as known to the Chinese in 1433, (ii) the Mao K'un map, (iii) ships, seamanship, navigation and related matters, (iv) the Lung ya strait, the course fol-lowed by Chinese merchant ships passing between Malacca strait and the south China sea in 1433, (v) the voyage from Kuala Pasai to Beru-wala, (vi) four Chinese stellar diagrams, (vii) the location of La-sa, on the coast of the Arabian peninsula, and (viii) the earliest European rutter of the voyage from Malacca to China, said to be derived from Tomé Pires and to be dated 1514.

Occasional publications

[1] Richard Hakluyt: his life and work. With a short account of the aims and achievements of the Hakluyt Society. An address delivered by Sir Clements Markham, K.C.B., F.R.S. (President), on the occasion of the fiftieth anniversary of the foundation of the society. 1896.

[2] Richard Hakluyt: his life and work...Address by Sir Clements Markham on the fiftieth anniversary of the foundation of the society (1896). Revised on the occasion of the sixty-fifth anniversary. 1911.

[3] A reproduction of the tablet erected in Bristol Cathedral to the memory of Richard Hakluyt, 1911. [1911.]

[4] An address on the occasion of the tercentenary of the death of Richard Hakluyt, with a note on the Hakluyt family. By Albert Gray, C.B., K.C. (President). 1917.

[5] The Hakluyt Society. A retrospect: 1846–1946. By Sir William Foster, C.I.E. Reprinted from Second Series 93 above. [1946.]

[6] Guide for editors of the Hakluyt Society's publications. 1958.

[7] Captain James Cook after 200 years. A commemorative address delivered before the Hakluyt Society by R. A. Skelton. 1969. [Published by the British Museum.]

Note: Extra Series. Volumes 1–12, 14–33, 37 and 38 appeared in commercial editions by other publishers, and only volumes whose binding contains the name of the Society were issued under its auspices. Volumes 13, 34–6, 39–42 were issued only by the Society.

The First Series was reprinted by Burt Franklin (subsequently Lenox Hill Corp. (Burt Franklin)), New York, 1963; the Second series, volumes 1–108, and Extra Series, volume 13, by Kraus Reprint (subsequently Kraus–Thomson Reprint), Nendeln, Liechtenstein, 1967

Index of books

An asterisk (*) indicates that the name is also a main entry in the General Index. Added entries will be found in the General Index. Italic numerals are used for references to CONTENTS AND SOURCES in volume II.

Valle, Pietro della, *Travels*, ed. E. Grey (1892), 623

Varthema, L., *Itinerario* (1510), 124–5, 176, 188, 215; *Travels*, ed. J. W. Jones and G. P. Badger (1853), 616; *see also* Willes, R.

Vaughan, E. V., *English trading expeditions into Asia* (1912), 606n

Veer, Gerrit de, *Waerachtishe Beschryvinghe* (1598), 257; *True and perfect description of three…voyages …by the shippes of Holland and Zeland*, tr. W. Phillip (1609), 42, 311, 323–4, 552, 553 (fig. 46); *True description*, ed. C. T. Beke (1853), 603n, 619; *Three voyages of William Barents*, ed. K. Beynen (1876), 603n, 619

Vergil, Polydore, *Anglicae historiae* (1570), 407, 408

Viaggi fatti alla Tane (1543), 216; *see* Stanley, H. E. J. (1873)

Vincentius, Bellovacensis (Vincent of Beauvais), *Myrrour of the worlde*, tr. W. Caxton (1481), 186–7

Virgil, *Eneydos*, tr. W. Caxton (1490), 23n

Virunio, L. P., *Britannicae historiae* (1585), 346

Vivian, J. L., *Visitations of Devon* (1895), 422

Voyagers' tales from the collections of Richard Hakluyt (1892), 584n

Vries, T. de, *Holland's influence on English language and literature* (1916), 604n

Wafer, L., *New voyage* (1699), 634; *New voyage*, ed. L. E. E. Joyce (1934), 634

*Wagner, H. R., *Sir Francis Drake's voyage round the world* (1926), 72n, 227–8, 231, 240n, 590n–591n, 609n; *Spanish voyages to the northwest coast of America* (1929), 232n; *Cartography of the northwest coast of America* (1937), 590n

Waldman, M., *Americana* (1925), 591n

Wallis, H., 'The first English globe' (1951), 67n, 591n; 'The Molyneux globes' (1951), 591n; 'Further light on the Molyneux globes' (1955), 67n, 72n, 591n; 'The Patagonian giants' (1964), 642; ed. *Carteret's voyage round the world* (1965), 642; 'English enterprise in the region of the Strait of Magellan' (1965), 597

Walpole, H., *Account of the giants lately discovered* (1776), 642

Walsingham, T., *Historia breuis* (1574), 347, 380, 384, 408, 412

*Warner, G. F., ed. *Voyage of Sir Robert Dudley…to the West Indies, 1594–95* (1899), 625

Warner, W., *A continuance of Albions England* (1606), 321; *Albions England* (1612), 321

*Waters, D. W., *Art of navigation in Elizabethan and early Stuart times* (1958), 200n, 591–2; 'Art of navigation in the age of Drake' (1972), 645

Watson, F., 'Richard Hakluyt and his debt to Spain' (1916), 584; 'Hakluyt and Mulcaster' (1917), 584, 591n; 'Richard Hakluyt: A pioneer of colonisation' (1917), 584; *Richard Hakluyt* (1924), 584–5

Watson, H. E., *The sailor in English fiction and drama, 1550–1800* (1931), 592n

Waxman, M., *History of Jewish literature* (1960), 177n

Weare, G. E., *Cabot's discovery of North America* (1897), 579n

Webbe, E., *Rare and most wonderfull things which E. Webbe hath seene* (1590?), 116

Welch, J., *List of scholars* (1788), 266, 280, 326

Wendt, H., *In search of Adam* (1956), 609n

General index

Britwell Court (S. R. Christie-Miller), 487
Broadhurst & Co., Southport, 488
Brockford, Suffolk, 327
Bromfield, Thomas, 459
Brooke sale (1678), 152
Brooklyn Public L., 518
Brotherton L., Leeds, 514
*Broughton, Hugh, 303, 312, 573
Broune, –, tutor at Christ Church, 266
Brown, John Carter, 145
Brown, Robert, 603n, 624
Browne, Oliver, 91
Browne, Thomas, 265
Brownlow, W. R., 181n
Brudenell, Sir Edmund, 275, 467
Bruun, Philip, 620
*Bry, Theodor de, 295, 298, 573
Buchau, Daniel Printz von, 163n–164n, 392
Buckden, Hunts, 326
Buena Guia, R., Calif., 445
Bukhara (Boghar), 109, 171, 173–4, 355, 381, 394
Burghley, Lord see Cecil, William
Burgoignon, Nicolas, 289, 442
Burma, 221
Burn, Sir Richard, 637
Burnell, A. C., 621
Burnet, Robert, 459
Burney, James, 646
Burrops farm, Eyton, 294
Burrough, Sir John, 33, 211
Burton, Richard F., 619
Burton, Robert and William, 481
Butrigarius, Galeacius, papal legate, 431
Button, Thomas, navigator, 624
Button, Thomas, servant to R. Hakluyt, 327
Butts, Thomas, 302
Buxton, J., 322
Bylot, Robert, 624
Byrd, William, of Virginia, 145n

Cabot, John, 6, 578; patent (1496), 244, 338, 371, 432, 461; voyages (1496–8), 371, 431, 612, 623, 641
Cabot, Sebastian, 91, 256; instructions (1553), 358, 392; pension, 372, 432; voyages, 239, 247, 338, 366, 372, 431, 455, 456; world map, 10, 51, 64, 371, 431
Cabral, Pedro Alvares, 635
Cadamosto, Alvise da, 635
Cadiz, 446; voyages (1587), see Drake, Sir F.; (1596), see Devereux, R., earl of Essex
Caesar, Julius, judge of Admiralty, 238, 249, 283, 328; dedications to, 183, 310, 327
Cairo, 345, 410, 415
Calais, siege of (1359), 384
California, 240, 245, 444–5, 456; cape of, 232, 444, 445; gulf of, 444, 445
California Hist. Soc. L., 484
Camargo, Alonso de, 629
Cambay, 209, 410
Cambodia, 617
Cambridge University L., 482, 513
*Camden, William, 3, 93, 134, 223, 275–6, 300, 303, 312
Camden Society, 146
Campeche, Yucatan, 450
Campion, Gaspar, 413
Canada, 280–1, 657; maps, 308; voyages to, 82, 286, 438
Canadian Public Archives, Ottawa, 483
Canary Is., 190–2, 194–5, 426, 451–2, 614, 618, 628, 644
Cancer, tropic of, 46
Canner, Thomas, 95
Cano, Bartholomew del, 444
Caño, I. of, 227
Cano, Sebastián del, 629
Canton, 631, 641
Cape Breton, 283, 367, 434–6
Cape Breton I., 68
Cape Verde, 456
Cape Verde Is., 118, 193, 201, 230, 345, 422, 452, 457

GENERAL INDEX

Nicaragua, *446, 456*, 616
Nicholas of Lynn, 5, 259, *354, 357, 379–80*, 608n
Nicholls, John, 93
Nichols, John, 31n
Nichols, J. G., 138n
Nichols, Thomas, 215, 216, 248
Nicols, William, 86
Niger, R., 12, 642, 643
Nikitin, Athanasius, 614
Nile, R., 12
Nisyros I., Greece, 183
Niza, Marcos da, 248, *442, 443*
Nodal, Bartolomé García de, 629
Nodal, Gonzalo de, 629
Noël, Jacques, *68, 438–9*; map, 52, 249
Nombre de Dios, *447*
Nonnia river, Guinea, *430*
*Nordenskiöld, A. E., 482
Norsk Polarinstituut, Oslo, 308
North America: on maps, 50–2; commodities, *340*, 462
North Carolina University L., 487
Northeast Passage, 107, 222, 254–5, 272, 307, *355, 357, 363–4, 366, 380, 399, 400, 402*, 599n, 613; on maps, 53
North Pole, *354, 357, 358, 380*
Northumberland, duke of *see* Dudley, John
Northwell, William de, *384*
Northwest Passage, 223, 232, 268, 601n; discourses on, 274–5, *338, 373*, 433; on maps, 52–3, 274, 284; voyages in search of, 90–2, *368–70, 376, 431–4*, 612–13, 619, 624–5
North-west Passage Company, 134, 326, 329
Norumbega, *436*
Norway, 171n, 255, 257, 308, *354, 378, 385–7, 389, 391*, 632
Norwich Public L., 514
Nottingham, earl of *see* Howard, Charles
Nova Scotia, 52; Provincial Archives, 483, 520

Novaya Zemlya, 90, 257, 307
Novgorod, *356, 381*
Nowell, Robert, 267
Nubia, 637
Nuremberg, 158
Nuttal, Derek, 491–2, 493

Ob, R., Russia, 90, 162, 255, 257, *382*
Odoric da Pordenone, 97, 209, 214, 216, 222, 309, *407*, 605, 616, 629
Offa, king of Mercia, *384*
Ohthere, *378–9*, 645
Olearius, Adam, map, 174n
Oliveira Lima L., Washington, D.C., 38
Oliver, S. Pasfield, 623
Oñate, Juan de, 95, 321
Ondegardo, Polo de, 618
Ontario, Lake (Tadouac), 68, 249
Orellana, Francisco de, 615
Oriel College L., Oxford, 512
Orinoco, R., 93, *452*
Orkney Is, *354, 378*
Ormuz, 111, 212, 345, *352, 410, 420*, 626
Orosius, Paulus, 378
Orsino, Allesandro, 94
*Ortelius, Abraham, 50n, 134, 214, 300; in London, 49, 268; world maps (1564), 48; (1587), 60–1, 66, 73
Osborne, Sir Edward, 184, 312, *349, 414*; letter (1584), *350, 416*
Oslo Universitetsbiblioteket, 521
Oudney, Dr Walter, 643
Oxenham, John, 223, 237, 241, 320, *368, 447*
Oxus, R. *see* Amu-Dar'ya

Pacific Ocean (South Sea), 73, 119–21, 215, 223, 231, 233, *368, 374, 447, 451, 456–8*, 616, 627, 634; voyages across, 224–5, 227, 232, 320–1, 445, 642–3
Painter, G. D., 259n

696

Sotheby & Co., 269, 286, 489, 515
Soto, Hernando de, 95, 249, 251, 323, 604
Southam, Thomas, *356, 381*
South America, 100, 119–21, 234, 241, 242, *370, 447–9, 451*; on maps, 70
Southern continent, 70, 72, 232
South Sea *see* Pacific
Sovin, Kuzma Petrovich, 644
Spain, 15–17, 21, 174, 637, 639; shipping, 18, 35, *424–5, 429, 460*
Spalding, Augustine, 43, 328, 569
Sparke, John, voyage to Russia, *356, 381*
Sparke, John, voyage to W. Indies, 203n, 245, *367, 426*
Sparrey, Francis, 93
Spaulding, William S., 485
Spert (Pert), Sir Thomas, *366, 447*
Spes, Guerau de, 18
Spitsbergen, 322, 614, 626, 632
Sreznevskiy, I., 170n
Stafford, Lady Douglas, 300, 303
Stafford, Sir Edward, 278, 281, 284, 598; correspondence *see* Walsingham
Stafford, Capt. Edward, 294, *369*
Stammer, P., 520
*Stanley, H. E. J., Lord Stanley of Alderley, 616–17, 619, 621
Stanley, Richard, *414*
Staper, Richard, 84, 160, 184, 303, 312, *348–51, 353, 373–4, 414, 425, 455*
Stationers' Company, 511
Staunton, George T., 603 613
Steelyard, London, *386*
stellar diagrams, 647
Stenning, A. H., 265
Sterling Library, 481
Stevens, George, F.R.S., 152
*Stevens, Henry, of Vermont, 145, 288, 467, 495
Stevens, John, 75
Stevens, Thomas, 607; letter (1579), 208, 215, 222, 276, *345, 423*
Steventon, Thomas, 277

Steward, Vulliamy and Watkins, of Ipswich, 327
Stoke, Leominster, 323
Stokes, I. N. Phelps, 286
Stone, Thomas, 487
Stone House, London, 286
Stoneman, John, 96
*Stow, John, *338, 372, 383*
*Strachey, William, 135, 575, 593, 594n
Strange, John, 466
Strange, Sarah, 481
Stransome, –, scholar at Christ Church, 266
Strasbourg Bibliothèque Universitaire, 520
Streeter, Frank S., 486, 489, 518
Streeter, Thomas W., 485, 489
Strongbow *see* FitzGilbert
Sturges, John, 484
Stukely, Thomas, 125, 193n, *423*
Suarez, Diego, of Lisbon, *455*
Suarez, Francis, of Brazil, *455*
Sudan, 195, 197
Suffolk subsidy of Armour, 323
Suleiman I, sultan, 302, *347, 412–13*
Sukham, 170n
Summerson, Sir John, 64n
Sunderland sale (1881–3), 152
Surat, 631, 637
Svaneti, Georgia, 169
Swann Auction Galleries, N.Y., 520
Sweden, *363, 391, 398*
Sweyn (Swanus), son of Godwin, *404*
Swynburne, Sir Thomas de, 182
Syr Darya (Jaxartes), 172
Syria, 181, 212, *341–3, 403, 406–7, 410,* 616, 637, 639

Tabaristan, 171n
Tadouac, lake *see* Ontario
Tafur, Pero, 170n
Tahiti, 629–30, 637, 640
Tahmasp I, of Persia, 172, *360*
Talbot L., Iowa, 484
Tartary, 169, 219, *343, 379*; on maps, 70
Tashkent, 173